AF540733

CADMIUM INDUCED ENVIRONMENTAL HAZARDS ON FRESH WATER FISH

CADMIUM INDUCED ENVIRONMENTAL HAZARDS ON FRESH WATER FISH

By

Dr. Lingaraj Patro

DISCOVERY PUBLISHING HOUSE PVT. LTD.
NEW DELHI-110 002

First Published-2008

ISBN 978-81-8356-325-3

Published by:

DISCOVERY PUBLISHING HOUSE PVT. LTD.

4831/24, Ansari Road, Prahlad Street,
Darya Ganj, New Delhi-110002 (India)
Phone: 23279245 • Fax: 91-11-23253475
E-mail: dphbooks@rediffmail.com
dphtemp@indiatimes.com
Website: www.discoverypublishinghouse.com

Printed at:
Arora Enterprises
Laxmi Nagar, Delhi–110 092

Preface

It is a very implicative research work which is on a burning topic of ecological imbalance on solid industrial wastes i.e. chloride. In other words, cadmium chloride is a combination of solid industrial wastes and chemical effluents merges by flowing into water bodies which is mentioned by testing scientifically in the laborotorical experiments with fish as sample. Because fish is the massive use of non-veg. food of the modern society. The hazards meant by pollutants flown to the aquatic environment including lake, river, sea, etc. causes the hazards to the living organs in the environment which also affects to the earth, air, ultimately to the living organs including human bodies. "Eco-Toxicology (ecological hazard) is the study of toxic affects (poisonous affects) of chemical and physical agents on living organism." The organic matters of domestic sewerage also mostly containing metabolic wastes, detergent formulations, consumer products, and trace elements, polythene materials are mostly bio-degradable and exceeds rate of environmental degradation. Modern agriculture with its rapid mechanism & spreading of fertilisers, pesticides causes herbicides, insecticides and fungicides which is an ever increasing pressure on natural environment.

Author

CONTENTS

1
INTRODUCTION

Threat to the very existence of mankind because of pollution has been well established. Man has been subjecting the earth to an increased variety of pollutants in the form of chemical substances and others since the time immemorial. This emission of pollutants has reached an alarming proportion due to rapid population growth, increasing urbanisation and industrial development. Pollution occurs when substances resulting from human activities are added to the environment, causing a detrimental alternation to its physical, chemical, biological or aesthetic characteristics. Of course all non-human organisms also produce wastes which are discharged to the environment but these are generally considered part of the natural system, whether they have detrimental effects or not. Our apparently limitless habitat has long been taken for granted with its supposedly vast capacity to absorb wastes. In recent years, it has become apparent that our environment has limitations to the waste and it can destroy or dilute or degrade to insignificance.

Pollution is intimately related to human activity. It stems from and gets augmented by human activities. Pollution is cause due to deliberate or accidental or inadvertent contamination of the environment with man's waste. Odum (1971) described "pollution as an undesirable change in the physical, chemical or biological characteristics of our air, land and water, that may or will harmfully affect human life or that of desirable species, our industrial processes, living conditions and cultural assets". Sax (1979) described pollution as a social phenomenon and according to him "the communal activities of man as a social being have created a new order of by-products which have increased in volume at a faster rate than population and has resulted in increasing contamination of the environment, where the natural purifying activities can no longer keep up with it and what was once contamination now becomes pollution. Eco-toxicology is the study of toxic effects of chemical and physical agents on living organisms. It includes the transfer pathways of these agents and their interactions with the environment and the study of the structural and functional effects of which they give rise to an ecosystem.

No doubt when man came to the earth, he was gifted with a balanced, pure, uncontaminated nature. He consumed a lot from the environment. He used and misused the natural resources. Today the process is continuing in a higher rate. And no doubt after some years man will not be able to lead a normal and simple life if the process still continue. We can call the reason in one word, it is POLLUTION. When man came to the earth he was mainly depended on his physical strength to gather food. He was just like the other animals of the earth, mostly from hunting he was collecting food. Then he discovered fire. He realised its true utility later on in eighteenth century after the invention of steam engine. Water was used since the beginning of civilisation. Wind energy was used much later. Then man came to know about the necessity of agriculture and animal husbandry. The problem of food was solved after this. Then he started playing with nature for agriculture, he had to cut trees or forests. As the food supply increased so did the storage facilities and social activities changed. Population increased, villages multiplied and became towns, cities, and nations. Then man started learning the use of fossil fuels, followed by the industrial revolution in Europe. The large-scale use of fossil fuels made transportation cheaper and helped spread industrialisation. In the hope of better living condition new technologies developed and the resources of the earth were used. As population increased, there was a demand in food supply, so as food production increased. Man cleared forests and introduced many chemicals into the environment to step up agricultural productivity (Sharma and Kaur, 1993).Today the main reason of environmental pollution is the over confidence of man who thought that just because of his brain he is the master of nature. The mad rat race between the developed countries and developing countries leads to rapid progress in agriculture, industry, transportation and technology. Such activities of man had created adverse effects on all living biota in the system. And this progress in modern living system left polluted rivers, contaminated soil, depleted wildlife and exhausted natural resources for us. Thus pollution is generally defined as the addition of undesirable constituents to water, air or land, which affect adversely to the natural quality of the environment. In some cases, pollution may involve removal, rather than addition of the constituents from the environment (Powell and Shaurrteleff, 1976). Today United States of America occupies the most polluted continent of the world. India occupies the 7th place among the industrialised developing countries and New Delhi is the 3rd most polluted metropolis in India. A rapid progress in atomic and nuclear energy had added a huge amount of radioactive substances to the atmosphere (Sasser, 1976). The developed countries dump a lot of effluents into the environment, polluting the whole earth. It would not be wrong if we will say that pollution has been exported to developing nations by the developed countries of the world. This is because of the fact that in well developed countries, citizens consume more food, use more fertilisers and pesticides, fuel, minerals, automobiles and other manufactured products of all kinds. In other words pollution means the addition of any foreign material like inorganic, organic, biological or radiological or any physical change occurring in nature which may harm or affect living organisms, directly or indirectly, immediately or after a long time. According to the U.S. President's Science Advisory Committee, Environmental Pollution is the unfavourable alteration of our surroundings, wholly or largely as a by-product of man's actions, through direct or indirect effects of changes in the energy pattern, radiation levels, chemical and physical constitution and abundance of organisms. It is not only the developed countries that are responsible for pollution by showing high resources consumption. Patterns that make them the real and bigger polluters. The developing countries are also similarly responsible for this. Their higher population growths, weak environmental regulations, use of outdated technologies are also dangerously polluting the environment.

Modern ecologists depict various factors for pollution, such as human population explosion, rapid industrialisation, deforestation, unplanned urbanisation, scientific and technological advancement etc.(Sharma and Kaur, 1993). Pollution is caused due to the addition of waste products of human activity to the environment. When the waste products are not efficiently assimilated, decomposed or otherwise removed by the natural, biological and physical process of the biosphere, adverse effects may result as the pollutants accumulate or get converted into more toxic substances. When the population growth rate increases the demand for food supply increases. Fertilisers were used to increase the food production. Fertilisers boosted the production of foodgrains and vegetables and an agricultural miracle or green revolution seemed in the making all over the earth. After sometime it was found that this revolution had another, costly and darker side. The fertilisers could even destroy the environment. The fertilisers did not stay entirely in the fields where they were utilised for the increase in production of foodgrains and vegetables. They were washed down into the aquatic system. These washed down fertilisers in the water stimulated the algae to luxuriant growth. The algae consumed oxygen dissolved in water much more than that returned to water in dissolved state. Scarcity of dissolved oxygen made it impossible for the fishes and other aquatic animals to live in water. So that the water surface started filling with slimy green of luxuriant growth of the algae. This results eutrophication. Pollutants today pollute everything. The rivers, seas, lakes and the land masses are polluted by wastes coming from various industries, the air by toxic effluents from thermal power plants and exhausts of automobiles and the land or soil by wastes, chemicals, fertilisers, pesticides, acid rains and insecticides etc. Along with other type of pollution the economic poisons such as herbicides, pesticides, fungicides, insecticides, rodenticides etc. are one of the major threat to the living system.

Pollution: Types and Sources

Pollution sources can be classified in various ways depending on the origin of pollutants, their main component, property and the effects etc. Very often the classification based on the origin of the pollutants is generally used, which categories, the pollution sources into domestic, agricultural, industrial and mining.

Domestic sewages mostly contain metabolic wastes, various detergent formulations, consumer products and significant amounts of trace elements, making them rich in organic matters and nutrients. The organic matters increase the BOD load of the receiving water bodies and render them unsuitable for the survival of the aquatic animals. The organic matters in the domestic sewages are mostly biodegradable and cause problem only when the rate of input into the environment exceeds the rate of degradation or dispersion. The addition of nutrients by the way of domestic sewage into the water bodies lead to eutrophication, which brings change in the community and the biological composition of inhabiting communities and populations.

Modern agriculture with its rapid mechanisation, and spreading of fertilises, besides the use of protective treatments such as herbicides, insecticides, and fungicides exert an ever-increasing pressure on the natural environment. Some of these chemicals are non-biodegradable, and hence, persist in the ecosystem. These chemicals can be absorbed and concentrated by the living organisms via any mechanism or pathway. This phenomenon is known as bioaccumulation and creates various problems, especially when the pollutants are of high toxic nature with high biological half-life time. This is because the level of pollutants in an organism increases with the increase in its distance from the primary producer in the food chain, *i.e.* with increase in the trophic levels. Thus, a result of biomagnification, the organisms placed at higher trophic levels usually accumulate a persistent pollutant in its tissues to a concentration much greater than those present in the surrounding habitat.

Industry is the third and the most important source of pollution. Over 75,000 chemicals are in common use today and several thousands of new compounds are being added to this figure each year (Cairns, 1980 and Miller, 1984). These chemicals are now, an inevitable part of the process of industrilisation and mostly they are produced and used by the industry to deliver finished goods. Some of these chemicals, the by-products and the waste discharges of the industry are released inadvertently or accidentally into the environment to such an extent that they really threaten the ecosystem in global scale. The mining operations also contribute significantly to the cause of pollution. The exploitation of ore deposits invariably exposes fresh rock surfaces and large quantities of waste rock or soil to accelerate weathering. In addition, ore processing, smelting and refining operations causes dispersion and deposition of large quantity of chemicals into the water, air and soil of the surrounding environment. Ramade (1977) has pointed out three principal causes of contamination of the environment. These are:

(*i*) The production of energy from combustible fossils or from atom, currently this forms the basis of almost all human activity industrialised countries and leads to many types of pollution;

(*ii*) The chemical industry and its extraordinary expansion over the last few decades, more than half of million chemicals are currently in use, all over the world;

(*iii*) Modern agriculture releases substantial quantities of chemicals into the environment by the use of fertilisers, herbicides, fungicides and mechanisation.

Entries of chemicals into the environment can be classified into three categories (Harris, 1976): point spills, chronic local releases and widespread releases. By point spill it is meant that a significant amount of chemical has entered an ecosystem at a point in both space and time and the effects of contamination are expected in a well defined more or less local area. Generally this happens when a substance stored in large quantity is released suddenly into the environment. The Bhopal gas tragedy can be an example of this category, wherein 2500 people died and thousands were seriously affected by the accidental release of methyl isocyanate, deadly poisonous gas, from a pesticide industry. Chronic local releases are cases in which discharges have taken place over such periods of time, and in such quantities, that a large region (for example, a river system, a catchments basin or the landscape downwind of a source) has been contaminated. Such a situation is association with a large industrial or municipal source (Holdgate, 1979). There can be no better example than the Minamata Bay and the Niigata tragedy of mercury poisoning, for this kind of release. Widespread releases are the release of substances in sufficient quantity and over a wide area. Such releases could result in a noticeable pollution of a significant part of the entire earth's surface. Though this type of release is yet to happen, there are examples of manufacture of a thousand substances in such quantities as to be capable of polluting the entire globe (Butler, 1978). One such situation of this type has arisen due to the increased release of Chlorofluorocarbons (CFCs) and Flurobromocarbons into the atmosphere. This has resulted in progressive destruction of the ozone layer up to 1.6 to 3 in the last decade, posing a serious threat to result global warming and Greenhouse effect. This threat has been responded well in time by the world in the Montreal Protocol, an international treaty that will eliminate CFC use by the year 2000 AD (Hoffman, 1990). Another situation, very close to this, has occurred in the recent Gulf war, where several oil wells in Kuwait caught fire emitting huge quantities of smoke and shoot. These were carried by the wind to the neighbouring states of Iraq and Iran covering most of their sky. Even shoot and carbon particles were found in the snowfalls on the Himalayas of the Indian subcontinent. The presence of matter or energy in an unintended place is considered as a pollutant.

The emission of pollutants into the environment is a complex phenomenon and cannot be limited to the fixed image of waste pipe spilling out its effluents into a lake or river. In almost all cases, substances discharged into the environment are going to be carried a long way from their source. Atmospheric and hydrologic circulation systems then disperse them progressively throughout the biosphere.

The pollutants act in many ways on the living systems. Acute and/or long term actions are the most obvious eco-toxicological impacts of a given pollutant. It results demoecological effects at population levels that are displayed through immediate or premature death, reduced reproductive success, reduced growth, and/or increased loss at the juvenile stages. These are ultimately reflected in the lower abundance and perturbed distribution of the exposed populations of sensitive species. The effect of the sub-lethal concentrations of some pollutants is by far; the most frequent eco-toxicological problem and it can be far more noxious in the long run for the exposed species resulting in chronic deterioration of the ecosystem. The persistent non-biodegradable pollutants are absorbed by riving organisms and are concentrated many times more than the concentration of the surrounding medium. Further these bio-accumulated pollutants are passed from one trophic level to another and exhibit increasing concentration in organisms related to their trophic status resulting in biomagnification.

Industry is responsible for creating a fantastic array of new chemicals every year all of which eventually find their way into the environment. For most of these chemicals, not even the chemical formula are known and much less is known about their acute, chronic or genetic effect on the living organisms. At present, the industry is the focus of attention, the world-over, as the most important source of pollution of the environment.

Chemical industry in India has grown up phenomenally since independence. There are today about 4000 chemical factories in India. They release large quantities of chemicals in the form of gas, liquid and solid wastes, into the environment. Many of these chemicals are toxic and create pollutional problem. The problem of toxic hazard has already reached alarming proportions in this country and is bound to grow with increasing industrialisation. India is the larges manufacturer of pesticides in the whole of South Asia and Africa. As many as 139 organic chemicals, heavy metals like zinc, lead, chromium, copper, mercury and various other compounds are used in the manufacture of dyes only. Sundaresan *et al.,* (1983) have given the growth of industries dealing with toxic chemicals and generating toxic and hazardous wastes during 1950s, 1970s and 1980s, in India.

Industries, which are known to produce potentially toxic and hazardous wastes, are pesticides, dyes and pigments, organo-chemicals, fertilisers, non-ferrous metals, steel and chlor-alkali plants. The major foci of such industries in India are Bombay, Calcutta, Kanpur, Delhi, Chandigarh, Jamshedpur, Bokaro, Hyderabad, Vishakhapatnam, Madras, Baroda, Cochin etc. The wastes from the industry are generally disposed by land filling or released into water bodies. Generally the toxic effluents from industry are neutralised before their discharge, but still they contain substantial amount of toxic substances that can cause pollution. At present it is believed that rivers are most severely polluted by industries followed by estuaries, lakes and ocean in declining order (Kumar, 1981).

Cadmium was recognised many years ago to be a highly toxic element but it was not until comparatively recently that concern began to be expressed over the possible effects on human health on long term exposure to low concentrations of this element. The discovery that Cadmium pollution from a base metal mining and smelting complex could cause series illness and possible death in a local community has led to widespread public anxiety (Kobayashi and Hagino,1965). Although industrial operations are major sources of Cadmium, many countries now show concern that disposal of metal which sewage sludge on land may adversely affect the fertility of the soil and render plants a health hazards if consumed by man and animals. Nevertheless, the increasing awareness of the political hazards of Cadmium contamination should not obscure the fact that Cadmium is present in natural ecosystems and an ubiquitous element in all living organisms. For the environmental impact of cadmium to be assessed, major steps in the bio-geo-chemical pathway must be outlined and gaps in our knowledge identified for future research undertakings. The concern over the public health implications of cadmium pollution has resulted in a considerable amount of research being carried out by regional and national laboratories and field stations throughout the world.

The most notable aspects of the geo-chemistry of cadmium with regard to its rock soil plant animal relationships is its low concentrations in the Earth's crust. Consequently, soil and plant contents of this element are generally low except where soils are formed on rocks with anomalously high concentrations of the metal, such as black shale, of where pollution has occurred. Plants and animals are unlikely to have evolved mechanisms to cope with relatively high concentrations of Cadmium, since these rarely occur in nature. However, with the increasing production of cadmium, pollution will assume a greater significance for soil plant animal pathways. Cadmium has an estimated crystal abundance of between 0.15 $\mu g.g^{-1}$ (Weast, 1969) and 0.2 $\mu g.g^{-1}$ Fleischer *et al.*, 1974) and thus occurs in sixty seventh position in an order of relative abundance (Aylett,1973). The estimated mean cadmium concentration in igneous rocks is 0.2$\mu g.g^{-1}$.With a range of 0-01-1.6$\mu g.g^{-1}$ Cadmium, but very few values of over 0.5 $\mu g.g^{-1}$ are found (Fleischer *et al.*, 1974). These low contents of Cadmium in igneous rocks accounts for its low crystal abundance. With the exception of ore bodies, trace elements occur as impurities in primary minerals, which form igneous rocks. They are substituted for one of the major ions in the crystal of a mineral without significantly attending the internal structure. This "isomorphous substitution" requires the potential replacing ion and the major ion to be replaced to have similar ionic radii. Similar charges unless other substitutions occur to maintain electrically neutrality, and similar electro-negativities or ionisation potentials (Siegel, 1974). Cadmium has the same valency and similar ionic radius as Calcium (Cd^{+2} 0.97 A°), but dose not commonly substitutes for Calcium in minerals such as the plagioclase or in secondary Calcium-containing minerals such as Calcite. This is probably due to Cadmium higher electrongativity (1.7) in comparison with that of Calcium (1.0) which implies that Cadmium has a greater tendency to form covalent bonds, whereas those formed by Calcium are predominantly ionic (Krausk opf, 1967). Therefore, since Cadmium is unable to substitute easily for a common constituent of primary minerals of concentration in igneous rocks is low.

Heavy metal contamination caused by either natural processes or buy human activities is one of the most serious eco-toxicological problems (Reddy and Prasad, 1990). Since, plants function as the principal entry point of heavy metals into the food chain leading to animals and man (Rauser,1990), the agricultural use of Cadmium containing fertilisers and of Cu as a fungicide is of major concern. Whereas, it is well established fact that Cadmium is more toxic to man amd other mammals than Cupper, the differential toxicity of these two heavy metal for plants is not clear (Galli *et al.,* 1996). The use of phosphate fertilisers will invariably increase at least to a slight extent, the Cadmium concentration in soils used for commercial agriculture as long as the accumulation exceeds the amount removed by crops harvested and leached from the plough layer (Alloway, 1990 and Singh,1994). Application of Cadmium containing fertilisers may not appreciably increase the plant cadmium concentration at present, but low annual application may result in elevated cadmium concentrations in the cultivated layer, especially where high Cadmium fertilisers are used. Some of the Cadmium added to soils will invariably be removed by the crop or by leaching with the former playing a more important role. The amounts of cadmium removed by the crop depend on the crop species or variety grown, the Cadmium concentration of the fertiliser used, the prevailing soil conditions and the magnitude of yields. Cadmium removal through leaching is generally of less importance than through crop remove, although reliable values are still missing (Jeng and Singh,1995). Knight and McGrath (1995)reported specifically that heavy metal accumulation in soil due to application of sewage sludge was found to reduce the number and genetic diversity of Rhizobium leguminosarum biovar trifolii. There was growing concern that the soil microbial community may not be adequately protected from the effects of metals in soils receiving sewage sludge. The main sources of Cadmium in streams are effluents from industries such as electroplating, paints, plastic, battery and zinc mining and refining. Because of its high toxicity, most countries include Cadmium among the "Priority pollutants "requiring suitable treatment prior discharge into the environment (Puranik *et al.,* 1995). The United States Environmental Protection Agency limits Cadmium levels in drinking water to 0.001 mg/1. In India, the permissible concentration, of Cd in the industrial effluents discharged into inland surface waters is 0.1 $mg.1^{-1}$. At present a variety of physico-chemical processes one employed to treat Cadmium containing effluents. These processes, however prove expensive when situations involving high volume and low metal concentration (typically less than 50 mg/1) are encountered (Puranik *et al.*, 1995). Various microorganisms are known to adsorb metals from dilute solutions and concentrate them several fold by the process of biosorption. The use of dead cell mass in metal sorption can be of great interest because of the large variety and low cost of these biological materials.

Heavy metals ions in small quantities are required for various physiological process and the normal functions of cells in plants and animals. Elevated levels of such metal ions are generally toxic and cause major damage to cells. In addition to the utilisation of metal ions as essential elements, adjustment of intracellular levels of free ions by binding to macromolecules or other mechanisms is indispensable if cells are to protect themselves against excessive metal ions or changes in levels of such ions in the environment. (Webb, 1987; Bremner and Beattie, 1990 and Mehra and Winge, 1991). Two different classes of cytoplasmic molecules that participate in binding of metal ions and thus, in resistance to metal ions have been identified in various plant and animal cells (Inouhe *et al.,1996*). Animal cells produce heavy metal binding protections known as metallothioneins (Kagi and Kojima,1987). Both types molecules are rich in cysteine residues as metal-binding sites but they are very different from each other in that the former are synthesised via an m-RNA transcript, while the latter are generated from GSH by PC synthase (Scheller *et al.,* 1987,Grill *et al.,*1989). Inouhe *et al.,* (1996)opined that it was important to determine, why such different systems became established and are exploited by plant and animal cells. Both MT and PC have been identified in several species of yeast and other fungi. This finding implies that fungi might be located at an intermediate position between plants and animals in terms of binding of heavy metal ions and thus in terms of the utilisation of such ions.

Cadmium is toxic to most living organisms. It occurs as part of different types of rocks, sedimentation sludges, coals and mineral oils in minerals, Cadmium (Cd) is frequently associated with zinc. It's worldwide presence and considerable industrial use has given size to an increase in its content in trophic food chains, which contribute mainly to human exposure. Oral absorption is relatively low and is influenced by the solubility of the compound type of diet, and individual nutritional state. Interest in Cadmium contamination began after the outbreak of itai-itai diseases in Japan. Evaluation of cadmium contamination has been carried out in all the countries of the European Economic Community and it has been estimated that in Spain emissions to the atmosphere and water are respectively 6.89 and 3.79 per cent of total emissions in the European communities(EC₵). When critical body concentration is reached, renal malfunction and damage are produced, proteinuria being the first sign, with increased urinary excretion of low molecular weight proteins such as B_2 microglobulin, Lysozyme, resinal binding proteins and immumoglobulin chains (Elinder *et al.,* 1985). After exposure, the kidney is the organ, which contains the highest concentrations of cadmium and retains it longest. Moreover studies carried out in humans not occupationally exposed to cadmium reveal that 50 per cent body burden is found in the Kidneys (Kjellstrom, 1979). In recent years, much research has focused on determining factors contributing to the level of exposure and degree of accumulation of cadmium in renal cortex (Spicket and Lazner, 1979; Blanusa *et al.,* 1985, Scott *et al., 1987).* Cadmium in the renal cortex increases with age, reaching a maximum between 40-50 years (Elinder,1985).

Heavy metals in soil occurs in various forms, each possessing different mobility and phyto-availability (Alloway, 1990; Kuo *et al.,* 1983; and Tuin and Tels,1990). Metals via aerial deposition in particulate form may enrich areas near industrial establishments. These particulates may come from varied sources such as automobile emission, combustion of fossil fuel, smelting and refining of metal ores and other. Because, these particulates arose from varying thermal conditions and matrices, they come in various forms *i.e.,* chloride, sulfate, carbonates, oxides etc. Excessive levels of metals in the soil can lead to elevated uptake by plants. Adverse consequences may ensure, such as phyto-toxicity or quality deterioration of edible portions from metal enrichment (Chlopecka, 1996). The same author indicted the existence of poor correlation between total metal content in the soil and plant uptake, whereas, better correlations have been observed for extractable form of metal. (Gupta *et al.,* 1975 and Xian, 1989). Cadmium can interfere with the root uptake process depending in turn on changes in growth rate and root system architecture (Barcelo and Poschenrieder, 1990), suberisation and damage to the external (root hairs) and internal structures can increase resistance to water uptake. At stem level, bean plants grown in the presence of Cadmium showed a reduction in the number of xylem vessels, their lumen was also reduced and this partial occlusion might be due to deposits of materials from the cells walls (Leita *et al.,* 1995). Studies on stomatal regulation of transpiration in whole plants treated with Cadmium through the root systems give contrasting results depending on metal concentration, exposure duration, timing of application and plant species. Three different stages of Cadmium stress are reported to interact with the uptake and movement or water in plants. The first short-term stage occurs within a few hours a exposure with primary effects on root metabolism and growth, an indirect effect was a stomatal opening generated by the increase of the leaf osmotic potential of the leaves. The second occurs after 24-48 hrs from Cadmium treatment. In this stage, Cadmium acted directly on the guard cells and severe root growth inhibition limits water uptake causing a decrease in RWC of the leaves and stomata closure (Leita *et al.,* 1995). In the third stage there was a general metabolic breakdown with loss of turgor and hydro passive stomatal closure, at very high cadmium supply or prolonged exposure time (Leita *et al.,*1995).

Cadmium is one of the most toxic metals occurring in nature. There is ample evidence in the literature that this metal is highly toxic to all living organisms (Yannai and Berdicevsky, 1995). In humans, chronic exposure to Cadmium causes, severe damage to the kidneys and it has been linked to enhanced ageing processes, as well as cancer Jentsch *et al.,*1993). Due to its many industrial uses such as an electroplating plants, dyestuffs industry and metallurgy and mining industries, this metal, cadmium has become widely employed and is now a major threat to man's environment. Numerous studies have demonstrated that the organic derivatives of metals are by far more toxic than their inorganic ions (Iverson and Brinckman, 1978). Further, the organic derivatives of heavy metals possess a much higher capability for absorption and accumulation in animal bodies than the inorganic ions (Venugopal and Luckey, 1978; Nakajima and Sakagnchi,1986; Gadd,1990). Little information is available on the formation of organic derivatives of Cadmium by environmental process. There were no findings in the literature of any direct evidence of such a process, except for a suggestion that a volatile cadmium compound, formed by a certain strain of *Pseudomonas,* may have been methylcadmium (Summers and Silver, 1978).

Commercial plastics use heavy metals in their formulation (Bode, 1992; Wagner *et al.,* 1992). Heavy metals are added to plastics for a number of reasons, namely as: stabilisers, plasticisers, antioxidants, coplourants and fire retardants (Bode, 1992 and Wagner *et al.,* 1992). Cadmium is widely used as a colourant and plasticiser (Tamaddon and Hogland,1993 ; Bergback *et al.,* 1994) and is often used in per cent amounts in PVC, Bode (1992) reports that they found Cd at levels up to 4 per cent in PVC. Other metals used in high concentrations in plastics formulations include Sb, Hg, Pb, Zn, Cr and Cu (Bode, 1992).

Pollution by Industry

Extensive literature on the pollution of surrounding biota through the discharges of effluents and sludges from chlor-alkali industries is available (Weiss *et al.,* 1971; Suckcharoen, 1979 and 1980; Lodenius, 1980; Suckcharoen and Nourteva, 1982; Lodenius and Tulisalo, 1984 and Shaw *et al.,* 1986). Studies on loss of mercury into the environment from the chlor-alklai industry were caried-out by Flewelling (1979), BOuveng (1968 and 1972), Ross (1974) and Shaw *et al.,* (1986). Turney (1970) reported contamination of river Detrait by mercury discharges from a chlor-alkali plant, similar studies were also conducted by Matida and Kumada (1969) on the river Agano of Japan, by Suobodova and Hejtmanek (1976) on the Ohre river and CArlos (1979) on the Jab river of Papua, Newguinea, Hattula *et al.,* (1978) indicated a severe pollution of the lake Paijane, which had received in past, the waste discharge from a caustic soda factory. Wallin (1976) reported fallout patterns of mercury in vegetation around five Swedish chlor-alkali plants. Lodenius (1981) reported the mercury fallout in terrestrial vegetation atound three Finnish chlor-alkali works. Lodenius and Tulisalo (1984) invetigated the geographical spread of mercury around achlor-alkali factory. Reports of mercury dispersion and contamination of Yatsushiro sea (Kudo and Miyahara, 1984), lake superior region (Glass *et al.,* 1986), and eight northern Minnesota lakes (Sorensen *et al.,* 1990) were available. Dylewski and Bradecks (1976) formulated methods of diminishing the contamination of natural environment by mercurial effluents and sludges of a chlor-alkali plant. Suckcharoen and Lodenius (1980) worked on the reduction of mercury pollution in the vicinity of caustic soda plant in Thailand; Thangappan (1972) investigated on the pollution and its prevention, by chlor-alkali plants. Perry (1974 a) worked out a method of purification of trade effluent containing mercury from electrolytic baths. Perry (1974 b) investigated recovery of mercury from contaminated water and sludges.

Literature pertaining to the effet of mercury and mercury contained industrial effluent on the plant systems are plentily availbale in comparison to animal systems. Reports on the effect of mercury and mercury contained effluents on plants, bioaccumulation of mercury and its tissue distribution arrre scanty. Suckcharoen (1978 and 1980) reported mercury in the vegetation, around a casutic soda plant in Thailand. Lodenius and Laaksovirta (1979) studied mercury content of Hypogymnia physodes and pine needles affected by a chlor-alkali works at Kusankoski, SE Finland. Huckabee *et al.,* (1983) studied the levels of mercury in vegetation around a mercury mine at Almads.

One hundred twnety four daily meals sampled at three different areas of Belgium were found to contain 6.5 mg of Hg in each meal (Buchet *et al.,* 1983). Shishido and Tsuguyoshi (1974) have investigated that in Japan the daily intake of inorganic, organic and total Hg ranged from 0.47 to 1.10, 2.68 to 70.04 and 3.25 to 70.92 mg respectively, in a diet by each Japanese. As per their gradation list on an average food, fish contained more amount of Hg than egg. The third position was assigned to boiled rice.

The purpose of acute toxicity test is to assess various abnormalities caused due to administration of a chemical to live systems on one occasion or other and to determine the order of lethality of the chemical. Many of the schemes are available at present, to test for adverse effects that may result when chemicals enter into the environment. In aquatic toxicology, acute lethal toxicity tests with the fish and invertebrates are usually intended to assess the numerical value of toxicity, to compare potenties of toxicants, to assess the effects of environmental variables on toxicity. Besides, statistical analysis of toxicity, is essentially a tool in all these studies. The rapid increase in contamination of aquatic environments with pesticide and industrial pollutants in recent years, has resulted in an escalation of scientific interests in the biological effects of pollution. Because of the importance of crop in the aquatic environment, any deleterious effect of the toxicant on this, is likely to be reflected on the entire ecosystem. Considerable information are available pertaining to residual toxicity levels in fresh water, estuarine and marine fishes but relatively very little work has been done on the mechanism of toxic action of mercurial compounds especially on studies concerning active transport across cellular membranes. It has been reported that a significant depression of (Na^+, K^+) ATPase activity is associated with excessive absoprtion of mercury (Jackim, 1974) and also suggested that the dearrangement of normal monovalent cation exchange induce by mercurial compounds across membranes. Although investigations have been conducted on blue-green algae (Sahu, 1987; Rath, 1991) and higher terrestrial vertebrates few researchers have studied the effects of mercury on the enzyme activity of fish (Armstrong, 1979; Passino, 1981; Panigrahi, 1980; Panigrahi, 1985 and Samant, 1989).

Na^+, K^+ - ATPases is well known to play an important role in nerve impulse generation and synaptic transmission (Ahuja and Subramanyam, 1978). Hewitt and Nicholas (1963) reported the indication of depressed or accelerated enzyme activity in aquatic organisms exposed to low concentrations of metals. Studies have shown that cadmium ion has damaging effects on respiration and ATPase activity of the pulmonary alveolar microphage (Cross *et al.*, 1970). Panigrahi (1980) reported depression of ATPase activity *in vivo* and *in vitro* in freshwater fishes following inorganic mercury intoxication. Panigrahi (1984) reported a similar trend in freshwater fishes exposed to mercury based fungicide. Metals can combine with enzymes in many ways among which are sulfahydryl binding, chelation and salt formation. A good number of references are available pertaining to the inhibitions of ATPase activity in fish by polychloride biphenyls (Desaiah *et al.*, 1972 and Koch *et al.*, 1972), Toxaphene (Desaiah and Koch, 1975); DDT (Desaiah *et al.*, 1975); Chlordane (Verma *et al.*, 1978) and by Kepone and Mirex (Desaiah *et al.*, 1975 and Dasaiah *et al.*, 1977). It is though that the ATPase may be involved in the transport of ions in the nerve and interfere with a variety of membrane-linked functions (Holan, 1969).

Metallic cations are highly essential for many enzymes to achieve their catalytic activity. These cations maintain the acid base balance; and are also highly essential for the ionic composition of the body fluids. Disturbance in electrolyte concentration are quite common in toxicity. Different studies on electrolyte change resulting from toxic status have produced a variety of diverse effects, because of differential size of toxic actions in the body. The reaction of mercury compounds with sulfahydryl groups has been well established (Hughes, 1957). A considerable decrease in succinic dehydrogenase activity of the mitochondrial fraction was reported by Syversen (1947 b), Bruin (1976) reported that cation movements within tissue cells originate from toxic effects on cellular membranes. Fungicides of diverse chemical structure are capable of changing mitochondria function, thereby making the membrane permeable to cation. Such cations are the mobile co-factors which are either firmly bound to metal called metaloenzymes or metal activated enzymes. Dawson (1979) reported decrease in plasma calcium and an increase in plasma sodium in winter flounder, when exposed to mercury chloride at the concentrations of 10 and 20 ppb Hg level. Mercurials have long been recognised as agents which interact with the poison proteins in general and enzymes in particular (Fox *et al.*, 1975).

The DNA molecule is a target site of most, if not all, carcinogenic and mutagenic agents. Additionally, a number of agents are acutely cytotoxic to cells because, they damage the DNA (Zwelling *et al.*, 1982 and Ikenaga *et al.*, 1981). Numerous chemical agents damage DNA *in vivo* (Ahmad *et al.*, 1977; Ahuja and Subrahamanyam, 1978). Geener and Jeener (1952) reported the reduced RNA synthesis due to methyl mercury intoxication. Rath and Misra (1980 b) reported changes in biochemical parameters of different organs of a freshwater fish exposed to dichlorvos. Panigrahi (1984) reported some biochemical changes induced by MEMC. Reports are available pertaining to the effects of pesticides on rat (Bhatia *et al.*, 1973); Pesticides induced DNA damage in cultured human cells (Ahmad *et al.*, 1977), reappraisal of lead on cell proliferation and influence of lead on nucleic acid metabolism in rat (Stevenson *et al.*, 1977), effects of inorganic mercury on different biochemical parameters of freshwater fish (Panigrahi, 1980).

Johanson and Jahil (1963) showed DDT induced chromosomal damages. Different aspects concerning the biochemical assessment of functional impairment in vital organs were explored in toxicological studies. Untoward effects can usually be traced back in the functional incompetence of organs. Whenever dysfunction occurs in a tissue it has its origin in biochemical abnormality may become apparent before the onset of morphological changes and precedes the development of chronic degenerative disease. Explanation of biochemical tests facilitates diagnosis of pretoxic condition in man and it may be valuable in the routine screening of chemicals in animal experimentation. Biochemical studies are the useful tools in aiding diagnostic pathology which covers a wide range embracing various organs and systems. Pesticides act either as a selective toxicant or may display rather a broad spectrum of adverse biological activities.

Toxicant effects on growth may be studied by examining macromolecules involved in growth, such as DNA, RNA and protein (Barron and Adelman, 1984). However, toxicant-induced changes in macromolecular content (RNA, DNA and protein) and RNA/DNA, RNA/protein, and protein/DNA ratios have received very little attention in fish (Barren and Adelman, 1984). Kearns and Atchison (1979) correlated RNA/DNA of young of the year yellow perch to growth rate and cadmium concentration in a metal contaminated lake. Mudge *et al.*, (1977) found reduced cell size and decreased cytoplasmic RNA content in the internal tissue of brooke trout acutely exposed to acid stress. Stroganov (1977) reported that cadmium, up to lethal concentrations, did not effect RNA or DNA tissue content.

Life depends on a complex network of chemical reactions brought about by a specific enzymes. The enzymes are the primary instruments for the expression of gene action. Enzymes are of biological importance in metabolic functions, which have the most highly specialised class of proteins. The change in metabolism can well be correlated with the disturbance in behaviour and action of the enzymes (Panigrahi, 1984). The reduction in active metabolism has been correlated with the toxic effective different types of toxicants. The disturbance in enzymatic action can be related to the specific action of certain toxicants by inhibiting the enzymes to act, bind the active sites of the enzyme and enzymes become non-functional due to disintegration. Inhibition of enzymes by chemical agents may be reversible or irreversible, competitive or non-competitive. There are many different mechanisms through which thiol groups of enzymes can be acted upon by heavy metals. The importance of enzymatic studies in the system lies in the functional interpretation of the pollutant causing different types of disorders. Membranes play a role in the structure and function of the cell and its organelles. One of the way by which membranes can affect cellular metabolism is by interacting with enzymes. Some membrane function as the organising matrix for enzyme systems, the micro environment in all these cases at or near the membrane surface may modulate the activities of the enzymes located in the region.

Cadmium, the Metal

Cadmium is a divalent metal, chemically similar to Zinc and Mercury. Although it is widely distributed in the lithosphere, cadmium is usually found at quite low concentrations in crystal rocks, the mean concentration being about 200-300 ppb (OECD, 1975). Sometime cadmium concentrations as high as 100 ppm found in phosphatic rocks (due to presence of fossilised fish teeth). Cadmium may also be leached from sulphide ores of zinc, copper and lead. The world production of cadmium is currently higher than 15,000 metric tons per year, about 50 per cent greater than the present rate of mercury production. The major producing countries are the U.S., Russia, Japan, Canada, Belgium and France. Cadmium is used in various industrial purposes *viz.*:

(*a*) for electroplating of steel, iron, copper, brass and other alloys to prevent corrosion;

(*b*) for colouring pigment production which are used in fabrics, textiles and paints etc.;

(*c*) for uses as plastic stabilisers;

(*d*) for manufacture of alloys;

(*e*) for manufacture of Ni-Cd batteries;

(*f*) for production of certain pesticides, luminiscent dials, X-ray screens etc.

Emissions to the Environment

The estimates of Cd emissions to the environment in different countries vary widely. There are a number of sources of Cadmium emission. An estimate as measured in US during 1968 is presented in the table 1.1.

Table 1.1 Estimated Cd Emissions (in Metric Tons) to the Environment during 1968 in the United States

Sources	*Air*	*Soil, Water*	*Total*
Extraction, refining and production	953	294	1,247
Industrial conversion	15	—	15
Consumption and disposal	186-927	909	1095-1836
Fossil fuel combustion	132-998	—	132-998
Application of fertiliser	—	23-227	23-227
Tires	5.2	—	5.2
Lubricating oils	0.8	?	0.8
Total	**1292-2899**	**1226-1430**	**2516 - 4329**

Source: OECD, 1975

Cadmium is a relatively rare heavy metals occurring naturally together with Zinc. Cadmium production increased rapidly during the 20th century until 1970. The increase was then temporarily halted due to environmental pollution problems. In the late 1979s, Cadmium productions increased again mainly due to the increasing demanded for rechargeable batteries (Eliner and Jarup, 1996). Only limited amounts of Cadmium products are reused. It has been estimated that only 50 per cent of the cadmium containing batteries sold in Sweden are returned after usage. Compared with most other countries, this is nevertheless a high percentage for recycling. The overall worldwide, recycling of the total amount of Cadmium produced annually is possibly less than 10 per cent Cadmium containing products are frequently dumped together with household waste, thereby contaminating the environment, in particular if the waste is burned. Cadmium emissions to the environment from mining and non-ferrous smelters are considerable and estimated to be about 7000 metric tons annually (Elinder and Jarup,1996) a proportion of all Cd emitted into the atmosphere will eventually be deposited on agricultural soils, additional amounts of Cadmium pollute the soil from the use of Cadmium contaminating sewage sludge and phosphate fertilisers.

Cadmium is readily available for uptake in grain, rice and vegetables and there is a clear association between the Cadmium concentration in soil and in the plants grown on the soil. The relative contribution to the Cadmium pollution of soil from fertilisers dependent on the type of fertliser, amount of Cadmium in the fertiliser as well as cadmium content in soil prior to fertilisation. Reports that Cadmium from fertilisers may add significant amounts to Cadmium to plants and thus add to human exposure, warrants attention. The uptake in plants increase with decreasing pH, thus, the acidification of the environment may increase the Cadmium content in grains.

Many environmental pollutants released into the atmosphere eventually reach the soil by direct deposition or by deposition on vegetation. In pollutants may be adsorbed and or assimilated by plants leaves before entering the animals food chain. A portion of the pollutants adsorbed onto plant leaves is washed off by rain. Chemically oxidised to other products or returned to the soil as the plant decay. The pollutants assimilated by vegetation may be translocated, metabolised and possibly Photo-degraded within the plant (Kummerova and Brandejsova, Lamdsnerger and Wu 1995). Pollution of the biosphere with this toxic metal has accelerated dramatically since the beginning of the industrial revolution (Nriagu, 1970) and Cadmium accumulation in soil and water now posses a major environmental and human health problem, which is in need of an effective and affordable solution. The use of metal accumulating plants to remove toxic metals including cadmium, from soil and aqueous streams has been proposed as a possible solution, to this problem (Salt *et al.,* 1995). This process of using plants for environmental restoration is termed "Phytoremediation". Cadmium is a particularly favourable target metal for this new technology, because it is readily transported and accumulated in the shoots of several plant species (Wagner, 1994). The primary point of entry for Cadmium into plants is through the roots, however, for its efficient removal from the soil, it must first be translocated to the harvestable parts of the shoot (Salt, 1995).

Cadmium is extremely toxic to organisms because it inhibits a large number of metabolic enzyme system, complexes with amino acids, peptides, and proteins and affects the conformation of polyriboadenylic acid and the physical properties of DNA (Conway, 1978). Algae bioaccumulate cadmium (Kelly and Whitton, 1989) and bioaccumulation ratios of about 10^4 have been reported in freshwater (Conway,1978) and marine (Cossa, 1996) diatoms. Although species-specific differences in sensitivity to Cadmium exist among algae (De Noyelles *et al.,* 1980, Zhang *et al.,* 1992) and at least one algae, a *Euglena gracilis,* is known to have Cadmium resistant strains(Bariand and Mestre, 1984).Cadmium is generally very toxic to algae. For example, $2\mu g.1^{-1}$ Cadmium decreased chlorophyll by about 10 per cent (Nalewajko, 1995). Cell suspension cultures of tomato were found to be more sensitive to excess copper than to similar concentrations of Cadmium, which was explained by the lack of synthesis of copper binding peptides by copper exposed cells. Indeed, these cells developed tolerance to 1 mM Cadmium after sub culturing with 100 mM

Cadmium induced the formation of cadmium binding pepticles (Inouhe *et al.,*1991). In cell suspension cultures of *Rawolfia serpurtina* Grill *et al.,* (1985) demonstrated the induction of heavy metal binding peptides of general structure (YEC) G not only by Cadmium but also by other heavy metal ions, such as copper, phytochelations (Galli *et al.,*1996). Grill *et al.,*(1989), showed that these peptides are synthesised from glutathione (GSH). Correspondingly, cell suspension cultures of *Datura innoxia* (Jackson *et al.,* 1992) and maize roots (Meuwly and Rauser, 1992 and Raegsegger *et al.,* 1992) showed a depletion of the GSH content after exposure to Cadmium. The function of phytochelations in the differential tolerance of plants to heavy metals, however is controversial and needs further confirmation by sepeated experimentation on different systems.

Plant metabolism may be affected by Cadmium in different ways. Cadmium is an effective inhibitor of chlorophyll biosynthesis (Stobart *et al.,* 1985), Photosynthesis (Weigel,1985), respiration and the activities of several enzymes (Lee *et al.,* 1976 and Bishnoi *et al.,* 1993). In winter wheat *(Triticum aestivum, L.* W.HvS) Cd^{+2} caused a growth retardation and changes in ion uptake. Immediate target of $Cd+^{2}$ in the cell membrane, where both the membrane composition and function can be altered and damaged (Fodor *et al.,* 1994). Popovic *et al.,* (1996) suggested several ways by which the plants can reduce these negative effect of Cd^{+2}. One of the possibilities suggested by them and that hypothesis has recently became very popular was that the heavy metals form chelates with sulphur rich proteins (Wagner, 1984). Besides, sulphur is a structural constitutent of amino acids and several co-enzymes and prosthetic groups such as ferrodoxine, which are important for nitrogen assimilation (Petrovic and Kastori, 1994).

Knowledge of the reactions of heavy metals with soils is necessary to accurately assess the future problems of food production and quality and to plant adequate counter measures. At moderate concentrations of heavy metals above the deficiency range, most natural soils act as a repository or sink for metals, without any effect of the metals on soil biological behaviour. In recent decades, there has been growing concern about the increasing concentrations of heavy metals in soils, because of the relative ease of their transfer from soil to plants (Carrillo Gonzalez *et al.,* 1996). Thus, the ability to predict metal concentrations in soils is vital to the adequate regulation of contaminated waste disposal and to present excessive uptake of heavy metals by plants and their transport to ground water. However, the extent of transfer of metals from soil to plant not only depends on plant species and the kind of metal involved, but also on such factors as soil solution composition, soil type, distribution of metals between solid and solution phase and chemical reactions controlling the mobility of heavy metals (Carrillo-Gonzaliez *et al.,* 1996).

The Food and Drug Administration in the USA has classed grain and cereals as being sensitive to cadmium uptake. This classification is based on the assumption that if a particular component contributes significantly to the overall exposure and markedly responds to a change in soil cadmium concentration, then it may be said to have a sensitive response (Jackson and Alloway, 1992). However, several studies have concluded that there is no evidence of a long term increase in the Cadmium content of wheat grain due to increased soil cadmium content (Mortvedt, 1987 and Jones and Johnston, 1989). Grain and cereal products generally contain moderate concentrations of Cadmium, but are consumed in relatively large amounts and therefore constitute a primary dietary source of this non-essential and toxic metal (Yost *et al.,* 1989). The amount of wheat based products consumed in the U.K by humans in 1992-93 was 5580 thousand tonnes (HGCA, 1993). On average, this is equivalent to about 260g of wheat based products per person each day. Using a median grain Cadmium concentration for 1992-1993 of 0.030 mg kg^{-1} this would result in a daily dietary intake of about 8 mg Cadmium per person or about 11 per cent of the German (BGA, 1986) limit of 70µg Cd d^{-1} . This value may be overestimated for children, but an underestimation for adults, since it assumes only average consumption of wheat. Also a large percentage of wheat based food is consumed as white flour, which contains less Cadmium than whole meal flour. Even so, this value is significantly lower than that given by Hutton (1982) for people in the European community of 30 to 40 per cent of the German's limit or of 20 per cent for the adults population, in the USA, by Yost *et al.*, (1980). Pb and Cd are the most abundant heavy metals polluting the environment. They are taken up by plants mostly through the root system (Cutler and Rains, 1974; Foy, 1978; Vojtechova and Leblova,1991) and partly in mud smaller amounts—through their leaves (Greger *et al.*, 1993). It was also proved that the composition of the culture solution can considerably modify the uptake and even the effect of these ions (Hardyman and Jacoby, 1984; Wozny *et al.*, 1990; Fodor *et al.*, 1996, Fodor *et al.*, 1996) reported that the most apparent symptom of Cadmium effects the chlorosis of the leaves. This is accompanied by the decrease in net photosynthetic activity, PS II activity, the overall inhibition of the dark reactions of photosynthesis and serious damages in chloroplast ultra-structure (Wozny *et al.*,1990; Mallik *et al.*, 1992). The toxic heavy metals can affects plant metabolisim and developement at several levels. Increasing levels of Pb in the nutrient solution, were reported to reduced root growth and the concentration of other elements in the needles of *Piecea abies* seedlings (Godbold and Kettner,1991). Cadmium was also found to inhibit K uptake into Oat roots (Keek, 1978) and reduced growth and iron content in different plants (Wong *et al.*,1984; Smith *et al.*, 1985). However, no clear-cut effect can be found, if one compares lower and higher concentrations of the applied heavy metals treatment (Godbold and Kettner, 1991), different plant species (Khan and Khan,1983) and the concentration of other elements in the root and shoot (Wong *et al.*, 1984 and Fodor *et al.*, 1996).

Accumulation of heavy metals in agriculture soils has become a major concern for food crop production. Of these metals, Cadmium is recognised as one of the most hazardous elements, which is not essential for plant growth (Kabata-pendias and Pendias, 1992). Since Cadmium is known to be easily taken up by plants and translocated within the plant (John *et al.*, 1972; Turner, 1973), a clear understanding of its bioavailabililty to plants is essential for reducing Cadmium entry into the food chain with potentially harmful effects on human health. It is well known that Cadmium concentrations in plant tissues is directly related to the concentration of plant available cadmium in soil (Braumemer *et al.*, 1986; Mench *et al.,* 1989). However, a number of soil factors can alter cadmium uptake and accumulation in plants. Soil cadmium speciation (Soltanpour, 1991), Soil pH (Xian and shokohifad, 1989) and soil organic matter concentration (Street *et al.,* 1977) are factors most frequently observed to affect Cd availability to plants. It has also been reported that concentration of cadmium in plants varies among species and cultures (Page *et al.,* 1981; F/orijn and Van Beusichem, 1993); Cieslinski *et al.,* 1996).

The toxic effects of Cadmium on plants have been described (Boddi *et al.,* 1995) and characterised in many physiological processes (Marschner, 1983). Among these, the chlorosis of leaves (Bishoni *et al.,* 1993; Ferretti *et al.,* 1993 and Siedlecka and Bazynski,1993) and the inhibition of various reactions of photosynthesis (Hamp *et al.,* 1996; Baszynski *et al.,* 1980) have been described. Boddi *et al.,* (1995) raised the question, whether the Cd^{2+} inhibits directly the chlorophyll biosynthesis and several reactions of photosynthesis or if it interacts with other metabolic processes and acts indirectly. $Cadmium^{2+}$ might induce iron deficiency (Marschner, 1983) which later causes the above mentioned symptoms (Siedlecka and Baszynski,1993). A further possibility is that the $cadmium^{2+}$ stimulates decomposition processes in the plants, resulting in the decrease of the chlorophyll contents and changes of the photosynthetic apparatus. Specific inhibitory effects of the Cd^{2+} have been observed by Boddi *et al.,* (1995), on the synthesis of 5-aminolevulinic acid and on the Pchlide photoreduction into chlide. Boddi *et al.,* (1995) opined based on his observations that the reaction of Cd^{2+} was concluded to interact with essential thiol groups of enzymes involved in those reactions. The inactivation of the tennary complex of the Pchlide-NADPH oxidoreductase complex was indicated by a blue shift of the absorption-maximum of dark grown leaves, if shifted from 650nm to 630-635 nm *(Stobart et al.,* 1985).

The concern for the transfer of the Cadmium within the food chain is greater than for other potentially toxic elements. This is due to trace principal factors: high toxicity, long time of retention in the human body and high mobility in the environment. Cadmium may be the more toxic heavy metal for plants at concentrations lower than for other metals, inhibiting the synthesis of chlorophyll hi barley and beans, the growth of sugar beet plant and the photosynthetic activity of tomato. Chlorophyll and Carotenoid content are parameters that allow to study the incidence of different Cadmium treatments on the growth and development of tomato plants (Gil *et al.*,1995). The uptake of Cadmium by plant roots and its subsequent translocation to the stem and leaves is influenced by several factors, including plant genetics, Cadmium concentration in the soil solution, ease of transport from root to shoot solution, ease of transport from root to shoot, dry matter production and management practised (Jarvis *et al.*, 1976; Eriksson,1990; Singh,1990). Addition of ammonium and phosphatic fertilisers tend to increase plant Cd concentration (Choudhury *et al.*,1994). Phytochelatins (Pcs) are low molecular weight peptides enzymatically produced by the plants, under the action of a specific phytochelatin synthase, in response to excessive uptake of heavy metals.(Grill *et al.*, 1989,Scheller *et al.*, 1987). They are cystein rich peptides with general stricture (γ-Glu-cys)n Gly(n=2 to 11) capable of binding metal ions via thiolate coordination. This reaction leads to the formation of an intracellular complex between a metal ion and Pcs (Grill *et al.*, 1985 and Grill *et al.*, 1987). These inducible metal binding complexes act as an effective hevy metal detoxifying mechanism, because they sequester metal ions in a form, which limits damage to metabolic processes (Mehasg, 1994; Gekeler *et al.*, 1988). Among the metal ions capable of inducing phytochelatin synthesis in plant cells, cadmium represents the best activator of the enzyme (Grill *et al.*, 1985 and 1987).

The Cadmium ion (Cd^{2+}) is believed to exert no toxic effect. In human system the efficiency cadmium absorption by the intestines is only about 5-6 per cent, but once ingested, Cadmium is transported to parts of the body by the blood stream. Although almost all organs probably absorb some Cd, the high concentrations are invariably found in the liver and kidneys. The toxic effects of cadmium are presumably associated with the metal's affinity for organic ligands containing sulphur, nitrogen or other electronegetive functional groups. The metal appears to be particularly attracted to enzyme containing Zinc. The most serious effects of Cadmium poisoning usually involve damage to the kidney, particularly the renal tubes. These symptoms are associated with proteinurea, glucosuria and high alkaline phosphatase in the blood. Cadmium poisoning is also associated' with bone softening, fatal lung damage, high rise of blood pressure and other heart diseases. As such as per the US drinking water standard Cd levels should not exceed 10 ppb. Chronic toxicity of cadmium is evident at 30-60 ppb in fresh water fish, 5 to 50 ppb at marine fishes. In general, Cadmium toxicity be partially reduced by user of Zinc. In 1955, two Japanese physicians reported the occurrence of a mysterious disease in the Jintsu bay of Japan near the city of Toyama. The disease was characterised by severe pain in the back, joints and lower abdomen, development of a waddling or duck like gait, kidney lesions, proteinurea, glycourea and loss of calcium from bones leading in some cases to multiple bone fractures. They designated the disease *'Itai-itai'* disease. Initial efforts to identify the cause of the diseases were unsuccessful, but they tried to link the same diseases with some nutritional toxicity. However, in 1970s, it was possible to identify that the same disease was due to chronic cadmium toxicity (EPA, 1972, 1976). The technology for removing Cd from industrial wastewater or from flue dust is well-established. In waste water, dissolved cadmium can be precipitated with sodium sulphide, cemented by the addition of zinc separated out by ion exchange. If the cadmium is incorporated into particulates, the cadmium can be dissolved by the addition of acid and then separated by one of the above techniques or the solids can be settled out the cadmium removed with the sludge. Cadmium released to the atmosphere via smoke stacks is primarily in the form of fine particulate materials, which can be separated from the stack gases by wet scrubbers, fabric filters or electrostatic precipitators (OECD, 1975). Removal of cadmium by any of the above technique may lead to a solids disposal problem if Cd is not to be recovered or recycled.

Dumping of cadmium or cadmium containing compounds at sea or in fresh water is prohibited. Land disposal is the obvious solution but only in areas where the soil is neutral or basic so that the cadmium is not mobilised by percolating groundwater.

Cadmium occurs in nature in association with zinc minerals. Growing plants require Zn and they also absorb and concentrate cadmium with the same biochemical apparatus. The outbreak of Cd poisoning occurred in Japan in the form of *itai itai* "Ouch ouch" disease. Many people suffered from this disease in which their bones became fragile. At high levels, Cd causes kidney problems, anaemia and bone marrow disorders. The major portion of cadmium ingested into our body is trapped in the kidneys and eliminated. A small fraction is bound most effectively by the body proteins, metallothionein, present in the kidneys, while the rest is stored in the body and gradually accumulates with age. When excessive amounts of Cd^{2+} are ingested, it replaces Zn^{2+} at key enzymatic sites, causing metabolic disorders. Cadmium concentrations in polluted paddy fields in Japan are generally below toxic levels to plants and rice plants can grow and produce brown rice. The behaviour of Cadmium in rice plants has become a major problem and has been studied in detail (Obata *et al.,* 1996) to avoid the accumulation of Cd in brown rice. However, levels of Cd may exceed toxic levels in areas near mines and smelters and in water of rivers which run through heavily polluted regions.

The toxic effect of Cd on plants remain to be clarified in order to remove toxic metals from polluted soil using accumulator plants, cover polluted ares with Cadmium tolerant plant, or to apply other measures. Obata *et al.,* (1996) initiated studies on the intracellular mechanism of Cadmium tolerance and found that Cd-tolerant plants produced higher levels of SH compounds and accumulated a considerable amount of Cadmium in root celols, when treated with Cadmium. It was assumed that Cadmium incorporated into the cells was detoxified by SH compounds (γEC) nG produced in proportion to the degree of Cd incorporation (Obata and Umebayashi, 1993). However, Schultz and Hutchinson (1988) indicated that the induction of thiol-rich protein by copper was not a major tolerance mechanism. De Knecht *et al.,* (1992) have also reported that the difference in the Cadmium tolerance mechanism in Silence vulgaris was not due to differences in the production of -SH compounds. The Cadmium tolerance mechanisms are complicated and several mechanisms may be involved in the cadmium tolerance of plants. Some of the toxic effects of $Cadmium^{2+}$ have been interpreted as cadmium effects on the permeability of membranes (De Fillippis, 1979; Strickland *et al.,* 1979). The plasma membrane is the first structure to encounter cadmium that penetrates into the cell. Lindberg and Wingstrand (1985) and Ross *et al.,* (1992) observed that plasma membrane ATPase activities in sugar beet and rice plant were inhibited by Cadmium. Cadmium is known to increase the permeability of cell membranes and thus cause metabolic cellular impairment (Grose *et al.,* 1987). It has also been recognised as a carcinogen through epidemiological studies. Cadmium is an important xenobiotic in aquatic ecosystems. As a non-degradable cumulative pollutant, Cadmium can alter aquatic trophic levels, for centuries and freshwater fish are particularly vulnerable to Cadmium exposure (Ricard *et al.,* 1998).

The purpose of acute toxicity test is to assess various abnormalities caused due to administration of a chemical to animals on occasion or other and to determine the order of lethality of the chemical. Many of the schemes are available at present to test for adverse effects that may result when chemicals enter into environment. Considerable efforts have been directed towards the establishment of short-cut procedure. In aquatic toxicology, acute lethal toxicity tests with fish or invertebrates are usually intended to assess the numerical value of toxicity, to compare potencies of toxicants, to assess the effect of environmental variables on toxicity. Besides, statistical analysis of toxicity is essentially a tool in all these studies. The rapid increase in contamination of aquatic environments with pesticides and toxicants in recent years has resulted in an escalation of scientific interests in the biological effects of heavy metals and pesticides in the environment; any deleterious effect of the heavy metal or any other toxicant on fish is likely to be reflected on the entire eco-system. Matida *et al.,* (1971) studied the effect of low concentration of methyl mercuric chloride on rainbow trouts, which showed poisoning symptoms. Macleod and Passah (1973) reported effects of temperature on mercury accumulation, toxicity and metabolic rate in rainbow trout *(Salmo garidneri).* Fathead minnows when exposed to low concentrations of methyl mercuric chloride (Olson *et al.,* 1975) showed no effect on survival at concentrations causing an acceptable residue. McKim *et al.,* (1976) reported long term effects of methyl mercuric chloride (MMC) on three generations of brook trot, *Salvelinus fontinalis.* Hannerz (1968) reported accumulation and distribution of several forms of mercury in aquatic animals. Amminikuty and Rege (1977) mentioned few toxicological effects of Agallol's (Methoxy ethyl mercuric chloride, (MEMC) on widow tetra *(Gymno-corymbus ternetzi).* Das and Misra (1982) studied the toxicity of MEMC (methoxy ethyl mercuric chloride) on *Cyprinus carpio* L. Panigrahi and Misra (1980) found severe poisoning symptoms in *Tilapia mossambica* exposed to inorganic mercury. The fish-pesticide Research Laboratory of the US Bureau of Sport Fisheries and Wildlife tested a large number of pesticide chemicals mainly on two species of fresh water fish, rainbow trout *(Salmo gairdneri)* and blue gills *(Lepomina macrochirus),* Huges and Davies (1963) tested the toxicities of several formulations of the phenoxy herbicides, such as, 2, 4-D and 2,4, 5-T to blue gills. Bond *et al.,* (1960) made a critical study on species like Chinook *(Oncorhynchus tshawytscha),* Coho salmon *(G. kisutch)* and large mouth bass *(Micropterus salmoides).* The toxicity of some combinations of insecticides to mosquito fish was studied by Ferguson and Bingham (1966) using DDT, endrin, toxaphene and methyl parathion. Richard (1966) studied the toxicity of Thiodan in several fish species and aquatic invertebrates. Doudoroff *et al.,* (1953) and Mathur (1969) demonstrated that insecticides such as aldrin, toxaphene, lindane, dieldrin, BHC and DDT were extremely toxic to fish. Amend (1974) made a comparative toxicity study of two iodophors on rainbow trout eggs. Caldwell *et al.,* (1978) reported the toxicity of the fungicides, "Captan" to the dungeneas crab, *Cancer magister.* Relative toxicity of Dichlorovos (DDVP) was studied by Rath and Misra (1979 a,b) on *Tilapia mossambica,* Peters belonging to 3 different age groups, Roald (1967) reported the acute toxicity of Lignosulphonates to rainbow trout. Gouda *et al.,* (1981) tested the toxicity of dimecron, sevin and lindax to *Anabas scandens* and *Heteropneustees fossilis.* Choudhury (1975) reported effects of organochloro insecticides (aldrin, dieldrin and endrin) on fish and other pond organisms. David *et al.,* (1976)studied the effects of heavy metals on juvenile bay scallop, *Agropectan irradians,* Ray and David (1962) studied the fish mortality caused by precipitation of ferric ion in the river Daha at Siwan (North Bihar). Reports on temperature induced changes in acute toxicity of zinc to Atlantic Salomon *(Salmo salar)* by Hodson and Spraque (1975), and Copper toxicity to embryos and larvae of 8 species of fresh water fish by McKim *et al.,* (1978) were available. Cadmium toxicry of gold fish, *Carassius auratus* by McCarty *et al.,* (1978), lethal and sub-lethal effects of Binary mixtures of cyanide and hexavalent chromium, zinc or ammonia to the fathead minnow *(Pimephales promelas)* and rainbow trout *(Salmo gairdneri)* by Broderius *et al.,* (1979); all these add to the knowledge of heavy metal toxicity on fishes. Hartung (1973) pointed out that much information was lacking in the due course of such changes during cadmium and other heavy metal toxicity assays. McCarty *et al.,* (1978) noted the accurate assessment of water quality criteria and data pertaining to heavy metal toxicity which are derived from static bioassay experiments is of much practical concern. McCarty *et al.,* (1978) studied the toxicity of cadmium to gold fish, *Carassius auratus* in hard and soft water. Panigrahi (1984) reported the toxicity of a mercury based pesticide (MEMC, Emisan - 6 Brand name) on a fresh water fish *Anabas scandens,* cuv. and val. Although adequate literature on acute toxicity of different pesticides and mercury based chemicals, pesticides and mercury contained effluents and solid wastes to fish is available, no adequate information is available regarding this metal, cadmium and its acute toxicity.

Long term sub-lethal effects resulting from chronic exposure of organisms to lower levels of toxicants probably have the most important on the aquatic organisms. Heavy metals and pesticides in the aquatic environment was recognised a century back as a serious problem. A good number of workers dealt this problem to find out the impact of heavy metals and pesticides on aquatic flora and fauna. Panigrahi (1980) reported the behavioural changes observed in inorganic mercury exposed fresh water fishes. Panigrahy (1984) reported that fishes showed a change in behaviour when exposed to Emisan-6 (MEMC). Macleod and Passah (1973) reported the behavioural changes induced by mercury in Rainbow trout. Larson and Lewander (1973) reported metabolic effects of starvation in the eel, *Anguilla anguilla* L., Gibilin and Massaro (1973) observed behavioural changes induced by methyl mercury in Rainbow trout. Stone *et al.,* (1977) reported changes in body weight, kidney and liver weight in Japanese Quail induced by lead. Bhatia *et al.,* (1973) reported behavioural changes induced by dieldrin in albino rats.

Aim of the Study

Keeping in view, the availability of heavy metal cadmium in the environment and discharge of industrial wastes of some industry containing cadmium compounds, entry of these chemicals into water bodies of the locality along with the irrigated waters or run-off waters in the rainy season; availability of cadmium in the air and consequent precipitation and entry of rain run-off water into water bodies; and their possible effect on the fresh water fishes surviving in the water bodies, this project was masterminded to evaluate the toxicological effects of Cadmium chloride on the toxicity, effect on the physiological parameters, biochemical metabolism and some blood parameters of the fish and its effect on few important enzymes of a freshwater fish, *Tilapia mossmbica,* Peters *(Oreochromis mossambicus,* Peters).

2

MATERIALS AND METHODS

Selection of the Toxicant: Cadmium Chloride [Cd Cl_2]

CADMIUM METAL

Physical Properties

Cadmium is a silvery-white metal with a bluish tinge; very thin foils appear blue-voilet in transmission. Selected physical properties are given in Table 2.1. The room temperature (γ) form of cadmium has a distorted hexagonal close neighbours in the close packed layer, and by three more remote atoms in each adjacent layer; the Cd-Cd distance are 298 and 329 pm, respectively. The vapour phase just above the boiling point is predominantly monatomic, but some 1 per cent exits as very weakly bonded diatomic species, Cd, [D(Cd-Cd)=12kJ mol^{-1}].

Table 2.1 Physical properties of cadmium metal*

Atomic weight	112.40
Mp, °C	320.9°
ΔH(fusion), kJ mol^{-1}	6.41
ΔS (fusion), J K^{-1} mol^{-1}	10.3
Bp,°C	767°
ΔH(vap.), kJ mol^{-1}	99.6
ΔS(Vap), J K^{-1} mol^{-1}	95.9
Vapour pressure	1 mm/394°; 10mm/484°; 100 mm/611^0
Density, g cm^{-1}	8.64/25°
Resistivity, μΩ cm	7.3/20°
Specific heat, J $kg^{-1}K^{-1}$	233/25°
Thermal conductivity,W m^{-1} K^{-1}	103/25°
Electronic ground states Cd $5s^2(^1S_0)$	$Cd^+5s^1(S_{1/2})$; Cd^{2+} $4d^{10}(S_0)$
Electronic transitions (Cd)	$5s(^1S_0)$ $Sp(^1P_1)$ 228.8
and corresponding wave length	$5s(^1S_0)$—$Sp(^1P_1)$ 326.1
μm	$5_P(^1Pi)$—$5d(^1D_2)$ 643.8

* Data from Aylett (1971)and Smithells (1976)

Chemical Properties

Cadmium reacts only slightly with dry air, while in moist condition a greyish-white film is produced which largely protects the metals from further attack. Oxidation by steam is quite rapid, and the powdered metal burns in air with a red flame. Dilute mineral acids dissolve the metals with evolution of hydrogen; concentrated sulphuric acid yields, SO_2, while moderately strong nitric acid and cadmium produce oxides of nitrogen and ammonia. Cadmium dissolves in strong aqueous NH_4NO_3 solution to give ammonium and cadmium nitrites. At room temperature, cadmium does not react with chlorine, bromine, iodine, sulphur or selenium, although the appropriate binary compounds are formed on heating. Unlike zinc, cadmium is unaffected by alkalies.

Alloys of Cadmium

Examination of phase diagrams and collected data (Smithells, 1976; Hanse, 1968; Elliott, 1965; Shunk, 1969; Hultgren, 1973; Amer. Soc. Metals, 1973) shows that cadmium is reluctant to form solid solutions; its mutual solubilities with Al, Be, Bi, Cr, Fe., Mn, Pb, Sn and Zn are low or zero. Eutecties'are formed with Bi(60 wt per cent Bi, 146°), Pb (82.6 wt per cent Pb, 248°), and Zn*17.4 atom per cent Zn, 226°), while the coinage metals yields a range of well defined compounds (*e.g.*, Cu_2Cd, AgCd and Au_3Cd), and cobalt and nickel from compounds M_5Cd_2 with the γ-brass structure. Large metal atoms form high co-ordination number phases, such as $CsCd_{13}$, and $LaCd_{11}$, in which the first named metal is surrounded by 24 and 22 cadmium atoms, respectively. A few alloy systems have commercial significance. For instance , large number of three-, four- and five-component systems are used as readily fusible alloys (Hewitt, 1977); a typical example is Wood's Metal (Bi, 50 per cent; pb, 25 per cent, Cd, 12.5; Sn, 12.5 per cent) which has melting range (solids-liquids) of 70-72°. This is used for heating baths and the sprinkler systems. A rather different application involve the addition of about 1 per cent of cadmium to copper: this has the effect of greatly improving the mechanical properties (*e.g.*, harder, more resistant to wear), while the electrical conductivity falls by only about 10 per cent.

METHODOLOGY

Maintenance of Fishes in Laboratory Aquarium

Oreochromis mossambicus [{Tilapia mossambica, Peters} *(Sarotherodon mossambica*, Peters)] of medium size (12-16 g) were collected from the local nursery of the Fisheries Department of Berhampur (Gânjam), Orissa. The fish were allowed to grow in the laboratory reservoirs for acclimatisation at least for 30 days before starting the experiment. The fish were maintained in aquarium of 60 × 60 cm. containing 50 litres of water. Chlorine-free tap water was used in both control and experimental aquarium. The water was changed daily. Air was bubbled through water of the aquarium to maintain the dissolved oxygen at 85 ± 5 per cent air saturation value. The physico-chemical quality of the water of both control and exposed aquarium were measured during the experimental period. (A.P.H.A., 1974) and maintained at the same level. Living earthworms from garden showing no contamination by any toxicant were collected and fed daily to both control and exposed fish initially and slowly the diet was changed to toxicant-free chopped goat liver and then to small slices of boiled eggs during holding and throughout the experimental exposure and recovery period. After acclimatisation, the fish were washed thoroughly with 1 per cent dilute Potassium permanganate ($KMnO_4$) solution, so as to prevent any infection.

Table 2.2 Water Quality of Both Control and Experimental Aquaria

Parameters	*Control*	*Exposed*
pH	7.1 ± 0.3	7.3 ± 0.4
Temperature	26 ± 2°C	26 ± 2°C
Illumination	2200 ± 200 lux	2200 ± 200 lux
Total hardness	65.4 ± 3.4 mg 1^{-1}	66.2 ± 2.2 mg 1^{-1}
Specific conductivity	3.58 × 100 μmho	3.59 × 100 μmho
Transparency	0.025 - 0.030	0.028 - 0.035

(Transparency was measured in terms of optical density at 550 nm taking double glass distilled water as standard).

The test solution of the experimental aquarium was changed daily so as to maintain the constancy of the heavy metal concentration. The experimental aquarium was washed thoroughly to remove any amount of heavy metal adhered to glass surface. Exposed fish were observed daily to record any change in behaviour, when compared to control fish. Test fish, *Tilapia* were collected, acclimatised in the laboratory as described above. A graded series of concentrations of Cadmium chloride ranging from 0.5 mg 1^{-1} to 15 mg 1^{-1} were prepared. 10 healthy fish were exposed to each concentration in 10 litre glass jars. The experiments were conducted in chlorine-free tap water at a room temperature of 26 ± 2°C.

The mortality rate of test-fish was studied following the method described by Shaw (1987). Observation on the toxicity of Cadmium chloride was made at 24, 48, 72, 96 hours and 28 days after the experimental animals were first exposed. Individuals showing no respiratory movements, no opercular movements and no response to a tactile stimulus were recorded as dead, and were immediately removed. The test fish exposed to lower range of the cadmium chloride was exposed for a period of five weeks to find out the maximum allowable concentration (MAC), where no mortality was noticed and this was expressed as mg 1^{-1}. Different values such as LC_{10}, LC_{50}, LC_{100}-were deduced from graphical interpolation (Finney, 1977). During the acute toxicity studies fish were observed for behavioural changes influenced by Cadmium chloride. Experimental fishes were sacrificed; brain, liver, kidney and gill were dissected out carefully and washed thoroughly with distilled water. The sacrificed fish were weighed. Brain, liver, kidney and gill were separated and weighed carefully in a single pan electric balance and the different somatic indices were calculated. The individual changes in body weight of both control and experimental fish were noted at 7-day interval and the per cent change in body weight was computed.

RESPIRATION

(*a*) Whole Animal Oxygen Uptake

The whole animal oxygen uptake rates of the test and control fish were measured using five wide mouth 2 liters capacity flasks. Each flask containing the test solution and a test fish was hermetically sealed. A reference flask was kept without fish to check any change of oxygen concentration during the experiments, due to the presence of microorganisms. Any change of oxygen concentration, caused by the microorganism was computed with the final data. After 30 minutes, the dissolved oxygen of all experimental flasks were determined according to the modified Winkler's method (Ashby, 1973 and Panigrahi, 1980). The same procedure was repeated for the control fish. The reduction of the dissolved oxygen concentration equals the amount of dissolved oxygen consumed by the fish in 30 minutes. The oxygen uptake was expressed as mg O_2 g^{-1} h^{-1} (Panigrahi, 1980).

The ventilation rate of both exposed and control *Tilapia* fish were counted by the number of opercular movements (strokes/ minute) per minute.

(*b*) Tissue Slice Respiration

Tissue and Medium: Both exposed and control fish were sacrificed. The brain, liver, muscle and gills were removed, washed in cold distilled water and kept in ice cold 0.25M sucrose solution. Tissue slices were prepared approximately 0.35 mm thick using a razor blade and recessed guide (McIlwain, 1951) and floated into Kreb's ringer phosphate medium pre-gassed with oxygen. One or two slices were picked up on a bent wire, drained of excess fluid and the surface was soaked with the help of Whatman filter paper and weighed in a single pan balance (Dhona, India) and transferred immediately to the medium. The weighed slices were subsequently transferred to the incubation medium in the Warburg flask.

The main compartment of the Warburg flask contained 3 ml incubation medium of the following composition: NaCl 124 mm; KCl-4, 8 m; $CaCl_2$-2.6 mm $MgSO_4$-1.2 mm; Na_2-HPO_4 16.0 mm; pH 7.4; and D-glucose, 10 mm. The pH of the medium was adjusted to pH 7.4 with NaOH and the medium was pre-gassed with oxygen. The center well of the flask had a filter paper wick and contained 0.2 ml of 0.3N-NaOH to trap the evolved CO_2. The oxygen uptake was considered equivalent to carbon dioxide evolved during respiration. The carbon dioxide after absorption created a vacuum in the flask. To fill up the vacuum the fluid present in the manometer rises (Panigrahi, 1980).

Both control and experimental tissues were subjected to the same effects of swelling, ionic shifts and other changes occurring during preparation of slices. These slices under control conditions were incubated in medium free of cadmium compound *in vitro* studies.

Incubation and Respiration: Incubation took place in a Warburg bath. Temperature was maintained at 37°C. The reading of oxygen uptake and the preparation of tissue extract involved at 15 minutes equilibration of the tissue in Warburg flask containing the incubation medium as mentioned above. Manometric reading of oxygen uptake or carbon dioxide evolution and preparation of tissue extracts were carried out by the methods reported by Patel *et al.*, (1973) and Fox *et al.*, (1975).

Analysis and Calculations: All calculations were made on the basis of wet weight of slices. Under our experimental conditions, dry weight of the tissues were calculated and presented below:

Brain tissue — 11.41 per cent of the wet weight

Liver tissue — 12.78 per cent of the wet weight

Muscle tissue — 16.24 per cent of the wet weight

(*c*) Ventillation Rate

Number of opercular movement per minute was counted in both control and Cadmium chloride exposed fishes. The fishes were not disturbed or excited. They were allowed to remain undisturbed. Opercular movements were counted from a safe distance.

ENZYME ANALYSIS

The fishes were sacrificed at 7 days interval (both control and exposed). Brain, liver and muscle tissues were removed, kept in watch glasses, and weighed separately. The tissues were kept in ice-cold 0.25M sucrose.

Method

100 mg of the wet tissue was taken and homogenised with 2.5 ml of 0.25M sucrose in a micro-tissue homogeniser. The homogenate was then centrifuged in a refrigerated centrifuge

at 15,000 rpm for 15 minutes. The supernatant was taken for enzyme extraction.

0.1 ml of the supernatant was added to two reaction vessels each (control and experimental) containing 5 ml Tris buffer (7.4 pH), 1 ml of 5 mm $MgCl_2$, 1 ml of 0.01, M ATP was added to the experimental vessel. Both the reaction vessels were incubated at 37°C for 60 minutes. After one hour, reaction was stopped by adding 7 ml of 10 per cent TCA to each vessel. Samples were then transferred for 15 minutes to a refrigerator at 5°C to allow complete precipitation of the homogenate proteins. The precipitate was then sedimented in a Remi (T30) centrifuge at 8000 rpm for 5 minutes.

Activity of ATPase was determined in fish tissues by measuring the amount of inorganic phosphate produced when adenosine triphosphate was converted to adenosine di-phoshphate. Total ATPase activity was measured with Na^+, K^+, Mg^{++}, in the reaction mixture.

Inorganic phosphate produced as a result of the cleavage of ATP to ADP was measured by the method of Fiske and Subbarao (1925) as modified by Martinek (1970). Colour development proceeded at room temperature for 30 minutes. Protein was determined by the procedure developed by Lowry *et al.*, (1951), using a spectrophotometer. The ATPase activity was expressed as m moles of inorganic phosphate liberated mg^{-1} of protein, h^{-1}.

ION ANALYSIS

Fishes were sacrificed and dissected after 28 days of exposure. Brain, liver, muscle and gill tissues of each fish were taken out, properly washed and weighed. Contamination of these tissues was avoided during autopsy. Soaking in Whatman filter paper, the tissues were then transferred to Kjeldahl flasks continuing Nitric acid (BDH, Analar grade) and Sulfuric acid (HNO_3, H_2SO_4 = 1:1) and digested to a nearly colourless solution. The total volume of the solution was diluted to an appropriate volume with double distilled water. The amount Na^+, K^+, Ca^{++}, were determined by a flame photometer taking NaCl, KCl and $CaCl_2$ as standards. For magnesium determinations, the procedure followed by Orange and Rhei

(1970) was adopted. The concentration of Mg^{++} was calculated from the standard curve.

Cadmium Residual Analysis

The brain, liver and muscle of both control and exposed fish was dissected, washed and separated carefully and digested with acid digestion [Nitric acid : Perchloric acid : Sulphuric acid at 10:4:1 ratio] mixture in a digestive chamber. The digested samples were sealed carefully in glass containers and analysed for Cadmium, in an Atomic Absorption Spectrophotometer (Perkin-Elmer—3110) at CIFA, Bhubaneswar. The amount of cadmium present was computed from the Standard curve and expressed in mg g^{-1} dry weight of the tissues.

Biochemical Analysis

The test fishes were sacrificed at 7 days interval (both control and exposed). Brain, liver and muscle tissues were removed carefully and kept in watch glasses and weighed separately. Care was taken to avoid contamination during autopsy. The tissues were taken and processed, for studying the change in DNA, RNA, protein and free amino acid content in brain, liver, and muscle of fishes exposed to Cadmium chloride at sub-lethal concentration.

Methods: 100 mg of the tissue was taken and homogenised with 5 ml of 70 per cent alcohol in micro tissue homogeniser and then centrifuged. One ml of supernatant was taken and 2 ml of Ninhydrin was added and heated for 10 minutes on a hot water bath. The volume was made upto 6 ml and optical density was measured. The free amino acid content was calculated from a standard graph. The standard curve was drawn taking glycine (Emerk) as standard.

The residue after centrifugation, was then suspended in ·5 ml of Ethanol and Ether (1:1) for 10 minutes and centrifuged. The supernatant was discarded. The residue was taken and heated on a boiling water bath for 30 minutes with 5 ml of 0.5N Perchloric acid. The residue was rejected. The supernatant was taken for DNA and RNA analysis. One ml of the supernatant was taken with 2 ml of double distilled waster land 5 ml of diphenylamine was added and heated in a boiling water bath for 30 minutes and cooled. The optical density was measured at 595 nm in a Spectrophotometer (Burton, 1956). The DNA content was calculated from the standard graph plotted, taking DNA (Sigma) as the standard. Two ml of the supernatant was taken and 3 ml of the Orcinol reagent was added and heated at 80°C for 30 minutes and cooled. The optical density was measured in a spectrophotometer. The amount of RNA was calculated from the standard graph, where RNA (Sigma) was take as standard (Volkin and Cohn, 1954). The concentration of DNA and RNA in tissues were expressed as mg g^{-1} of wet tissue.

The protein content in the homogenate was estimated following the method of Lowry *et al.*, (1951). The standard graph was plotted taking BSA (Sigma) as standard.

HAEMATOLOGY

Collection of Blood

Since unclotted blood samples are required for haematological studies and the anticoagulant should have no influence on the red cells or other cells, heparin, one of the most powerful anticoagulant was used for the collection of blood (Hurkat and Mathur, 1976). Blood was collected from each fish by cardiac puncture. The sample was transferred gently into a glass vial containing the anticoagulant and frozen until further use. This was used in all experiments. The same procedure was followed at each procedure and recovery period.

Blood was directly collected from the ventral aorta with a heparinised syringe and a drop of blood was spread on a clean slide following the usual procedure described by Dacie and Lewis (1970). The blood smear was prepared, stained with Leishman's stain, washed thoroughly with distilled water and examined under a good trinocular microphotographic attachment microscope (Olympus).

Haemoglobin Percentage (Hb.%)

The haemoglobin percentage was measured with the aid of a Spectrophotometer by acid hematin method (Sievered, 1964).

RBC Count

Red blood corpuscle (RBC) counts were made by drawilng blood into a standard RBC diluting pipette diluting 1:200 with Haem's fluid and the counting was conducted by the aid of a Neubauer's haemacytometer and a research microscope. The results were expressed as number of cells × 10^6 mm^{-3}. (Balxhall and Daisley (1972, 1973)).

Haematocrit Percentage (Hct.%)

The haemotocrit percentage or packed cell volume of blood was determined following Wintrobe's method (Dacie and Lewis, 1970). Heparinised blood from the glass vial was filled in Micro Wintrobe's tube with the help of a glass capillary pipette. After the filing was over, the Micro-Wintrobe's tube was centrifuged (T-8 Remi) at 3000 rpm for 30 minutes. The height of the solution in the Micro-Wintrobe's tube was recorded and expressed on the percentage of total volume of blood.

Estimation of Oxygen Carrying Capacity of Blood

Oxygen carrying capacity of blood (ml/100 ml blood) was determined by multiplying the haemoglobin concentration with that of oxygen combining power of 1.25 ml of oxygen per gram of haemoglobin (Johanson, 1970). Hb per cent, RBC count, Haematicrit per cent and oxygen carrying capacity were estimated after exposure periods of 7,14,21 and 28 days. Then the exposed fish were transferred to toxicant free clean tap water and the recovery of the above parameters were studied after 14 and 28 days.

AChE Activity

Both the control and exposed fishes were sacrificed at a 7 day interval. Brain, liver and muscle tissues were dissected out carefully and weighed seaprately. The tissues were homogenised and centrifuged at 10,000 rpm at less than 8°C. The supernatants were analysed for acetylcholinesterase activity using Hestrins (1949) technique as modified by Sudderuddin (1973). The substrate volume per assay was 2.9 ml and the volume of $FeCl_3$ was reduced to 0.1 ml. Activity of AChE was dtermined in fish tissues by measuring the amount of Acetylcholine chloride (Koch-light) hydrolysed in 30 mts. The AChE activity was expressed as μmoles of Ach. Hydrolysed mg^{-1} of tissue hr^{-1}. To determine the rate of recovery of acetylcholinesterase activity, a number of fishes were kept in cadmium free tap water. The rate of recovery was measured at 14 d interval for 28 days.

STATISTICAL ANALYSIS

All data were analysed using students 't ' test. Independent data represent mean ± standard deviation. Correlation coefficient (r) analysis was carried out between days of exposure *vs* exposure period. Analysis of variance ratio test conducted for all the data of all the tables to find out significance levels (Misra and Misra, 1984).

3

RESULTS

The obtained data showed that the MAC value of Cadmium chloride was found to be 1.05 $mg.1^{-1}$ for 30 days and to be on the safe side 1.00 $mg.1^{-1}$ was considered for 28 days of the exposure and 28 days of recovery (Table 3.1) for sub-lethal physiological studies. The observations showed LC_{10} values at 24 hours to be 3.2 $mg.1^{-1}$ and at 48 hours to be 3.0 $mg.1^{-1}$. The results showed that the LC_{50} values for test fish were 7.5 $mg.1^{-1}$ at 24 hours, 7.2 $mg.1^{-1}$ at 48 hours. The result also indicated that the LC_{100} values for test fish were 10.5 $mg.1^{-1}$at 24 hours and 9.8 $mg.1^{-1}$ at 48 hours. The LC_{10}, LC_{50}, LC_{90} and LC_{100}, values after 28 days were recorded to be 1.2, 1.85, 2.75 and 3.5 $mg.1^{-1}$ of Cadmium chloride. No mortality was observed in the control set.

All the exposed fish appeared lethargic after exposure to Cadmium chloride. The major clinical symptoms such as inappetance and ataxia appeared after 2 to 3 days exposure. At higher concentration of the Cadmium chloride, the exposed fish showed erratic movements. The other signs of toxicity such as loss of equilibrium, gradual onset of inactivity, erratic swimming with irregular collision to the inner glass walls of the aquarium were observed. Restlessness and least feeding was observed. The exposed fish shed fins and disintegration of dermal mucous layer was marked. Ulceration of the gill lamellae was observed in the exposed fish. Some symptoms were similar to the preliminary symptoms of Epizootic Ulcerative Syndrome (BUS) and was marked in the exposed fish Infection of eyes. Bleeding of gills were not marked as observed by Harichandan (2002). Exophthalmia and involusions of test fish were not observed when compared to results obtained by Panigrahi and Misra (1978) Panigrahi (1980) and

Table 3.1 Showing different lethal concentration values at different exposure periods

Lethal concentration value	*Cadmium chloride toxicant concentration (mg.l^{-1})*	
	24 h	*48 h*
LC_{10}	3.2 mg.l^{-1}	3.0 mg.l^{-1}
LC_{50}	7.5 mg.l^{-1}	7.2 mg.l^{-1}
LC_{100}	10.5 mg.l^{-1}	9.8 mg.l^{-1}
Exposure period 30 days		
MAC		1.05 mg.l^{-1}
Used concentration		1.00 mg.l^{-1}
LC Value after 30 days of exposure		
LC_{10}		1.20 mg.l^{-1}
LC_{50}		1.85 mg.l^{-1}
LC_{90}		2.75 mg.l^{-1}
LC_{100}		3.50 mg.l^{-1}

Panigrahy (1984). Exposed fish could not regain their pre-exposed activity after transferring the exposed fish to toxicant free water in recovery studies. In the present investigation, peculiar symptoms were marked. The cadmium chloride exposed fish showed initial symptoms like mercury poisoning but later on the exposed fish became overexcited and periodic outbursts in irratic swimming was noted, ultimately the excited fish died of suffocation. When the excited fishes were heavily oxygenated and kept in undisturbed water survived. The movement of the fish slowed down and became sluggish. The exposed fishes showed high level of sensitivity. Under the influence of any stimulus, the sluggish fish instantly started vigorous movement and many a times colloided with the inner glass of the aquarium frequently and showed circular movements. . After 1/2 minutes, the movements slowed down and the fish became senseless, ventillation rate almost stops. If heavily oxygenated, the fish survives otherwise the exposed fish dies. During this later period of slowing down the movement, the colour of the fish becomes black due to dispersion of melanin pigment. This black colour disappears, when the exposed system was heavily oxygenated. At times, the shocked fish automatically returns to normalcy, and the black colour disappears. This type of self recovery was only in 20 per cent of the cases. Heavy oxygenation can help to around 60 per cent suffered fishes to survive but the rest of the excited fish die instantly and never recover from the shock. In cadmium exposed fish lesions develope on the fins and later the skin erodes and the bones were clearly visible and shedding of fins were noted in few exposed fish towards later period of exposure or at higher exposure period. This seems to be an important symptom in cadmium exposure, which was not marked in mercury or pesticide exposure.

Body weight of the control fish increased by 1088 per cent after 28 days and by 18.6 per cent after 56 days of exposure. Whereas, the body weight of the exposed fish gradually decreased during the exposure period and a maximum of 5.52 per cent decrease was observed after 28 days of exposure (Fig. 3.1 and 3.2 and Table 3.2), when compared to control fish. Control fish did not show any signs of toxicity. Partial insignificant recovery by 1.04 per cent and 1.84 per cent on 14 and 28 days of recovery in body weight was marked, when the exposed fish was transferred to toxicant free normal medium. No further depletion over the 28 days exposure value was marked, on 28th day of recovery (Table 3.2 and Figs. 3.1 to 3.5). Recovery studies clearly indicated that transferring the exposed fish to normal water medium has no direct effect. Rather higher depletion in body weight was marked (Figs. 3.3 to 3.5). The two-way analysis of variance ratio test conducted on the basis of Table-3.2 data, related to body weight of the control and exposed fish, indicated the existence of non-significant difference between rows, and columns (Table-I). The body weight showed a linear increase showing the existence of significant positive correlation ($r = 0.987$, $P \leq 0.05$) with the exposure period in the control set. Whereas, a significant negative correlation was observed between the exposure period and body weight. With the increase in exposure period, the body weight significantly ($r = -0.991$, $p \leq 0.01$) declined (Table-3.2, Figs. 3.3 to 3.5).

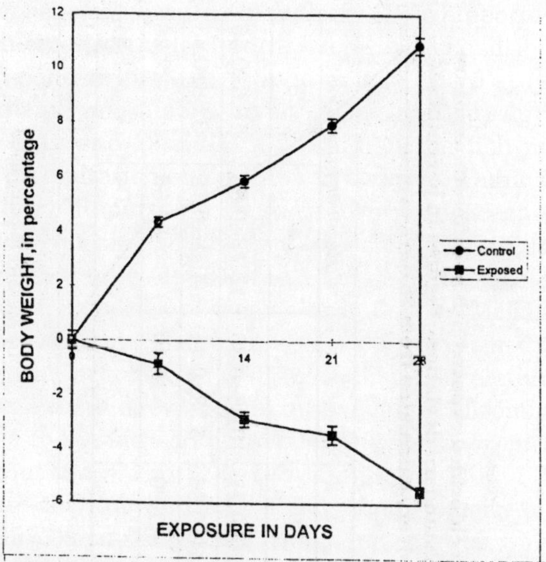

Fig. 3.1 Showing changes in body weight of the control and Cadmium chloride exposed fish at different days of exposure

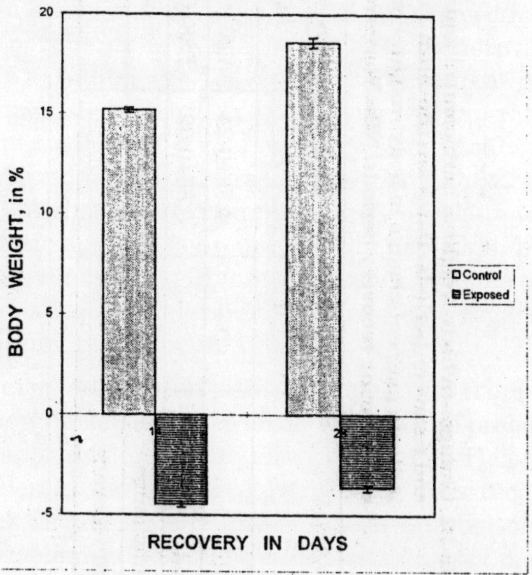

Fig. 3.2 Showing change in body weight of the control and Cadmium chloride exposed fish at different days of recovery

Table 3.2 Changes in body weight of both control and Cadmium chlorided exposed fish at different exposure and recovery periods. Dates are the mean 5 samples ± standard deviation. Figures in parentheses indicate per cent change in body weight. Per cent recovery calculated from 28 days exposure value during recovery periods. NR= No recovery.

Status of Fish	*Exposure in days*					*Recovery in days*	
	0	*7*	*14*	*21*	*28*	*14*	*28*
Control	—	4.35±0.24	5.86±0.19	7.95±0.21	10.88±0.35	15.18±0.85	18.6±0.36
Exposed	—	0.85+0.09	-2.88+0.42	-3.44±0.36	-5.52±0.44	-4.48±0.72	-3.68±0.55
Per cent change	—	-5.20	-8.74	-11.00	-16.40	-19.66	-22.28
Per cent recovery						1.04	1.84

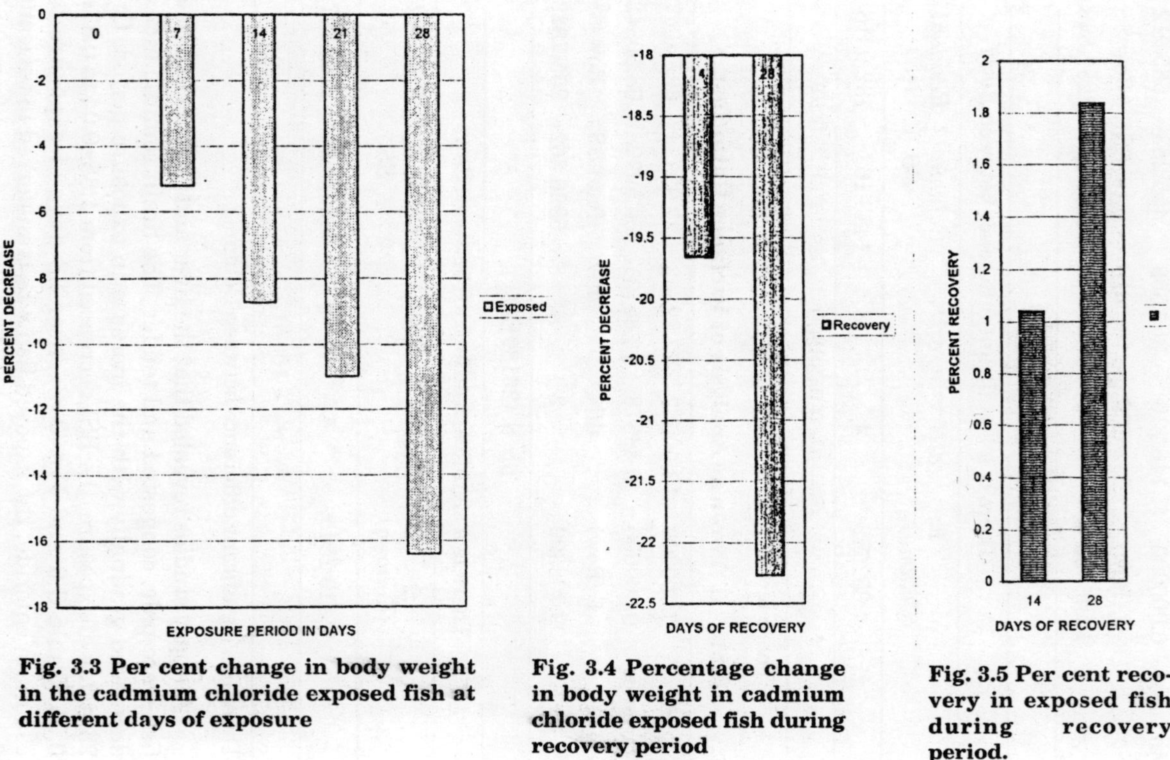

Fig. 3.3 Per cent change in body weight in the cadmium chloride exposed fish at different days of exposure

Fig. 3.4 Percentage change in body weight in cadmium chloride exposed fish during recovery period

Fig. 3.5 Per cent recovery in exposed fish during recovery period.

Table I Two-way Analysis of Variance Ratio Test

Mean	0.000000	-15.93333	-17.71667	-25.87334	-28.28000
Variance	0.000000	146.736	350.359	455.283	555.012
	F (Row)	dfN	dfD	Total SS	Row SS
	12.45326	2	8	4499.942	2281.848

p = 3.49325E-03

There is a significant difference between Rows

F (Column)	*dfN*	*dfD*	*Column SS*	*Residual*
4.052662	4	8	1485.162	732.9316

p = 0.0438509

There is not a significant difference between Columns

Table - II Two-way Analysis of Variance Ratio Test

Mean	0.000000	-13.00667	-22.22333	-27.93334	-62.74667
Variance	0.000000	40.40578	13.86731	60.59998	68.60842
	F (Row)	dfN	dfD	Total SS	Row SS
	9.202399	2	8	6996.362	255.7822

p = 8.426189E-03

There is a significant difference between Rows

F (Column)	*dfN*	*dfD*	*Column SS*	*Residual*
119.2545	4	8	6629.399	111.1807

p = < 10(-6)

There is a significant difference between Columns

Autopsy studies revealed that the liver and brain of exposed fish were pale, congested and tender. The brain somatic index decreased gradually with the increase in exposure period. On 28th day of exposure, the BSI decreased from 1.85±0.04 to 0.87± 0.05 (Table 3.3 and Fig. 3.8). After 28 days of exposure to cadmium chloride, the exposed fish was transferred to toxicant free medium for recovery studies. The BSI increased from 0.87 to 0.94 on 14th day of recovery. Interestingly, on 28th day of

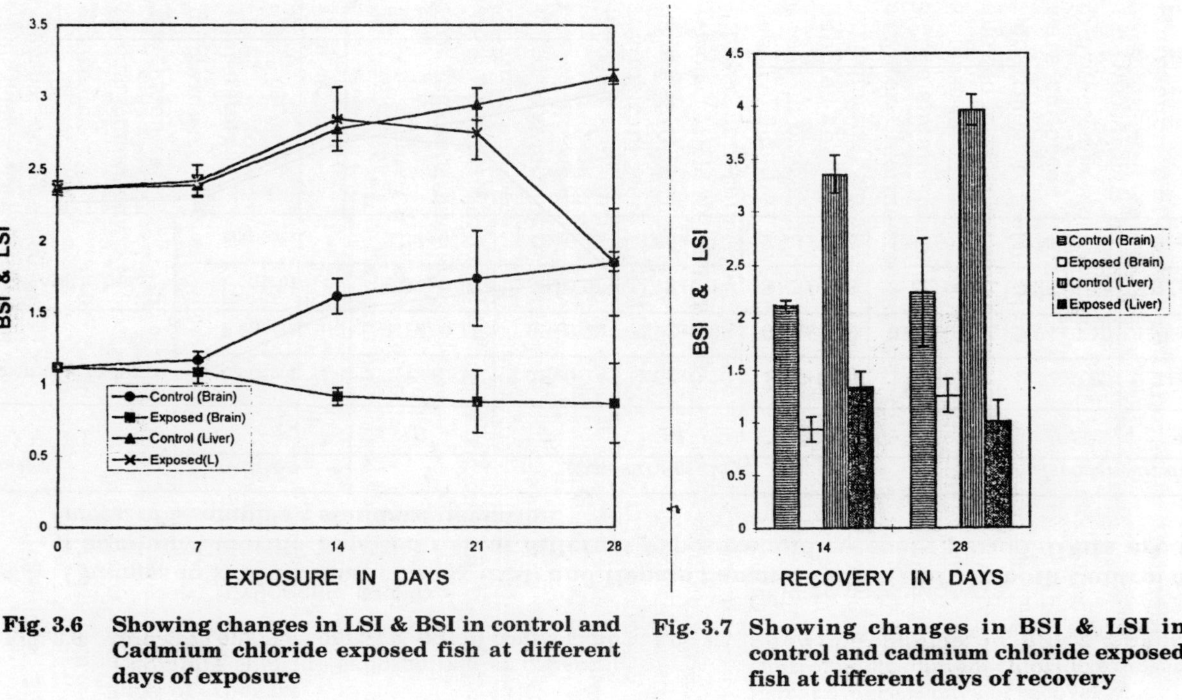

Fig. 3.6 Showing changes in LSI & BSI in control and Cadmium chloride exposed fish at different days of exposure

Fig. 3.7 Showing changes in BSI & LSI in control and cadmium chloride exposed fish at different days of recovery

Table-3.3 Changes in Brain Somatic Index (BSI) and Hepato Samatic Index (HSI), in both Control and Cadmium Chloride Exposed fish at different exposure and recovery period. (Data are the mean of 5 samples ± standard deviation

Tissue	*Condition*	*Exposure in days*					*Recovery in days*	
		0	*7*	*14*	*21*	*28*	*14*	*28*
P[illegible] Somatic Index	Control	1.12±0.11	1.18±0.14	1.62±0.10	1.74±0.08	1.85±0.04	2.12±0.05	2.24±0.10
	Exposed	1.12±0.11	1.09±0.22	0.92±0.08	0.88±0.09	0.87±0.05	0.94±0.10	1.26±0.14
Hepato Somatic Index	Control	2.37±0.13	2.39±0.06	2.78±0.14	2.95±0.13	3.14±0.08	3.36±0.14	3.97±0.05
	Exposed	2.37±0.13	2.42±0.12	2.85±0.10	2.75±0.15	1.86±0.12	1.35±0.09	1.01±0.08

recovery, the BSI increased to 1.26 but the value was less than the control value (Table 3.3 and Figs. 3.6 and 3.7). The Hepato Somatic Index (HSI) remained almost at the same level in the control fish throughout the experimental period. The HSI gradually and significantly increased with the increase in exposure period upto 14 days. After 21 days of exposure, the HSI in exposed fish decreased significantly. The value depleted from 3.14±0.08 to 1.86±0.12 on 28th day of exposure (Figs. 3.8 to 3.10 and Table 3.3). No recovery was noted on 14th day of recovery. On 28th day of recovery, partial recovery by 9.2 per cent was noted in BSI. The HSI value initially increased significantly by 6.7 per cent on 21st day of exposure and 40.7 per cent decrease was noted on 28th day of exposure (Figs. 3.8 to 3.10 and Table-3.4).

The liver somatic index and brain somatic index decreased ($r = -0.985, p \leq 0.01$ and $r = -0.948, p \leq 0.05$) with the increase in exposure period, when compared to control fish ($r = 0.636$, p = NS and $r = 0.340$, p = NS). The per cent inhibition of HSI intitially increased and after 21 days of exposure the HSI and BSI decreased in exposed fish with the increase in exposure period (Table 3.4 and Figs. 3.8 to 3.9). The control fish remained clinically healthy throughout the period of experiment. Table-3.4 indicate the per cent decrease in BSI and LSI in exposed fish, when compared to control fish. The per cent decrease of BSI, increased with the increase in exposure period and a maximum decrease of 52.9 per cent was recorded on 28th day of exposure (Fig. 3.8). When the exposed fish was transferred to toxicant free medium 9.2 per cent recovery was noted on 28 days of recovery in BSI (Fig. 3.10). In case of LSI, a similar trend was observed but here the index decreased maximum by 40.7 per cent, when compared to control fish, after 28 days of exposure (Table-3.4 and Fig. 3.8). The HSI initially increased by 6.7 per cent on 21st day of exposure. When the exposed fish was transferred to toxicant free medium, no recovery was marked after 14 and 28 days of recovery (Figs. 3.9 and 3.10). Instead of any recovery, further depletion of the index was noted and a maximum depletion by 33.8 per cent was noted on 28 days of recovery (Fig. 3.10). The values clearly indicated that during exposure, the liver was drastically damaged and no recovery was possible even though the exposed fish was

Table-3.4. Per cent change in BSI and HSI in exposed fish, when compared to control fish, at different days of exposure and recoveiy. (Data calculated from the mean of the samples).

Tissue	*Exposure Period in Days*					*Recovery Period in Days*	
	0	*7*	*14*	*21*	*28*	*14*	*28*
Brain Somatic Index	–	–7.6	–43.2	–49.4	–52.9	–55.6	–43.7
Per cent Recovery during Recovery Period						NR (-2.7)	9.2
Hepato Somatic Index	–	1.2	2.5	6.7	–40.7	–59.8	–74.5
Per cent Recovery during Recovery Period						NR (–19.1)	NR (–33.8)

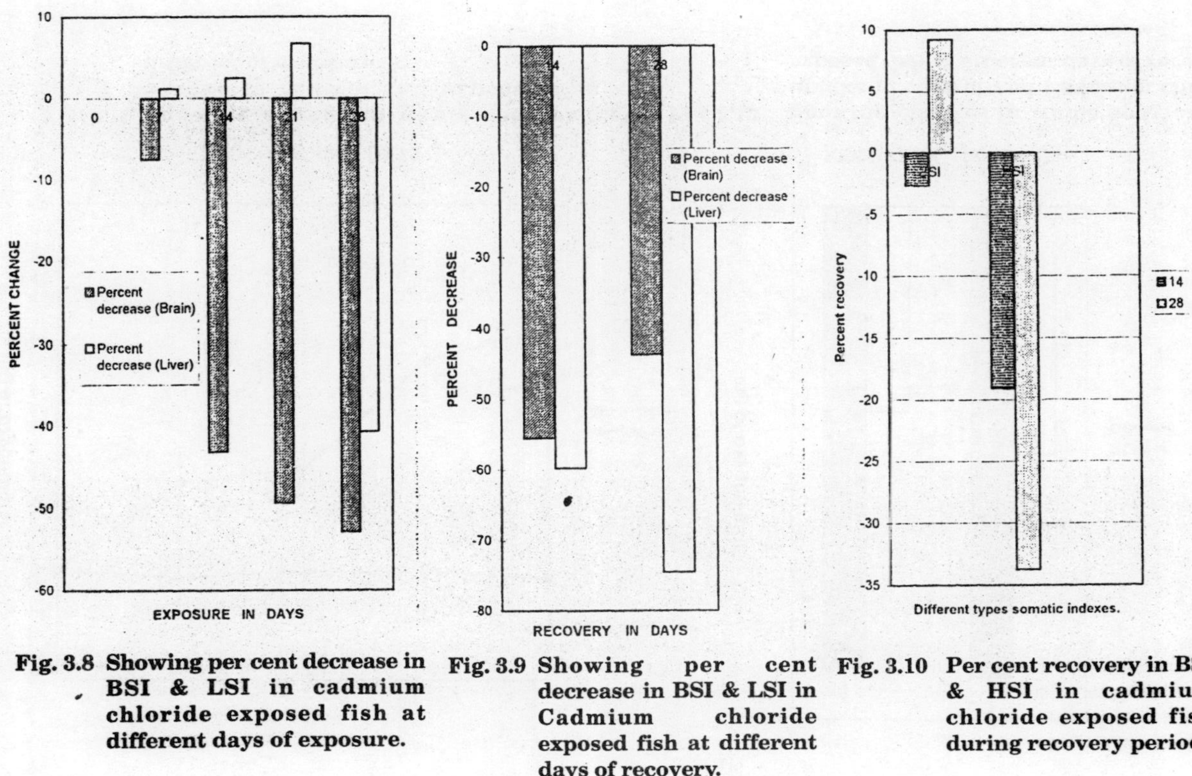

Fig. 3.8 Showing per cent decrease in BSI & LSI in cadmium chloride exposed fish at different days of exposure.

Fig. 3.9 Showing per cent decrease in BSI & LSI in Cadmium chloride exposed fish at different days of recovery.

Fig. 3.10 Per cent recovery in BSI & HSI in cadmium chloride exposed fish during recovery period.

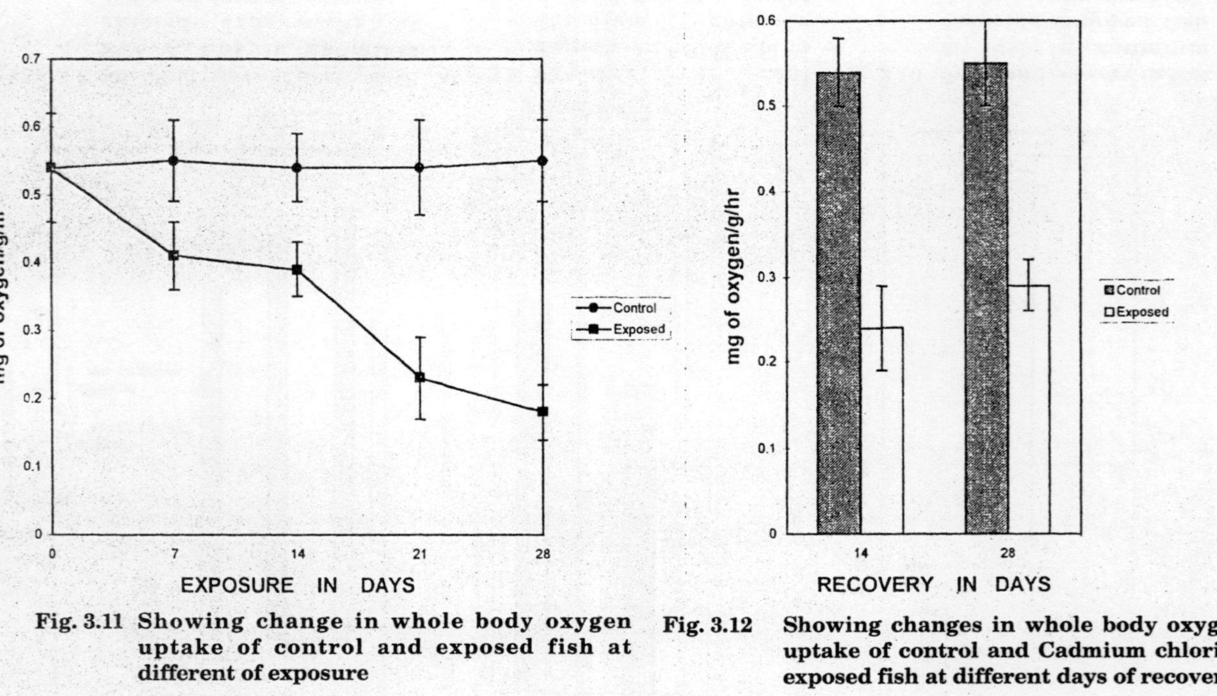

Fig. 3.11 Showing change in whole body oxygen uptake of control and exposed fish at different of exposure

Fig. 3.12 Showing changes in whole body oxygen uptake of control and Cadmium chloride exposed fish at different days of recovery

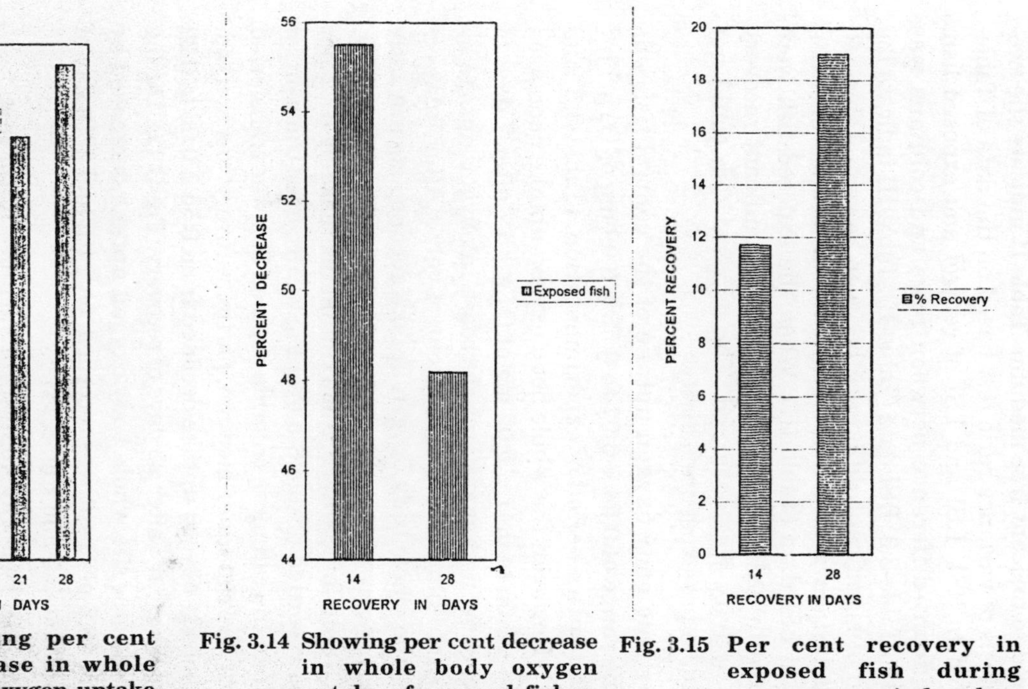

Fig. 3.13 **Showing per cent decrease in whole body oxygen uptake of exposed fishes, when compared to control at all exposure periods.**

Fig. 3.14 **Showing per cent decrease in whole body oxygen uptake of exposed fishes, when compared to control during recovery period.**

Fig. 3.15 **Per cent recovery in exposed fish during recovery period, when compared to 28 d exposed value.**

transferred to toxicant free medium. Table II indicate the two-way analysis of variance ratio test based on the data of Table-3.3 related to BSI, KSI and LSI of control and exposed fish. No significant difference between rows and columns was observed in Table-3.3, BSI data (Table-II). Table-III indicate the existence of significant difference between rows of Table-3.3, KSI and LSI data and non-significant difference between columns of LSI data (Table-III). When the exposed fish were transferred to toxicant free tap water, no significant recovery in their activity was observed. The exposed fish could not recover to its pre-exposure activity.

The whole body oxygen uptake of the control fish was within the range of 0.54 ± 0.07 to 0.55 ± 0.09 mg of O_2 g^{-1} h^{-1} during the entire period of experimentation. (Table-3.5, and Fig. 3.11). However, the whole body oxygen uptake decreased from 0.55 ± 0.05 to 0.41 ± 0.07 mg of O_2 g^{-1} h^{-1} after 7 days of exposure, showing a maximum decrease in oxygen uptake by 25.4 per cent (Table-3.5) over the control value. After 7 days of exposure, the whole body oxygen uptake declined significantly to 0.18 ± 0.06 mg of O_2 g^{-1} h^{-1} after 28 days of exposure (Fig. 3.11 and Table-3.5), where, a maximum decrease by 67.2 per cent, was recorded (Table 3.5 and Fig. 3.13), over the control value. When the cadmium chloride exposed fish was transferred to toxicant free tap water medium, partial recovery was marked. The whole body oxygen uptake declined from 0.55 ± 0.06 to 0.29 ± 0.08 mg Oa g^{-1} h^{-1} after 28 days of recovery (Fig. 3.12). During recovery studies the whole body oxygen uptake decreased by 55.5% and 48.2 per cent was recorded, on 14th and 28th day of recovery (Table-3.5 and Fig. 3.14).

Table III Two-way Analysis of Variance Ratio Test

Mean	0.000000	–8.210000	–17.36333	–27.14000	–37.75667
Variance	0.000000	7.223688	23.20142	10.67981	207.744
	F (Row)	df N	df D	Total SS	Row SS
	2.746861	2	8	3179.91	202.6289

p = 0.1235472

There is not a significant difference between Rows

F (Column)	*df N*	*df D*	*Column SS*	*Residual*
18.18018	4	8	2682.212	295.0698

p = 4.441142E-04

There is a significant difference between Columns

Table IV Two-way Analysis of Variance Ratio Test

Mean	18.18000	17.42500	17.11500	15.92500	15.04000
Variance	0.000000	1.711364	2.808410	9.461216	9.331179
	F (Row)	df N	df D	Total SS	Row SS
	9.923302	1	4	35.78711	16.61475

p = 0.0345099

There is a significant difference between Rows

F (Column)	*df N*	*df D*	*Column SS*	*Residual*
1.862715	4	4	12.4751	6.697266

p = 0.2808205

There is not a significant difference between Columns

Table V Two-way Analysis of Variance Ratio Test

Mean	108.000	116.500	121.000	105.500	99.500
Variance	0.000000	112.500	200.000	24.50001	144.500
	F (Row)	df N	df D	Total SS	Row SS
	103124	1	4	1076.899	12.10156

p = .7641911

There is not a significant difference between Rows

F (Column)	*df N*	*df D*	*Column SS*	*Residual*
1.268429	4	4	595.3985	469.3985

p = .4116649

There is not a significant difference between Columns

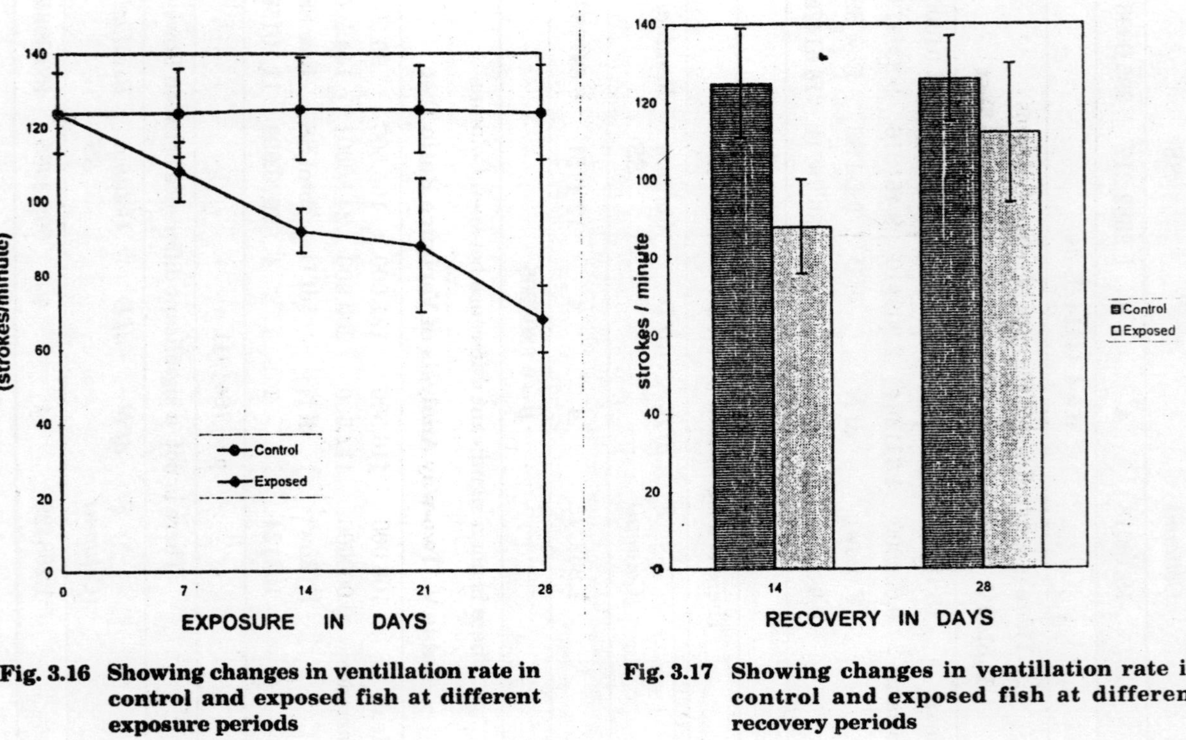

Fig. 3.16 Showing changes in ventillation rate in control and exposed fish at different exposure periods

Fig. 3.17 Showing changes in ventillation rate in control and exposed fish at different recovery periods

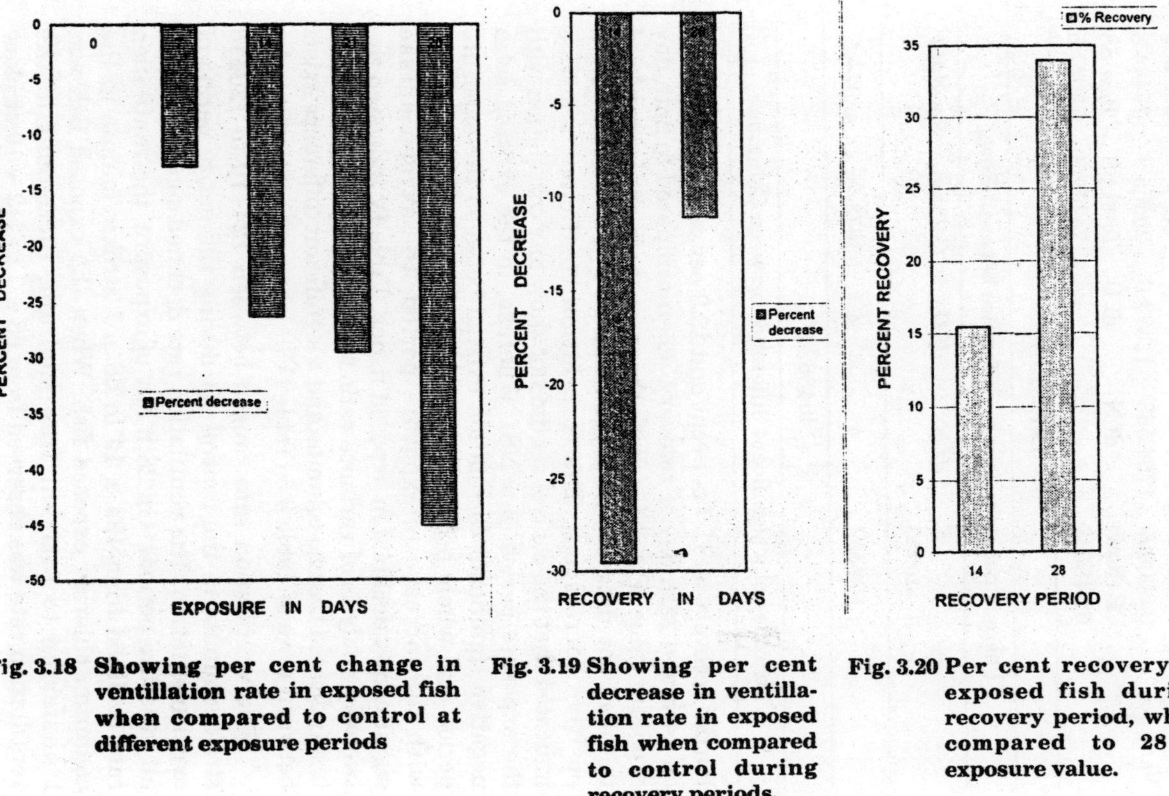

Fig. 3.18 **Showing per cent change in ventillation rate in exposed fish when compared to control at different exposure periods**

Fig. 3.19 **Showing per cent decrease in ventillation rate in exposed fish when compared to control during recovery periods.**

Fig. 3.20 **Per cent recovery in exposed fish during recovery period, when compared to 28 d exposure value.**

Table VI Two-way Analysis of Variance Ratio Test

Mean	558.600	539.680	486.840	431.350	359.580
Variance	0.000000	1766.563	12494.6	29655.9	77444.8
	F (Row)	df N	df D	Total SS	Row SS
	6.045588	1	4	174440.8	73037.5
	p = 6.978315E-02				
	There is not a significant difference between Rows				
	F (Column)	*df N*	*df D*	*Column SS*	*Residual*
	1.098382	4	4	53078.75	48324.5
	P = .4648624				
	There is not a significant difference between Columns				

Partial recovery by 11.7 per cent and 19.0 per cent was recorded on 14th and 28th day of recovery, when compared to 28th day exposure value (Fig. 3.15). With the increase in exposure period the per cent decrease in oxygen uptake increased showing a positive correlation. The correlation coefficient analysis indicated that the control set did not show any correlation with the exposure period (p = NS). Whereas, in the exposed set a negative significant correlation existed between the exposure period and whole body oxygen uptake ($r = -0.993$, $p < 0.01$). with the increase in exposure period, the oxygen uptake significantly declined in exposed fishes. Table IV indicated the two way analysis of variance ratio test based on Table 3.5. The test indicated that no columns and a significant difference exists between rows of Table 3.5 (Table IV).

The ventillation rate ranged between 124±10 to 126±10 strokes/minute in the control set during the entire period of experimentation. The ventilation rate declined significantly at all exposure periods. On 28th day of exposure, the ventilation rate declined from 124 ± 15 to 68 ± 7 strokes/minute in the cadmium chloride exposed fish. When the exposed fish was transferred to toxicant free medium, increment in the ventillation rate was observed from 68 ± 7 to 112 ± 10 strokes/minute on 28 days of recovery, when compared to 28 days exposure value (Figs. 3.16-3.17 and Table-3.6). The ventillation

Table-3.5. Effect of Cadmium chloride on control and exposed fresh water fish, *Tilapia mossambica* at different days of exposure and recovery. [Whole body oxygen uptake (mg of O_2 g^{-1} hr^{-1})]

Status of fish	*Exposure in Days*					*Recovery in Days*	
	0	*7*	*14*	*21*	*28*	*14*	*28*
Control	0.54±0.07	0.55±0.05	0.54±0.08	0.54±0.05	0.55±0.09	0.54±0.08	0.55±0.06
Exposed	0.54±0.07	0.41±0.07	0.39±0.05	0.23±0.07	0.18±0.06	0.24±0.04	0.29±0.08
Per cent Change over control	—	–25.4	–27.7	–57.4	–67.2	–55.5	–48.2
Per cent recovery during recovery period						11.7	19.0

Table-3.6. Changes in ventillation rate (strokes/minute) in both control and exposed fish at different exposure and recovery periods. Per cent change values were calculated from the mean of the samples, when compared to respective control values. Per cent recovery was calculated from 28 days exposure value. Data are mean of 5 samples ± standard deviation

Status of fish	*Exposure in Days*					*Recovery in Days*	
	0	7	14	21	28	14	28
Control	124±10	124±12	125±13	125±14	124±15	125±16	126±10
Exposed	124±10	108±12	92±8	88±10	68±7	88±9	112±10
Per cent change when compared to control	0	–12.9	–26.4	–29.6	–45.1	–29.6	–11.1
Per cent recovery, when compared to 28 days exp. value	—	—	—	—	—	15.5	34.0

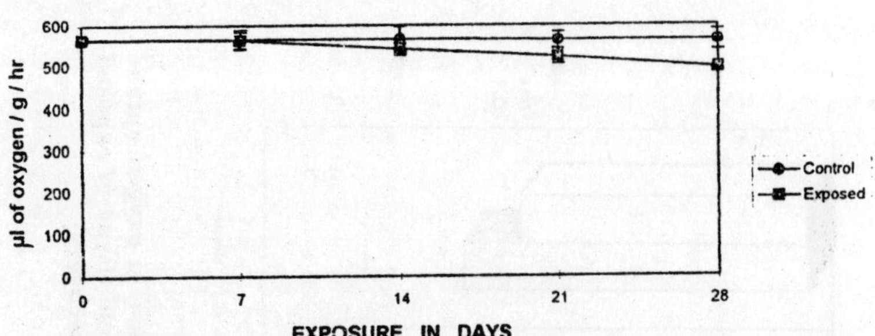

Fig. 3.21 Showing changes in oxygen uptake by brain tissue of control and exposed fish at different exposure periods

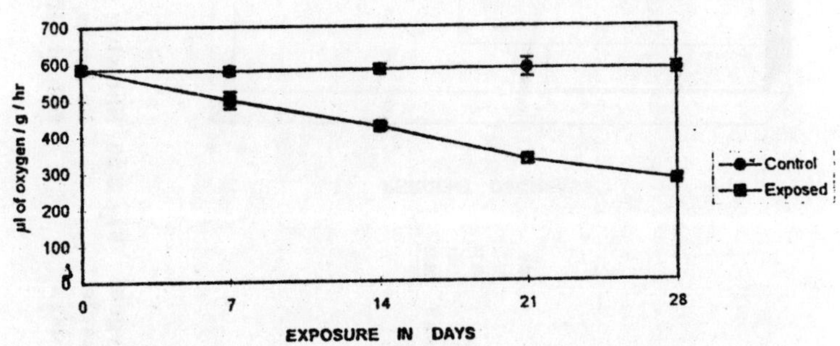

Fig. 3.22 Showing changes in oxygen uptake by liver tissue of control and exposed fish at different exposure periods

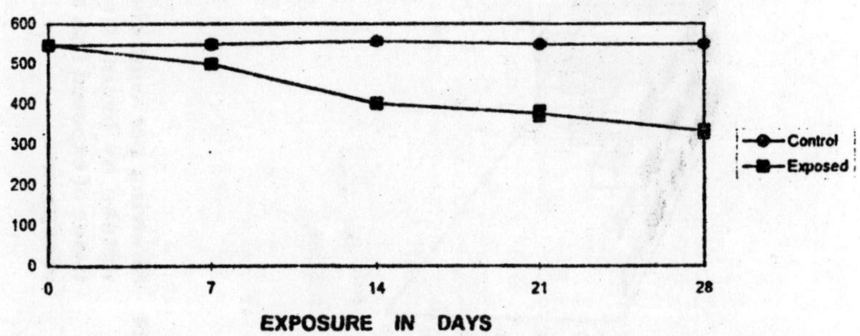

Fig. 3.23 Showing changes in oxygen uptake by muscle tissue of control and exposed fish at different exposure periods

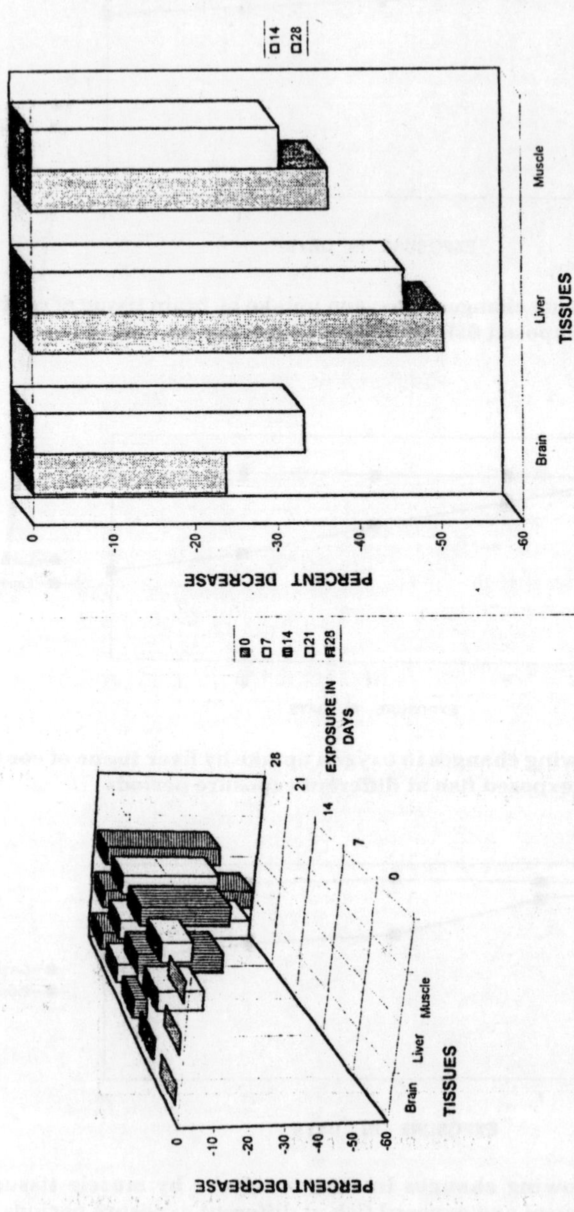

Fig. 3.24 Showing per cent change in oxygen uptake by brain, liver and muscle tissue of exposed fish at different days of exposure

Fig. 3.25 Showing per cent decrease in oxygen uptake by brain, liver and muscle tissue of exposed fish at different days of recovery

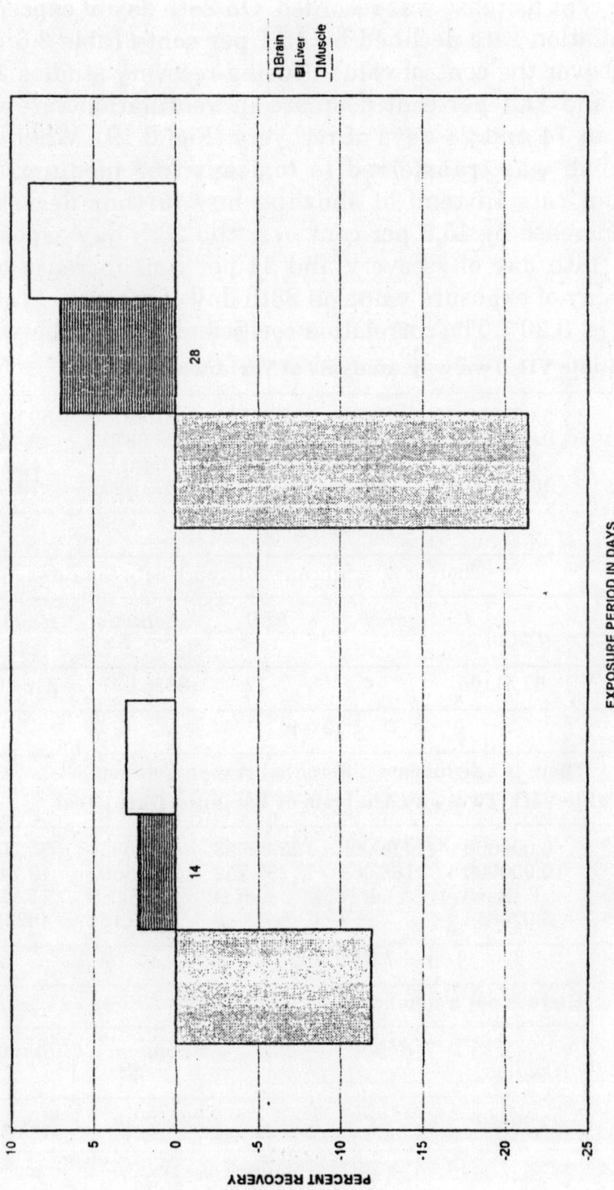

Fig. 3.26 Per cent recovery in oxygen uptake by brain, liver and muscle of exposed fish, when compared to 28 days exposure value, during recobery studies

rate of the exposed fish showed a higher value, when compared to the control fish up to 2 days of exposure, where a maximum of 8.5 per cent increase was recorded. On 28th day of exposure, the ventillation rate declined by 45.1 per cent (Table-3.6 and Fig. 3.18) over the control value. During recovery studies 29.6 per cent and 11.1 per cent decrease in ventillation rate was observed in 14 and 28 days of recovery (Fig. 3.19). When the exposed fish was transferred to toxicant free medium, the ventilation rate instead of showing any further decrease, showed increase by 15.5 per cent over the 28th day exposure value on 14th day of recovery and 34 per cent increase over the 28th day of exposure value on 28th day of recovery (Table-3.6 and Fig. 3.20). The correlation coefficient analysis between

Table VII Two-way Analysis of Variance Ratio Test

Mean	0.000000	–21.99000	–38.51750	–47.39750	–59.91750
Variance	0.000000	143.810	79.56315	98.38737	49.42644
	F (Row)	df N	df D	Total SS	Row SS
	10.09095	3	12	9797.207	797.461

p = 1.334667E-03

There is a significant difference between Rows

	F (Column)	*df N*	*df D*	*Column SS*	*Residual*
	82.41106	4	12	8683.637	316.1094

P =< 10 (–6)

There is a significant difference between Columns

Table VIII Two-way Analysis of Variance Ratio Test

Mean	0.000000	–14.96000	–23.02333	–41.20334	–58.26667
Variance	0.000000	168.063	297.252	36.15601	19.74512
	F (Row)	df N	df D	Total SS	Row SS
	3.670858	2	8	7246.161	498.8487

p = 7.393736E-02

There is not a significant difference between Rows

	F (Column)	*df N*	*df D*	*Column SS*	*Residual*
	22.82559	4	8	6203.736	543.5771

P = 1.971126E-04

There is a significant difference between Columns

exposure period and the ventillation rate of the control fishes did not show the existence of any significant correlation (P = NS). It seems the ventillation rate has slowed down when the fish was kept in a stagnant water for a prolonged period, with the same type of food throughout the experimental period. Rather during this holding period, little depression in the rate was observed. Whereas, in the cadmium chloride exposed set, the ventillation rate initially increased significantly up to 2 days of exposure, than the ventillation rate declined significantly. The correlation coefficient analysis between days of exposure and ventillation rate in the exposed fish, indicated, the existence of a significant negative correlation ($r = -0.965$, $P \leq 0.05$). This indicated that with the increase in exposure period, the ventilation rate significantly declined. The initial increase in ventilation rate might be due to the stress. The fish probably out of suffocation, tried to pump more amount of water through the gills, either to trap more oxygen or to wash the gills. The analysis of variance ratio test indicated the existence of non-significant differences between columns and significant difference exists between rows of Table 3.6 (Table V).

Table 3.7 and 3.8 and Figs. 3.21 to 3.25 indicated the changes in oxygen uptake (μl of O_2 g^{-1} h^{-1}) by brain, liver and muscle tissue slices of control and cadmium chloride exposed fish. In case of brain tissue slices, significant decrease in oxygen uptake was marked on 28th day of exposure. The O_2 uptake declined from 563.7 ± 9.5 to 496.4 ± 11.8 μl of O_2 g^{-1} h^{-1}, (Fig. 3.21) where a maximum of 11.9 per cent decrease was marked over the control value (Fig. 3.24 and Table 3.8). When the exposed fish was transferred to toxicant free medium, the oxygen uptake did not improve showing 23.8 per cent after 14 days and 33.3 per cent further decrease after 28 day of recovery, respectively (Table-3.8 and Fig. 3.25). In case of brain, the oxygen uptake declined from 562.2 ± 9.4 to 374.8 ± 7.8 μl of O_2 g^{-1} h^{-1}, where a maximum of 33.3 per cent decrease was marked over the control value, after 28 days of recovery (Figs. 3.24 and 3.25). No recovery by was marked on 28th day of recovery. The correlation coefficient analysis between days of exposure and the oxygen uptake of brain tissue slices of the control set indicated the existence of a non-significant

Table 3.7 **Changes in oxygen uptake (µl of O_2 g^{-1} hr^{-1}) by brain, liver and muscle of control and Cadmium chloride exposed fish, at different days of exposure and recovery. Data are mean of 5 samples ± standard deviation**

Tissue		*Exposure in Days*					*Recovery in Days*	
	Condition	*0*	*7*	*14*	*21*	*28*	*14*	*28*
Brain	Control	564.6±9.5	565.2 ± 11.2	565.5 ± 12.6	562.5 ± 10.6	563.7 ± 9.5	565.8 ± 6.2	562.2 ± 9.4
	Exposed	564.6±9.5	562.8 ± 7.4	541.2 ± 11.5	522.9 ± 10.6	496.4 ± 11.8	430.8 ± 9.2	374.8 ± 7.8
Liver	Control	585.6±6.5	580.2 ± 9.1	582.6 ± 9.8	586.8 ± 8.4	584.5 ± 8.6	586.9 ± 10.5	586.5 ± 8.6
	Exposed	585.6±6.5	501.5 ± 11.4	426.4 ± 9.8	332.6 ± 11.2	276.6 ± 11.2	291.4 ± 9.5	318.6 ± 11.2
Muscle	Control	546.4±6.5	548.4 ± 8.8	556.2 ± 7.9	548.2 ± 9.4	549.4 ± 5.2	548.2 ± 6.2	556.6 ± 9.4
	Exposed	546.4±6.5	498.8 ± 7.6	401.8 ± 9.2	376.5 ± 10.8	332.5 ± 5.6	348.6 ± 7.9	386.4 ± 9.0

Table 3.8 **Per cent change in oxygen uptake by the brain, liver and muscle of exposed *Tilapia* fish at different days of exposure and recovery. '–' indicate decrease. Values in parentheses indicate per cent recovery. (Data calculated from the mean of the samples) NR = No recovery**

Tissue	*Exposure in Days*					*Recovery in Days*	
	0	*7*	*14*	*21*	*28*	*14*	*28*
Brain	0	–0.4	–4.2	–7.0	–11.9	–23.8(NR)	–33.3(NR)
Liver	0	–13.5	–26.8	–43.3	–52.6	–50.3(2.3)	–45.6(7.0)
Muscle	0	–9.0	–27.7	–31.3	–39.4	–36.4(3.0)	–30.5(8.9)

correlation ($r = -0.445$, P = NS), but the brain tissue slices of the cadmium chloride exposed fish, showed the existence of a significant ($r = -0.981$, $P \leq 0.05$) negative correlation with the exposure period. The two way analysis of variance ratio test indicated that a significant difference exists between rows and no significant difference exists between columns of the data based on Table 3.7 (Table VI). The per cent decrease in oxygen uptake by brain tissue slices of the exposed fish, indicated the existence of a positive and significant correlation.

The liver tissue slices showed the maximum decrease in oxygen uptake. The values declined from 584.5 ± 8.6 to 276.6 ± 11.2 µl of O_2 g^{-1} h^{-1} on 28th day of exposure, showing a maximum decline by 52.6 per cent (Figs. 3.22 and 3.24 and Table-3.7 and 3.8). With the increase in exposure period, the oxygen uptake steadily and significantly declined during the entire period of experimentation. When the exposed fish was transferred to cadmium chloride free medium, a partial recovery by 2.3 per cent and 7 per cent was marked after 14 and 28 days of recovery (Table-3.8 and "Figs. 3.24 and 3.25). In case of liver, the oxygen uptake declined from 586.5 ± 8.6 to 318.6 ± 11.2 µl of O_2 g^{-1} h^{-1}, where a maximum of 45.6 per cent decrease was marked over the control value, after 28 days of recovery (Fig. 3.24). A partial recovery by 7 per cent was marked on 28th day of recovery, in case of exposed liver (Fig. 3.25). The correlation coefficient analysis between the exposure period and the oxygen uptake of liver tissue slices of the control fish indicated the existence of non-significant correlation. Whereas, the liver slices of exposed fish showed the existence of a significant negative correlation ($r = -0.965$, $P \leq 0.01$) between days of exposure and oxygen uptake of liver tissue slices. The two way analysis of variance ratio test based on table 3.7 (liver) indicated the existence of significant difference between columns (Table-VII). The per cent decrease in oxygen uptake in liver tissue slices indicated the existence of a negative and significant ($r = -0.992$, $P \leq 0.001$) correlation with the exposure period. Table-3.7 and 3.8 and Figs. 3.23 to 3.25 indicated the changes in oxygen uptake (µl of O_2 g^{-1} h^{-1}) by muscle tissue slices of control and cadmium chloride exposed fish. In case of

Table IX Two-way Analysis of Variance Ratio Test

Mean	0.000000	–20.14750	–27.57750	–40.14000	–55.17500
Variance	0.000000	49.37074	150.521	130.323	98.96451
	F (Row)	df N	df D	Total SS	Row SS
	5.77226	3	12	8206.953	760.5235

p = 1.110476E-02

There is a significant difference between Rows

F (Column)	*df N*	*df D*	*Column SS*	*Residual*
39.38797	4	12	6919.41	527.0196

P = <10 (–6)

There is a significant difference between Columns

Table-X Two-way Analysis of Variance Ratio Test

Mean	0.000000	–19.96250	–17.82500	–32.33250	–48.40250
Variance	0.000000	29.64576	152.069	275.633	629.031
	F (Row)	df N	df D	Total SS	Row SS
	1.97011	3	12	8438.766	1075.5

p = .1723418

There is not a significant difference between Rows

F (Column)	*df N*	*df D*	*Column SS*	*Residual*
7.116068	4	12	5179.631	2183.635

p = 3.551245E-03

There is a significant difference between Columns

muscle tissue slices, significant decrease in oxygen uptake was marked on 28th day of exposure. The O_2 uptake declined from 549.4 ± 5.2 to 332.5 ± 5.6 µl of O_2 g^{-1} h^{-1}, (Fig. 3.23) where a maximum of 39.4 per cent decrease was marked over the control value on 28 days of exposure (Figs. 3.23 and 3.24 and Table-3.7 and 3.8). When the exposed fish was transferred to cadmium chloride free medium, the oxygen uptake improved showing 3.0 per cent and 8.9 per cent after 14 and 28 days of recovery, respectively (Table-3.8 and Fig. 3.25). In case of muscle, the oxygen uptake declined from 556.6 ± 9.4 to 386.4 ± 9.0 μl of O_2 g^{-1} h^{-1} (Fig. 3.24) where a maximum of 30.5 per cent decrease was marked over the control value, after 28 days of recovery (Fig. 3.25). A partial insignificant recovery by 8.9 per cent was marked on 28th day of recovery (Fig. 3.26). The muscle tissue slices in the exposed fish showed gradual decrease in oxygen uptake with the increase in exposure period, showing an inverse relationship. The oxygen uptake in muscle tissues declined significantly and a maximum of 39.4 per cent decrease was marked on 28th day, when compared to its control value (Fig 3.24 and Table-3.8). The exposed fish could recover insignificantly after 14 day and 28 day, respectively (Table-3.8). The correlation coefficient analysis conducted between days of exposure versus the oxygen uptake of muscle tissue slices of the control fish indicated the existence of a negative, non-significant (r = –0.398, P = NS) correlation, whereas, a negative but highly significant (r = –0.983, P ≤ 0.01) correlation existed between days of exposure and the oxygen uptake rate of the exposed fish. The regression analysis between days of exposure versus the per cent decrease in oxygen uptake by muscle tissue indicated a significant (P ≤ 0.01), negative correlation. The existence of an inverse relationship indicated the effect of stress on the animal. The two-way analysis of variance ratio test indicated the existence of non-significant difference between rows and columns. The analysis of variance ratio test based on Table-3.8), pertaining to the per cent change in oxygen uptake by exposed fish brain, liver and muscle indicated the existence of significant difference between rows and a non-significant difference between columns (Table-VII).

The residual cadmium analysis of different tissues like brain, liver, and muscle of control and cadmium chloride exposed fish was carried out. The control fish brain, liver, and muscle did not show any accumulation of cadmium indicating absence of any background cadmium and also indicated that the control system was uncontaminated. The residual accumulation of cadmium or retention of cadmium in different exposed fish tissues was presented in Table 3.9 and Fig. 3.27. The brain of the exposed fish accumulated significant amount of cadmium interestingly. On 7th day of exposure, the brain of the exposed

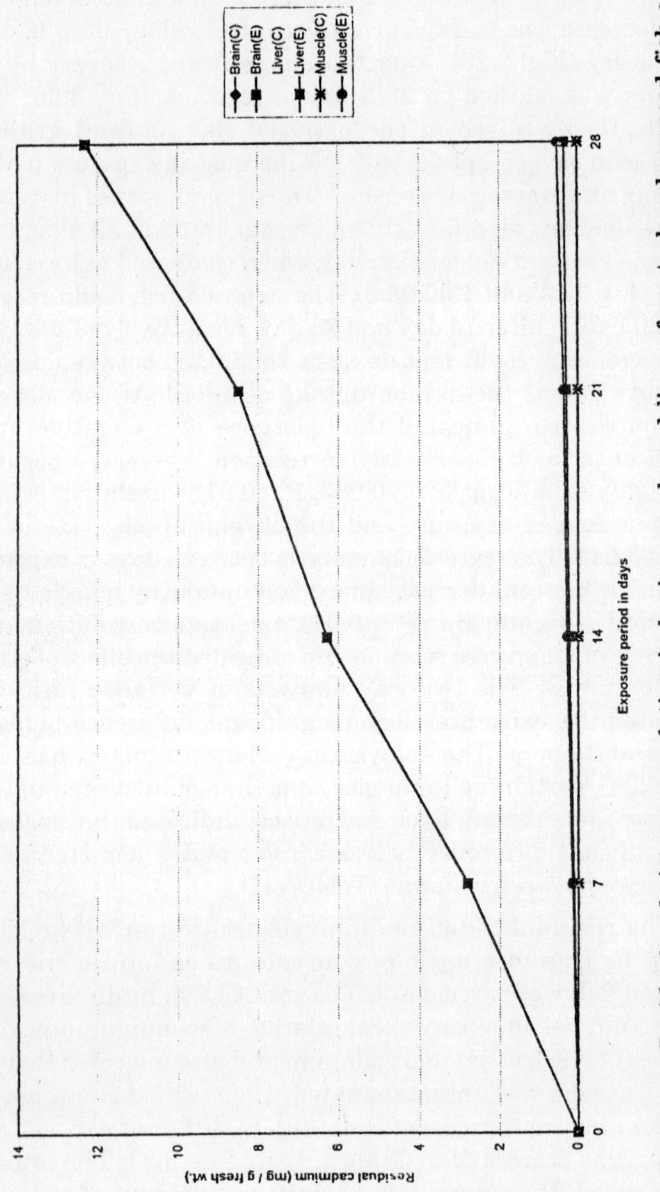

Fig. 3.27 Residual cadmium accumulation in brain, muscle and liver of control and exposed fish at different days of exposure

Table 3.9 **Residual cadmium accumulation in brain, liver, and muscle of control and exposed *Tilapia* fish at different exposure periods. Data represents mean of 5 estimations by Atomic Absorption Spectrophotometer**

Tissue		*Exposure in Days*				
	Condition	*0*	*7*	*14*	*21*	*28*
Brain	NT	NT	NT	NT	NT	NT
	Exposed	NT	0.11	0.22	0.29	0.33
Liver	Control	NT	NT	NT	NT	NT
	Exposed	NT	2.81	6.30	8.5	12.30
Muscle	Control	NT	NT	NT	NT	NT
	Exposed	NT	0.14	0.28	0.36	0.51

fish accumulated 0.11 mg of cadmium gm^{-1} tissue. On 14th day of exposure, the brain of the exposed fish accumulated 0.22 mg of cadmium gm^{-1} tissue. On 21st day of exposure, the brain of the exposed fish accumulated 0.29 mg of cadmium gm^{-1} tissue. On 28th day of exposure, the brain of the exposed fish accumulated 0.33 mg of Cadmium gm^{-1} tissue (Fig. 3.27 and Table-3.9). The residual cadmium level in exposed liver increased with the increase in exposure period. On 7th day of exposure, the liver of the exposed fish accumulated 2.81 mg of cadmium gm^{-1} tissue. On 14th day of exposure, the liver of the exposed fish accumulated 6.30 mg of cadmium gm^{-1} tissue. On 21st day of exposure, the liver of the exposed fish accumulated 8.5 mg of cadmium gm^{-1} tissue. On 28th day of exposure, the liver of the exposed fish accumulated 12.3 mg of cadmium gm^{-1} tissue (Fig. 3.27 and Table-3.9). On 7th day of exposure, the muscle of the exposed fish accumulated 0.14 mg of cadmium gm^{-1} tissue. On 14th day of exposure, the muscle of the exposed fish accumulated 0.28 mg of cadmium gm^{-1} tissue. On 21st day of exposure, the muscle of the exposed fish accumulated 0.36 mg of cadmium gm^{-1} tissue. On 28th day of exposure, the muscle of the exposed fish accumulated 0.51 mg of cadmium gm^{-1} tissue (Fig. 3.27 and Table-3.9). It was observed that the exposed fish liver and muscle accumulated the highest amount of cadmium when compared to exposed fish brain. Cadmium accumulated faster in liver and muscle, when compared to other tissues of the exposed fish. The exposed fish liver showed the highest accumulation and brain showed the least accumulation of cadmium. When we compare the data of table-3.9, it seems liver being the most active sites of action accumulated more amount of cadmium, when compared to other tissues.

The changes in Total ATPase activity in brain, liver and muscle of control and cadmium chloride exposed fish at different days of exposure and recovery and it's per cent changes were shown in Table 3.10 and 3.11 and Fig. 3.28 to 3.32. The brain tissue showed a maximum decrease by 44.4 per cent (Fig. 3.28) and the enzyme activity declined from 62.1 ± 4.8 to 34.5 ± 8.8 μmole of ip liberated mg^{-1} of protein hr^{-1} on 28th day of exposure (Fig. 3.28). When the exposed fish was transferred to toxicant free medium, the ATPase activity declined from 62.5 ± 9.5 to 31.8 ± 6.6 μmole of ip liberated mg^{-1} of protein hr^{-1} on 14th day of recovery and from 61.9 ± 7.8 to 39.2 ± 8.2 μmole of ip liberated mg^{-1} of protein hr^{-1} on 28th day of recovery (Fig. 3.29). This enzyme activity decreased by 49.1 per cent on 14th day recovery and decreased by 36.6 per cent over the 28th day exposure value, after 28 days of recovery, indicating a partial recovery (Table-3.11 and Fig. 3.30). The exposed fish brain enzyme activity could recover partly by 7.8 per cent on 28th day of recovery (Fig. 3.32). Partial recovery in the brain enzyme activity was marked on 14 days of recovery, rather no further depletion in the enzyme activity was noted (Fig. 3.32). The changes in total ATPase activity in liver of control and cadmium chloride exposed fish at different days of exposure and recovery and it's per cent changes were shown in Tables 3.10 and 3.11 and Figs. 3.28 to 3.32. The liver tissue showed a maximum decrease by 69.2 per cent and the enzyme activity declined from 38.4 ± 7.6 to 11.8 ± 9.2 μmole of ip liberated mg^{-1} of protein hr^{-1} on 28th day of exposure (Fig. 3.28). When the exposed fish was transferred to toxicant free medium, the ATPase activity declined from 38.4 ± 3.8 to 16.2 ± 4.3 μmole of ip liberated mg^{-1} of protein hr^{-1} on 14th day of recovery and from 38.6 ± 4.7 to 19.6 ± 5.6 μmole of ip liberated mg^{-1} of protein hr^{-1} on 28th day of recovery (Fig. 3.29). This enzyme activity decreased by 57.8 per cent on 14th day recovery and decreased by 49.2 per cent over the 28th day exposure value, after 28 days of recovery, indicating a partial recovery (Table-3.11 and Fig. 3.31). The exposed fish liver enzyme activity could recover partly by 11.4 per cent and 20 per cent on 14th and 28th day of recovery (Fig. 3.32). The changes in total ATPase, activity in muscle of control and cadmium chloride exposed fish at different days of exposure and recovery and it's percent changes were shown in Tables 3.10 and 3.11 and Figs. 3.28 to 3.32. The muscle tissue showed a maximum decrease by 76.1 per cent of the enzyme activity (Fig. 3.29) on 28th day of exposure, when compared to control and the enzyme activity declined from 45.9 ± 6.8 to 10.5 ± 8.4 μmole of ip liberated mg^{-1} of protein hr^{-1} on 28th day of exposure (Fig. 3.28). When the exposed fish was transferred to toxicant free medium, the ATPase activity of muscle declined from 45.4 ± 7.4 to 19.6 ± 7.1 μmole of ip liberated mg^{-1} of protein hr^{-1} on 14th day of recovery and from 46.8 ± 6.2 to 24.5 ± 5.2 μmole of ip

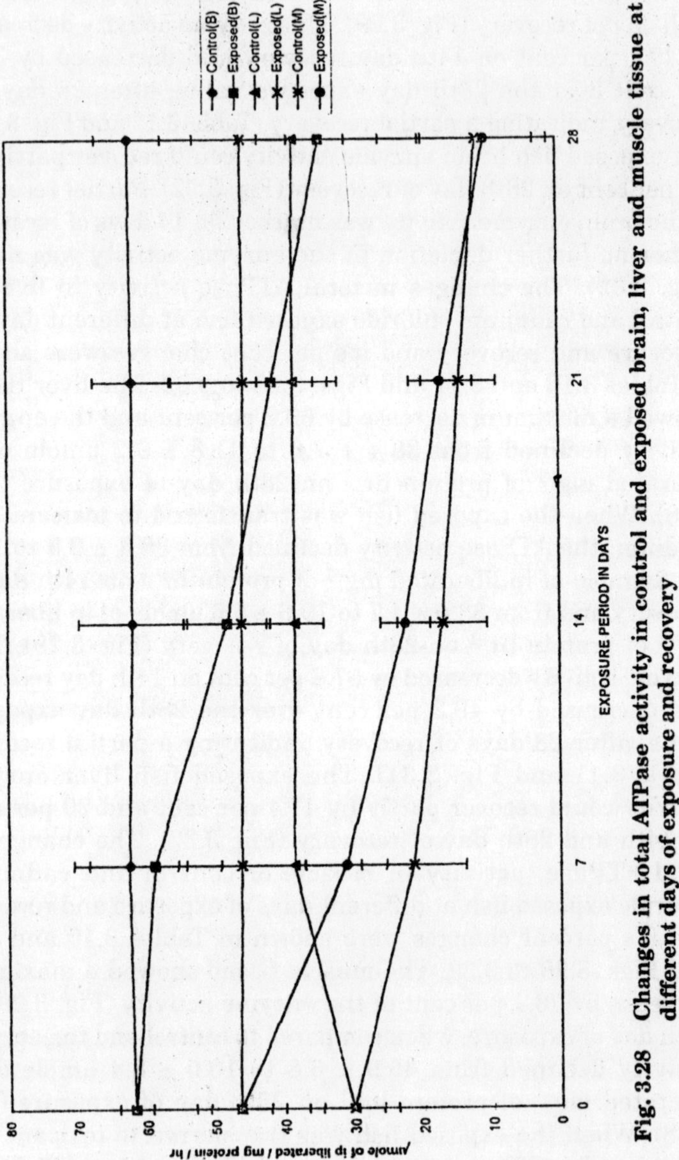

Fig. 3.28 Changes in total ATPase activity in control and exposed brain, liver and muscle tissue at different days of exposure and recovery

Table-3.10 Changes in total ATPase activity(μ moles of ip liberated mg^{-1} protein hr^{-1}) in control and Cadmium chloride exposed fish brain, liver and muscle at different days of exposure and recovery

Tissue		*Exposure in Days*					*Recovery in Days*	
	Condition	*0*	*7*	*14*	*21*	*28*	*14*	*28*
Brain	Control	61.7±2.4	62.4±8.2	61.8±7.9	61.9±5.6	62.1±4.8	62.5±9.5	61.9±7.8
	Exposed	61.7±2.4	58.7±9.6	48.2±6.2	41.64±9.5	34.5±8.8	31.8±6.6	39.2±8.2
Liver	Control	30.2±4.4	38.6±7.2	38.4±4.1	38.6±5.1	38.4±7.6	38.4±3.8	38.6±4.7
	Exposed	38.2±4.4	21.4±5.9	17.1±3.6	14.5±4.6	11.8±9.2	16.2±4.3	19.6±5.6
Muscle	Control	46.5±6.5	46.2±9.2	46.1±8.4	45.8±10.2	45.9±6.8	45.4±7.4	46.8±6.2
	Exposed	46.5±6.5	31.2±7.6	22.4±6.5	17.2±5.5	10.5±8.4	19.6±7.1	24.5±5.2

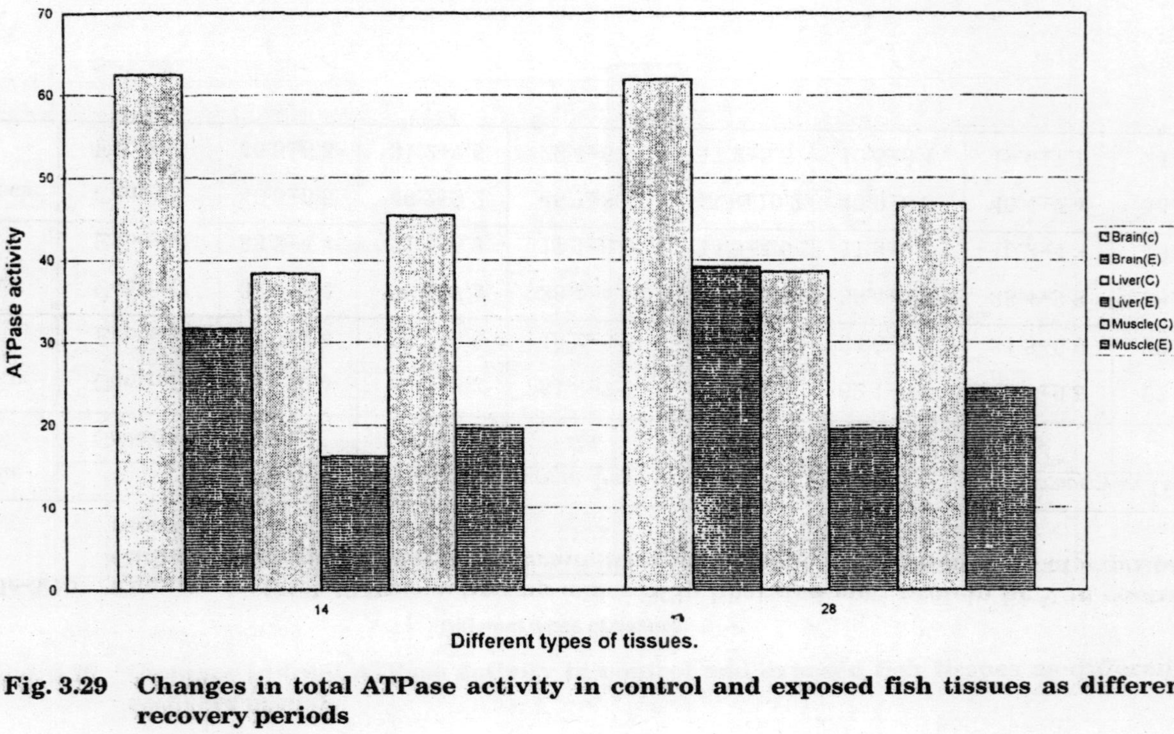

Fig. 3.29 Changes in total ATPase activity in control and exposed fish tissues as different recovery periods

liberated mg^{-1} of protein hr^{-1} on 28th day of recovery (Fig. 3.29). This enzyme activity decreased by 56.8 per cent on 14th day recovery and decreased by 47.6 per cent over the 28th day exposure value, after 28 days of recovery, indicating a partial recovery (Table-3.11 and Fig. 3.31). The exposed fish muscle enzyme activity could recover partly by 19.3 per cent and 28.5 per cent on 14th and 28th day of recovery (Fig. 3.32). The correlation coefficient analysis between days of exposure and Na^+, K^+, Mg^{++} dependent ATPase activity in control fish brain showed a positive but non-significant correlation, whereas, the exposed fish brain showed a significant negative correlation ($r = -0.979$, $P \leq 0.01$). The control set showed positive but insignificant correlation. The per cent change in the enzyme activity in the exposed fish brain when compared to control fish brain showed the

Table XI Two-way Analysis of Variance Ratio Test

Mean	492.320	450.760	398.400	321.140	307.340
Variance	0.000000	5128.782	18709.5	58797.1	72367.3
	F (Row)	df N	df D	Total SS	Row SS
	8.073285	1	4	206455.8	103648.9

p = .0468036

There is a significant difference between Rows

F (Column)	*df N*	*df D*	*Column SS*	*Residual*
1.001925	4	4	51452.88	51354

P = .4992787

There is not a significant difference between Columns

Table-XII Two-way Analysis of Variance Ratio Test

Mean	471.800	387.300	357.080	360.740	302.060
Variance	0.000000	15410.7	22404.2	26348.9	54489.6
	F (Row)	df N	df D	Total SS	Row SS
	12.37311.	1	4	149379.6	89666

p = 2.450431E-02

There is a significant difference between Rows

F (Column)	*df N*	*df D*	*Column SS*	*Residual*
1.059987	4	4	30726.25	28987.38

P = .4781661

There is not a significant difference between Columns

Table 3.11 Per cent change in total ATPase activity in cadmium chloride exposed *Tilapia* fish brain, liver and muscle at different days of exposure and recovery values in parentheses indicate per cent recovery

TISSUE	*Exposure in Days*					*Recovery in Days*	
	0	*7*	*14*	*21*	*28*	*14*	*28*
Brain	—	–5.9	–22.0	–32.7	–44.4	–49.1 (–5.0)	–36.6 (7.8)
Liver	—	–44.5	–55.4	–62.1	–69.2	–57.8 (11.4)	–49.2 (20.0)
Muscle	—	–32.4	–51.4	–62.4	–76.1	–56.8 (19.3)	–47.6 (28.5)

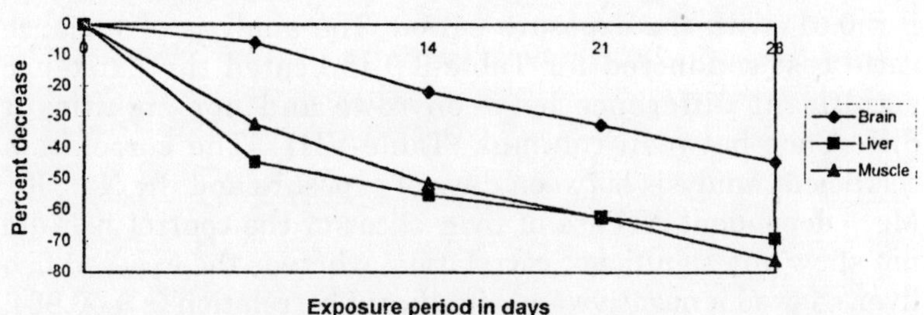

Fig. 3.30 Per cent decrease in ATPase activity in exposed brain, liver and muscle tissue, when compared to control

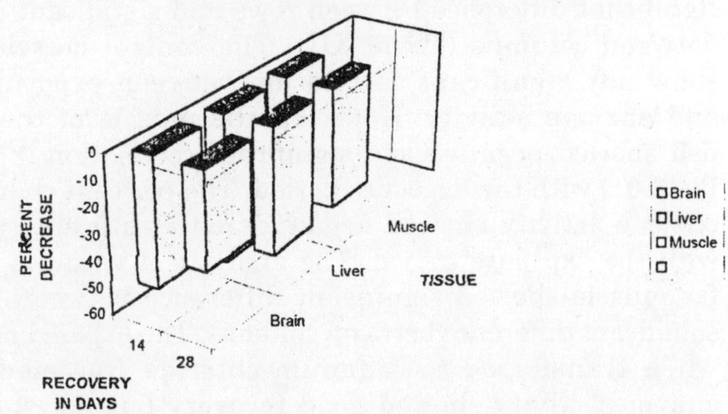

Fig. 3.31 Showing per cent decrease in Total ATPase activity in brain, liver and muscle of cadmium chloride exposed fish at different recovery periods

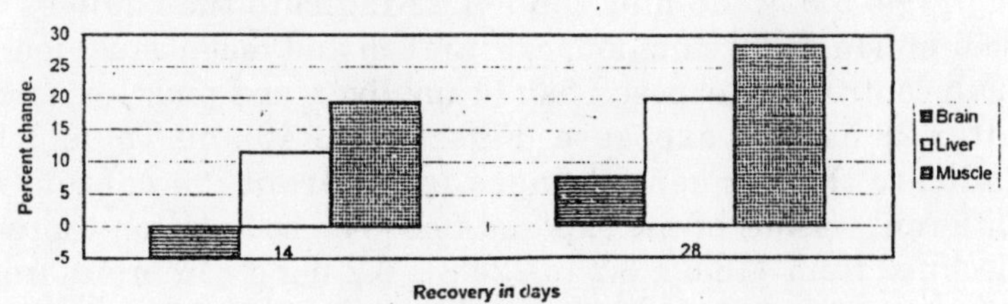

Fig. 3.32 Per cent recovery in total ATPase activity in brain, liver and muscle of exposed fish during recovery period

existence of a negative significant correlation (r = –0.981, P ≤ 0.01) with the exposure period. The analysis of variance ratio test conducted for Table-3.9 indicated the existence significant difference between rows and non-significant difference between columns (Table-VIII). The correlation coefficient analysis between days of exposure and the Na^+, K^+, Mg^{++} dependent ATPase of liver slices of the control fish did not show any significant correlation, whereas the exposed fish liver showed a negative and significant correlation (r = –0.984, P ≤ 0.01) with the exposure period. The per cent change in ATPase activity showed the existence of a negative, significant correlation (r = –0.985, P ≤ 0.01) with the exposure period. The analysis of variance ratio test indicated the existence of significant difference between rows and significant difference between columns (Table XII). The control muscle did not show any significant correlation between exposure period and enzyme activity. However, the muscle of the exposed fish showed negative and significant correlation (r = –0.985, P ≤ 0.01) with the exposure period. The per cent change in the enzyme activity showed negative and significant correlation with the exposure period. The analysis of variance ratio test for muscle showed significant difference between rows and significant difference between columns. The exposed fishes were when transferred to cadmium chloride free medium, the enzyme activity showed good recovery but not statistically significant. Muscle showed the highest recovery (28.5%), brain showed the lowest recovery by 7.8 per cent and liver showed recovery by 20 per cent in the recovery fishes, after 28 days of recovery (Table-3.11 and Fig. 3.32).

Figs. 3.33-3.36 and Table-3.12 indicate the changes in sodium ion, potassium ion, calcium ion and magnesium ion of both control and exposed fish brain, liver, and muscle tissues after 28 days of exposure. Figs. 3.37-3.40 and Table-3.13 indicate the per cent changes in different ion content of different tissues of the exposed fish. The sodium ion content declined from 416.6 ± 8.2 to 224.8 ± 6.2 mg g^{-1} in brain, from 452.2 ± 8.6 to 218.9 ± 6.4 mg g^{-1} in liver, from 378.4 ± 8.8 to 296.5 ± 7.6 mg g^{-1} in muscle (Fig. 3.33) after 28 days of exposure showing maximum d[illegible]ase by 46 per cent, 51.5 per cent and 21.6 per cent in brain, liver, muscle and kidney tissues,

Table 3.12 Changes Na^+, K^+, Ca^{++} and Mg^{++} ion concentration in control and exposed fish brain, liver and muscle after 28 days of exposure

TISSUE	*Condition*	*Ion Concentration*			
		Na^+	*K^+*	*Ca^{++}*	*Mg^{++}*
Brain	Control	416.6±8.2	409.2±4.6	193.6±8.8	236.5±8.2
	Exposed	224.8±6.2	289.8±4.5	174.4±2.4	114.2±9.6
Liver	Control	452.2±8.6	385.6±7.2	202.4±6.6	249.2±8.5
	Exposed	218.9±6.4	216.4±4.6	171.3±5.9	151.8±7.6
Muscle	Control	378.4±8.8	392.6±6.4	206.5±8.8	231.4±8.4
	Exposed	296.5±7.6	284.5±5.4	156.2±6.5	184.5±9.5

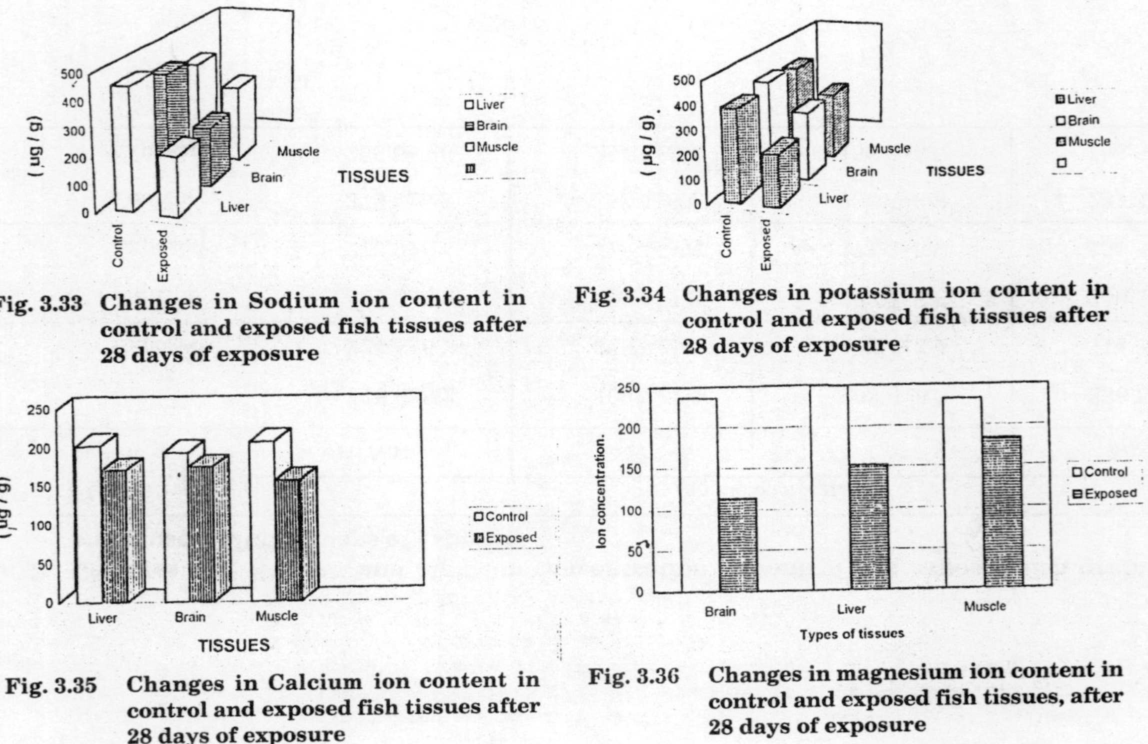

Fig. 3.33 **Changes in Sodium ion content in control and exposed fish tissues after 28 days of exposure**

Fig. 3.34 **Changes in potassium ion content in control and exposed fish tissues after 28 days of exposure**

Fig. 3.35 **Changes in Calcium ion content in control and exposed fish tissues after 28 days of exposure**

Fig. 3.36 **Changes in magnesium ion content in control and exposed fish tissues, after 28 days of exposure**

respectively (Fig. 3.37). The liver showed the highest per cent decrease, when compared to muscle and brain tissues of the exposed fish (Table-3.13). The potassium ion content declined from 409.2 ± 4.6 to 289.8 ± 4.5 mg g^{-1} in brain, from 385.6 ± 7.2 to 216.4 ± 4.6 mg g^{-1} in liver, and from 392.6 ± 6.4 to 284.5 ± 5.4 mg g^{-1} in muscle, respectively, after 28 days of exposure (Table-3.12 and Fig. 3.34). Brain, liver, and muscle of the exposed fish showed 29.1 per cent, 43.8 per cent, and 27.5 per cent decrease in potassium ion content, when compared to the control value, where liver was highly affected showing the maximum depletion (Fig. 3.38 and Table-3.13). Significant ($P \leq 0.01$) decrease in potassium ion content in brain, liver, and muscle of exposed fish, compared to the control fish, was marked. Significant variation was marked in the calcium ion content in different tissues of the exposed fish, when compared to control fish tissues. The calcium ion content, decreased from 193.6 ± 8.8 to 174.4 ± 2.4 mg g^{-1} in brain, from 202.4 ± 6.6 to 171.3 ± 5.9 mg^{-1} in liver and from 206.5 ± 8.8 to 156.2 ± 6.5 mg g^{-1} in muscle (Fig. 3.35 and Table-3.12) after 28 days of exposure. Maximum depletion by 24.3 per cent in muscle tissues, 15.3 per cent in liver tissue and least depletion by 9.9 per cent in brain tissues of the exposed fish, when compared to control fish tissues were recorded (Fig. 3.39 and Table 3.13). The magnesium ion content, decreased from 236.5 ± 8.2 to 114.2 ± 9.6 mg g^{-1} in brain, from 249.2 ± 8.5 to 151.8 ± 7.6 mg g^{-1} in liver and from 231.4 ± 8.4 to 184.5 ± 9.5 mg g^{-1} in muscle (Fig. 3.36 and Table 3.12) after 28 days of exposure. Maximum depletion by 51.7 per cent in brain tissues, 39 per cent in liver tissue and least depletion by 20.2 per cent in muscle tissues of the exposed fish, when compared to control fish tissue was recorded (Fig. 3.40 and Table 3.13). Out of the four ions studied in the exposed fish tissues, significant decrease was recorded in sodium ion and potassium ion content and highly significant differences were observed in potassium ion content in all the tissues studied. Out of the four tissues studied liver was the most affected than the least affected was brain for some ion and for the rest of the ions the muscle was least affected (Fig. 3.33 to 3.40 and Tables 3.12 and 3.13). The analysis of variance ratio test

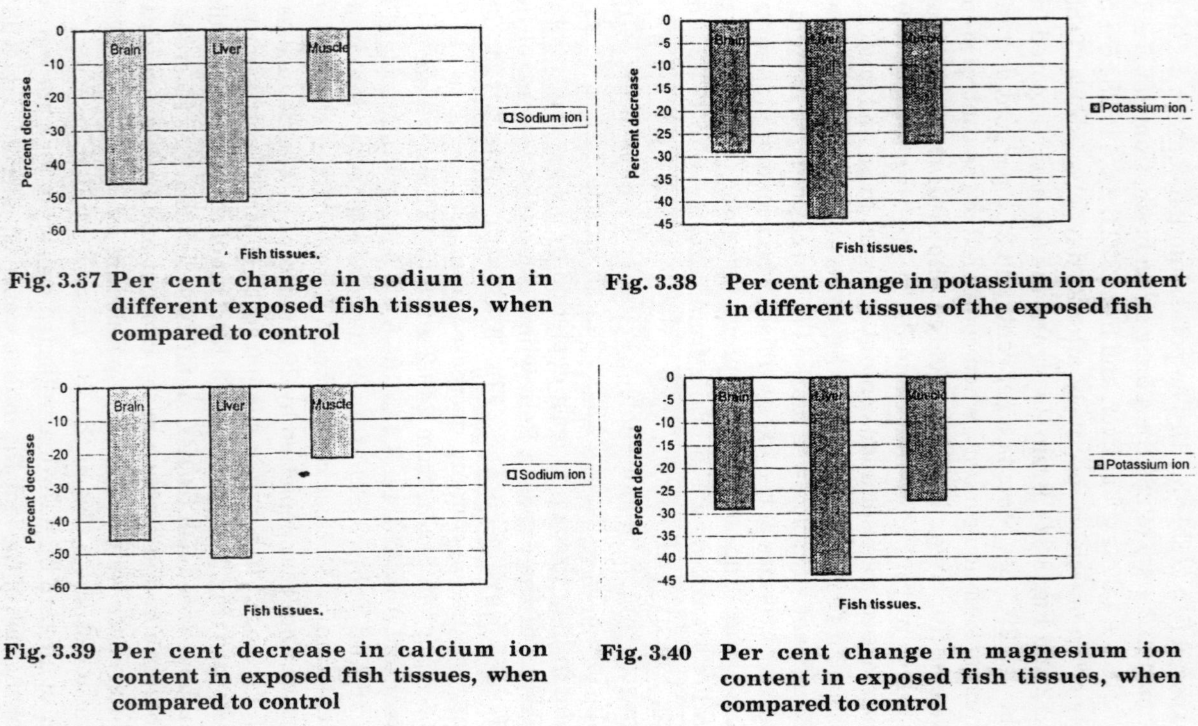

Fig. 3.37 Per cent change in sodium ion in different exposed fish tissues, when compared to control

Fig. 3.38 Per cent change in potassium ion content in different tissues of the exposed fish

Fig. 3.39 Per cent decrease in calcium ion content in exposed fish tissues, when compared to control

Fig. 3.40 Per cent change in magnesium ion content in exposed fish tissues, when compared to control

Table 3.13 Per cent changes in Na^+, K^+, Ca^{++} and Mg^{++} ion concentration in control and $CdCl_2$ exposed fish brain, liver, muscle and gill, after 28 days of exposure, when compared to control. Per cent change calculated from the mean of the samples

Tissue	*Condition*	*Ion Concentration*			
		Na^+	*K^+*	*Ca^{++}*	*Mg^{++}*
Brain	Control	NC	NC	NC	NC
	Exposed	–46.0	–29.1	–9.9	–51.7
Liver	Control	NC	NC	NC	NC
	Exposed	–51.5	–43.8	–15.3	–39.0
Muscle	Control	NC	NC	NC	NC
	Exposed	–21.6	–27.5	–24.3	–20.2

Table-3.14 Changes in total DNA content (mg. g^{-1} dry weight) in control and exposed fish brain, liver and muscle at different days of exposure and recovery.(Data are the mean of 3 samples ± standard deviation)

Tissue	Condition	Exposure in Days					Recovery in Days	
		0	7	14	21	28	14	28
Brain	Control	3.5±0.3	3.5±0.2	3.5±0.2	3.5±0.3	3.5±0.4	3.5±0.2	3.5±0.3
	Exposed	3.5±0.3	3.5±0.3	3.4±0.3	3.2±0.4	3.1±0.1	3.1±0.3	3.1±0.1
Liver	Control	3.5±0.2	3.5±0.2	3.5±0.4	3.5±0.3	3.5±0.4	3.5±0.1	3.5±0.1
	Exposed	3.5±0.2	3.0±0.1	2.9±0.2	2.7±0.3	2.2±0.2	2.1±0.2	2.6±0.2
Muscle	Control	3.4±0.6	3.4±0.4	3.4±0.3	3.4±0.4	3.4±0.1	3.4±0.1	3.4±0.3
	Exposed	3.4±0.6	3.0±0.1	2.8±0.3	2.5±0.5	2.2±0.2	2.4±0.3	2.6±0.39

Table 3.15 Per cent change in DNA content in exposed fish brain, liver and muscle at different exposure and recovery periods, when compared to respective controls. Values in parentheses indicate per cent recovery. (Data calculated from the mean of the samples)

Tissue	Exposure in Days					Recovery in Days	
	0	7	14	21	28	14	28
Brain	—	00	–2.8	–8.5	–11.4	–11.4 (NR)	–11.4 (NR)
Liver	—	–14.2	–17.1	–22.8	–37.1	–40.0 (–2.9)	–25.7 (11.4)
Muscle	—	–11.7	–17.6	–26.4	–35.2	–29.4 (5.8)	–23.5 (11.7)

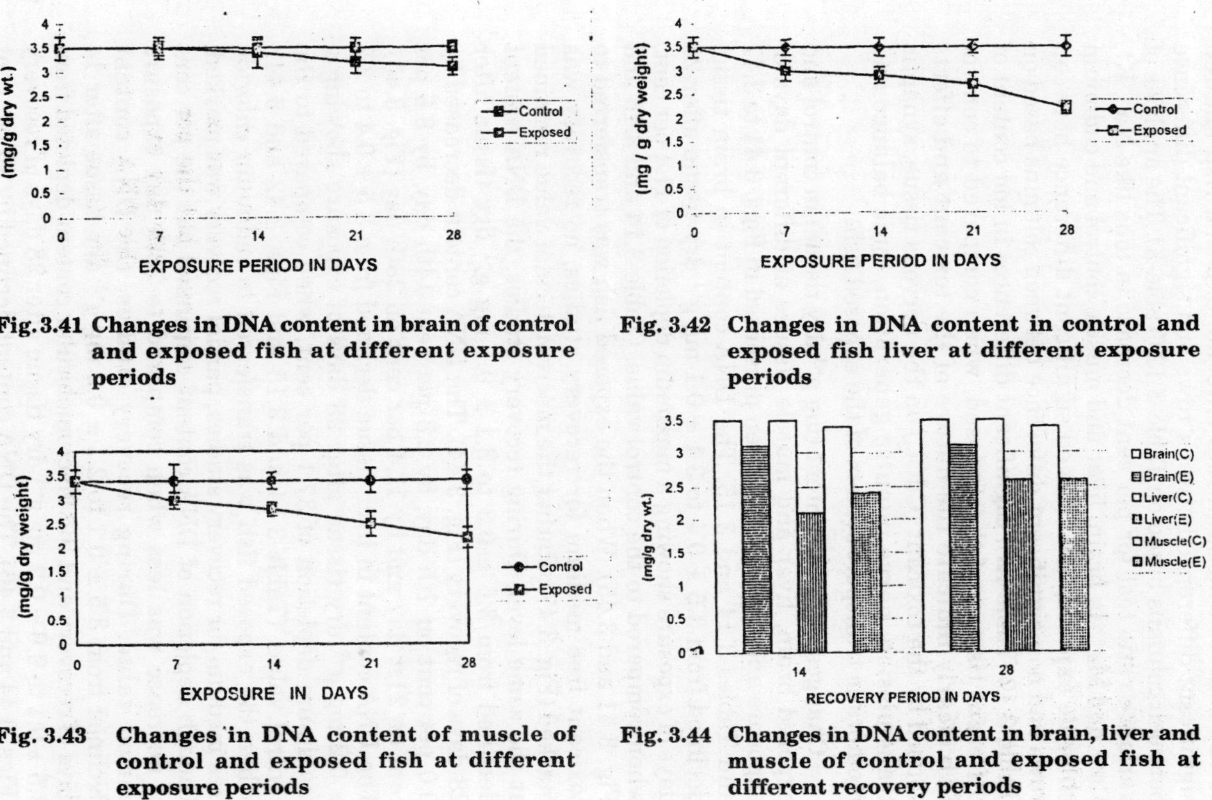

Fig. 3.41 Changes in DNA content in brain of control and exposed fish at different exposure periods

Fig. 3.42 Changes in DNA content in control and exposed fish liver at different exposure periods

Fig. 3.43 Changes in DNA content of muscle of control and exposed fish at different exposure periods

Fig. 3.44 Changes in DNA content in brain, liver and muscle of control and exposed fish at different recovery periods

for ions like Na^+, K^+, Ca^{++} and Mg^{++} in brain, liver and muscle of the control and cadmium chloride exposed fish showed significant difference between rows and significant difference between columns based on Table-3.12 (Table-X). The analysis of variance ratio test for per cent decrease in ions like Na^+, K^+, Ca^{++} and Mg^{++} in brain, liver and muscle control and cadmium chloride exposed fish showed significant difference between rows and non-significant difference between columns based on Table-3.12 (Table-XI). Significant differences in ion content of different tissues of the exposed, when compared to control fish clearly indicate the nature of the toxicant and effects caused by the toxicant ($CdCl_2$) on the nervous tissue, synaptic transmission, nerve impulse generation, ionic balance and membrane transport system of the exposed fish.

Changes in DNA content (mg g^{-1} dry tissue) in control and exposed brain, liver and muscle tissues at different days of exposure and recovery has been presented in Figs. 3.41 to 3.47 and Tables-3.14 and 3.15. The DNA content in brain tissue declined from 3.5 ± 0.4 to 3.1 ± 0.1 mg g^{-1} dry tissue after 28 days of exposure showing a maximum depletion of 11.4 per cent, when compared to the control value. (Table-3.14 and 3.15 and Fig. 3.41 and 3.45). When the exposed fish was transferred to toxicant free medium for recovery studies, no recovery was marked (Fig. 3.47). Rather the macromolecular value remained at the same level. During recovery studies, the DNA content declined from 3.5 ± 0.3 to 3.1 ± 0.1 mg g^{-1} dry tissue after 28 days of recovery (Fig. 3.44). The DNA content decreased by 0.0 per cent on 7th day, by 2.8 per cent 14th day, by 8.5 per cent on 21st day and by 11.4 per cent on 28th day (Fig. 3.45). The DNA content in liver tissue declined from 3.5 ± 0.4 to 2.2 ± 0.2 mg g^{-1} dry tissue after 28 days of exposure showing a maximum depletion of 37.1 per cent, when compared to the control value. (Table-3.14 and 3.15 and Figs. 3.42 and 3.44). When the exposed fish was transferred to cadmium chloride free medium for recovery studies, partial recovery was marked. Though depletion of DNA content continued but the per cent of decrease was less when compared to 28th day exposure period value. During recovery studies, the DNA content declined from 3.5 ± 0.1 to 2.1 ± 0.2 mg g^{-1} dry tissue after 14 days of recovery and the macromolecular content depleted from 3.5 ± 0.1 to 2.6 ± 0.2 mg g^{-1} dry tissue after 28 days of recovery (Figs. 3.44 and 3.46). The DNA content declined by 40 per cent and 25.7 per cent on 14th and 28th day of recovery (Fig. 3.45).

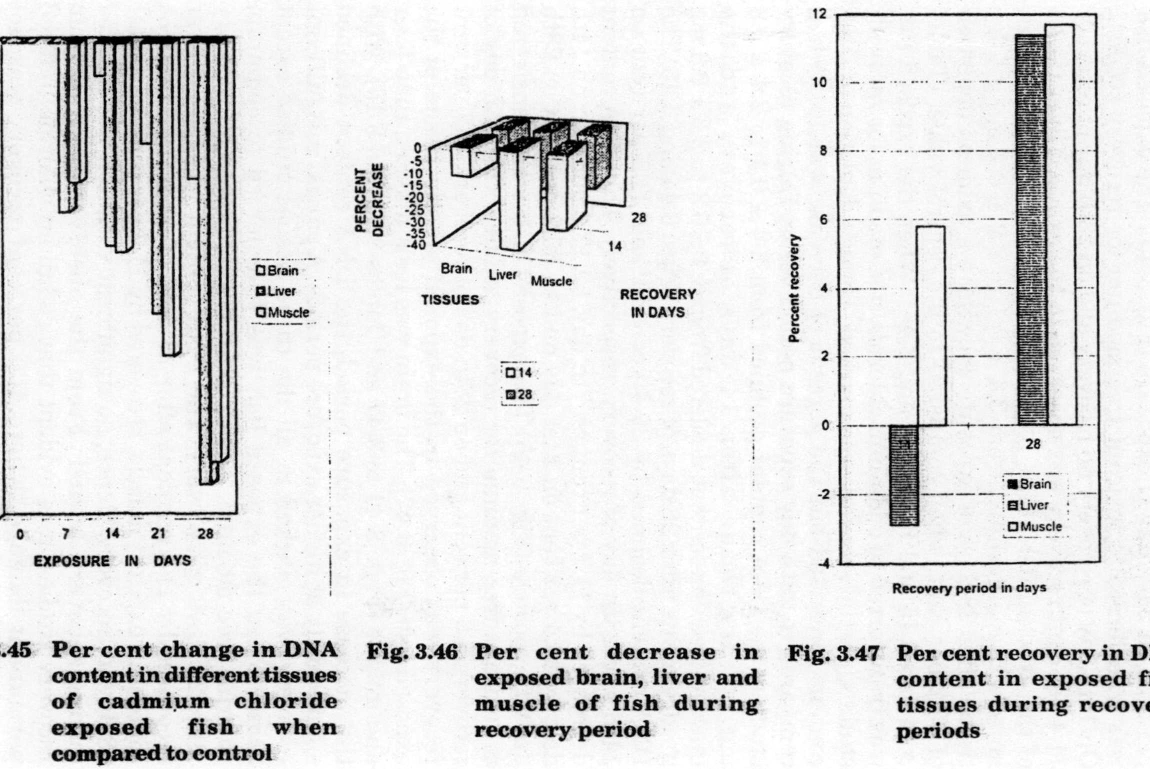

Fig. 3.45 Per cent change in DNA content in different tissues of cadmium chloride exposed fish when compared to control

Fig. 3.46 Per cent decrease in exposed brain, liver and muscle of fish during recovery period

Fig. 3.47 Per cent recovery in DNA content in exposed fish tissues during recovery periods

The DNA content decreased by 14.2 per cent on 7th day, by 17.1 per cent on 14th day, by 22.8 per cent on 21st day and by 37.1 per cent on 28th day of exposure (Fig. 3.45). The exposed fish was transferred to toxicant free medium for recovery studies. On 14th day of recovery no recovery and on 28th day of recovery 11.4 per cent recovery was observed in the exposed liver tissue of the exposed fish (Figs. 3.46 and 3.47). The DNA content in muscle tissue declined from 3.4 ± 0.1 to 2.2 ± 0.2 mg g^{-1} dry tissue after 28 days of exposure showing a maximum depletion of 35.2 per cent, when compared to the control value. (Table-3.14 and 3.15 and Figs. 3.43 and 3.45). When the exposed fish was transferred to cadmium chloride free medium for recovery studies, partial recovery was marked. Though depletion of DNA content continued but the percent of decrease was less when compared to 28th day exposure period value. During recovery studies, the DNA content declined from 3.4 ± 0.1 to 2.4 ± 0.3 mg g^{-1} dry tissue after 14 days of recovery and the macromolecular content depleted from 3.4 ± 0.3 to 2.6 ± 0.3 mg g^{-1} dry tissue after 28 days of recovery (Figs. 3.44 and 3.46).The DNA content declined by 29.4 per cent and 23.5 per cent on 14th and 28th day of recovery, respectively. The DNA content decreased by 11.7 per cent on 7th day, by 17.6 per cent on 14th day, by 26.4 per cent on 21st day and by 35.2 per cent on 28th day of exposure (Fig. 3.45).The exposed fish was transferred to toxicant free medium for recovery studies. On 14th day of recovery 5.8 per cent and on 28th day of recoveiy 11.7 per cent recovery was observed in the exposed muscle tissue of the exposed fish (Fig. 3.47). The brain was least affected than liver and muscle (Figs. 3.41 to 3.47 and Tables-3.14 and 3.15). With the increase in exposure period, the DNA content declined significantly at higher exposure periods. A partial insignificant recovery was marked in all the three tissues studied except brain, when the exposed fish was transferred to cadmium chloride free medium. The exposed brain showed no recovery after 28 days of recovery. The DNA content of exposed liver recovered by 11.4 per cent after 28 days of recovery. The DNA content in exposed muscle, recovered by 11.7 per cent only, after 28 days of recovery. Hence, no significant variation was marked during recovery period. From the observations and from recovery studies, it is evident that cadmium chloride induced permanent damage, where 100 per cent recovery was not possible under experimental conditions. The correlation coefficient analysis between days of exposure and changes in the DNA content of brain of the control fish, showed (P = NS)

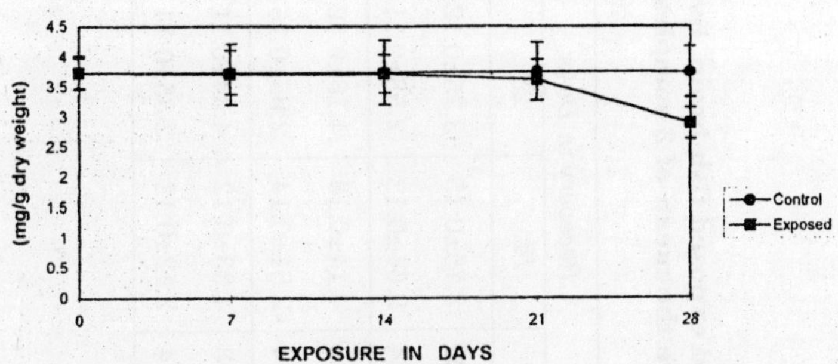

Fig. 3.48 Changes in RNA content of brain of control and exposed fish at different exposure periods

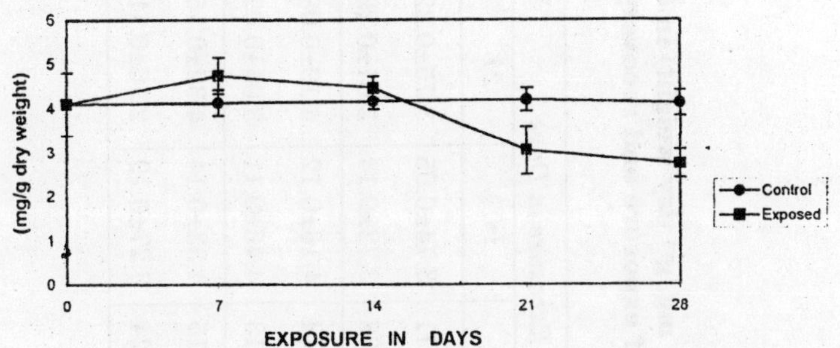

Fig. 3.49 Changes in RNA content of liver of control and exposed fish at different exposure periods

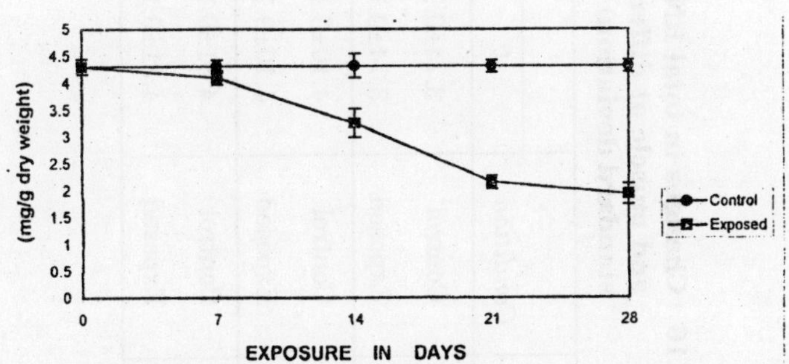

Fig. 3.50 Changes in RNA content of muscle of control and exposed fish at different exposure periods

Table 3.16 Changes in total RNA content(mg. g^{-1} dry weight) in control and exposed fish brain, liver and muscle at different days of exposure and recovery. (Data are the mean of 3 samples ± standard deviation)

Tissue	*Condition*	*Exposure in Days*					*Recovery in Days*	
		0	*7*	*14*	*21*	*28*	*14*	*28*
Brain	Control	3.74±0.12	3.74±0.11	3.74±0.05	3.75±0.22	3.74±0.21	3.75±0.15	3.75±0.12
	Exposed	3.74±0.12	3.71±0.08	3.72±0.14	3.61±0.22	2.88±0.14	2.64±0.12	2.58±0.11
Liver	Control	4.10±0.14	4.13±0.14	4.16±0.12	4.19±0.08	4.12±0.12	4.14±0.13	4.16±0.12
	Exposed	4.10±0.14	4.74±0.13	4.46±0.11	3.04±0.09	2.74±0.14	2.81±0.14	2.98±0.16
Muscle	Control	4.31±0.11	4.32±0.15	4.33±0.14	4.32±0.15	4.32±0.13	4.33±0.12	4.34±0.11
	Exposed	4.31±0.11	4.11±0.24	3.27±0.19	2.16±0.11	1.94±0.14	2.12±0.12	2.35±0.14

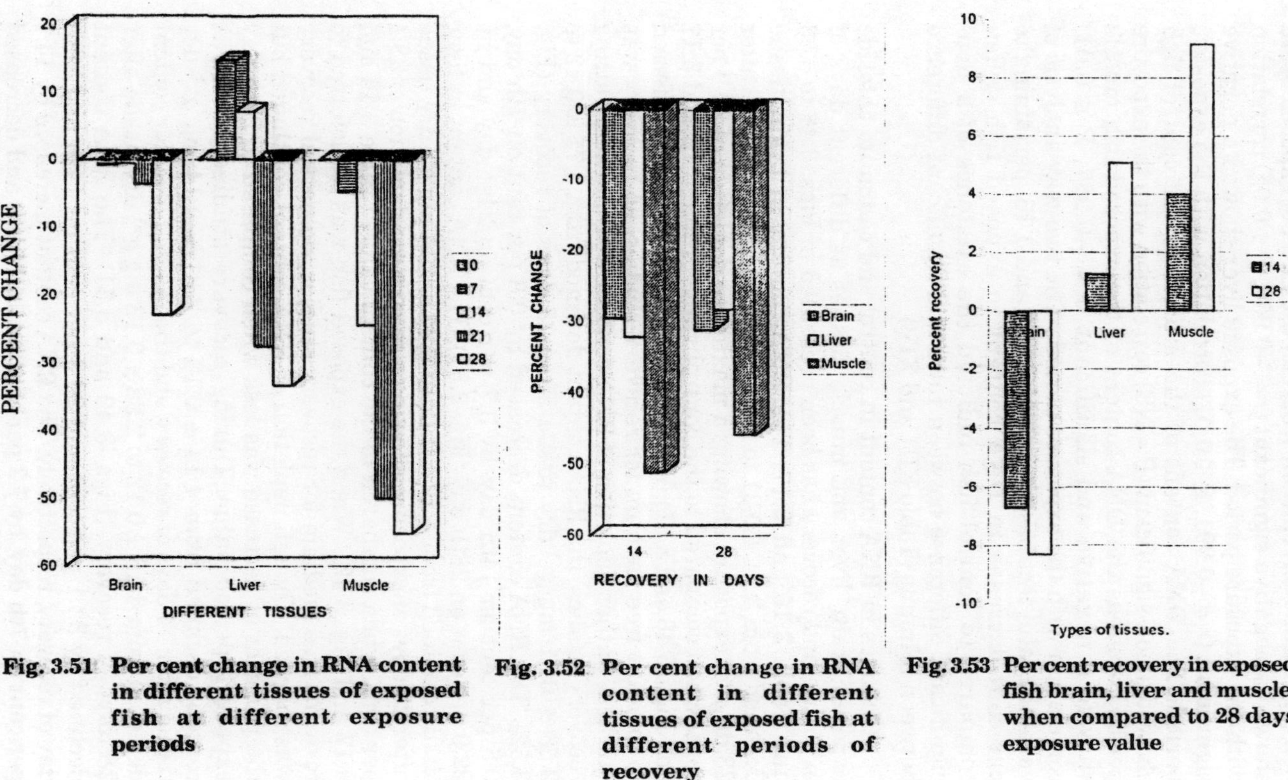

Fig. 3.51 **Per cent change in RNA content in different tissues of exposed fish at different exposure periods**

Fig. 3.52 **Per cent change in RNA content in different tissues of exposed fish at different periods of recovery**

Fig. 3.53 **Per cent recovery in exposed fish brain, liver and muscle, when compared to 28 days exposure value**

non-significant correlation, whereas the DNA of exposed brain showed a negative significant ($r = -0.956$, $P \leq 0.05$) correlation with the exposure period. The exposed liver showed a negative significant ($r = -0.991$, $P \leq 0.01$) correlation with the exposure period. The DNA content of the muscle of the control fish showed a non-significant (P = NS) correlation with the exposure period, whereas the DNA content of the exposed fish muscle showed a negative and significant ($r = -0.987$, $P \leq 0.01$) correlation with the exposure period . The two-way analysis of variance ratio test based on Table-3.15 and 3.16, pertaining to per cent decrease in DNA content in exposed fish, when compared to control fish indicted the existence of a non-significant difference between rows and significant difference between columns (Table XIII and XIV).

Changes in RNA content in control and cadmium chloride exposed brain, liver and muscle tissues at different days of exposure and recovery has been presented in Figs. 3.48 to 3.53 and Table 3.16 and 3.17. The RNA content in brain tissue declined from 3.74 ± 0.21 to 2.88 ± 0.14 mg g^{-1} dry tissue after 28 days of exposure showing a maximum depletion of 22.9 per cent, when compared to the control value (Table-3.16 and 3.17 and Figs. 3.48 and 3.51). When the exposed fish was transferred to toxicant free medium for recovery studies, no recovery was marked. Rather depletion of RNA content was marked. During recovery studies, the RNA content declined from 3.75 ± 0.12 to 2.58 ± 0.11 mg g^{-1} dry tissue after 28 days of recovery (Fig. 3.52). The RNA content decreased by 0.8 per cent on 7th day, 0.5 per cent on 14th day, by 3.7 per cent on 21st day and by 22.9 per cent on 28th day (Fig. 3.51). The RNA content in liver tissue declined from 4.12 ± 0.12 to 2.74 ± 0.14 mg g^{-1} dry tissue after 28 days of exposure showing a maximum depletion of 33.4 per cent, when compared to the control value. (Table 3.16 and 3.17 and Fig. 3.49). When the exposed fish was transferred to toxicant free medium for recovery studies, no partial recovery was marked. Though depletion of RNA content continued but the per cent of decrease was less when compared to 28th day exposure period value. During recovery studies, the RNA content declined from 4.14 ± 0.13 to 2.81 ± 0.14 mg g^{-1} dry tissue after 14 days of recovery and the macromolecular content depleted from 4.16 ± 0.12 to 2.98 ± 0.16 mg g^{-1} dry tissue after 28 days of recovery (Figs. 3.49 and 3.51). The RNA content declined by 32.1 per cent and 28.3 per cent on 14th and 28th day of recovery, respectively. The RNA content increased by 14.7 per cent on 7th day, by 7.2 per cent on 14th day, and decreased by 27.4 per cent on 21st day and by 33.4 per cent on 28th day of exposure (Fig. 3.51). The exposed fish was transferred to toxicant free medium for recovery studies. On 14th day of recovery 1.3 per cent and on 28th day of recovery 5.1 per cent recovery was observed in the exposed liver tissue of the exposed fish (Fig. 3.53). The RNA content in muscle tissue declined from 4.32 ± 0.13 to 1.94 ± 0.14 mg g^{-1} dry tissue after 28 days of exposure showing a maximum depletion of 55 per cent, when compared to the control value. (Table 3.16 and 3.17 and Figs. 3.50 and 3.51). When the exposed fish was transferred to toxicant free medium for recovery studies, insignificant partial recoveiy was marked. Though depletion of RNA content continued but the per cent of decrease was less when compared to 28th day exposure period value. During recovery studies, the RNA content declined from 4.33 ± 0.12 to 2.12 ± 0.12 mg g^{-1} dry tissue after 14 days of recovery and the macromolecular content depleted from 4.34 ± 0.11 to 2.35 ± 0.14 mg g^{-1} dry tissue after 28 days of recovery. The RNA content declined by 51 per cent and 45.8 per cent on 14th and 28th day of recovery (Fig. 3.52). The RNA content decreased by 4.8 per cent on 7th day, by 24.4 per cent on 14th day, by 50 per cent on 21st day and by 55 per cent on 28th day of exposure (Fig. 3.51). The exposed fish was transferred to toxicant free medium for recovery studies. On 14th day of recovery 4 per cent and on 28th day of recovery 9.2 per cent recovery was observed in the exposed muscle tissue of the exposed fish (Fig. 3.53). The brain was least affected than liver and muscle (Figs. 3.48 to 3.53). With the increase in exposure period, the RNA content declined significantly at higher exposure periods (Tables 3.16 and 3.17). A partial insignificant recovery was marked in all the three tissues studied except brain tissue, when the exposed fish was transferred to cadmium chloride free medium. The exposed brain showed decrease in the value from the 28 days exposure value after 28 days of recovery. No recovery was marked in the exposed brain tissue, rather further depletion in RNA content was noted. The RNA content of exposed liver recovered by 5.1 per cent after 28 days of recovery. The RNA content in exposed muscle, recovered by 9.2 per cent only, after 28 days of recovery. Hence, no significant variation was marked during recovery period. From the observations and from recovery studies, it is evident that the cadmium chloride induces permanent damage, where 100 per cent recovery was not possible under experimental conditions. The exposed liver showed a negative significant ($r = -0.989$, $P \leq 0.01$) correlation

Table 3.17 Per cent change in RNA content in exposed fish brain, liver and muscle at different exposure and recovery periods when compared to respective controls. Values in parentheses indicate per cent recovery. (Data calculated from the mean of the samples)

Tissue	*Exposure in Days*					*Recovery in Days*	
	0	*7*	*14*	*21*	*28*	*14*	*28*
ın	0.0	–0.8	–0.5	–3.7	–22.9	–29.6 (NR)	–31.2 (NR)
Liver	0.0	+14.7	+7.2	–27.4	–33.4	–32.1 (1.3)	–28.3 (5.1)
Muscle	0.0	–4.8	–24.4	–50.0	–55.0	–51.0 (4.0)	–45.8 (9.2)

with the exposure period. The two-way analysis of variance ratio test based on Tables-3.16 and 3.17, pertaining to change and per cent decrease in RNA content in exposed fish, when compared to control fish indicted the existence of a non-significant difference between rows and significant difference between columns. The correlation coefficient analysis between days of exposure and changes in the RNA content of brain of the control fish, showed (P = NS), non-significant correlation. The RNA content of the exposed fish muscle showed a negative significant correlation ($r = 0.985$, $P \leq 0.01$) with the exposure period. Whereas, the RNA content in exposed fish liver showed a significant negative correlation ($r = -0.974$, $P \leq 0.05$) with the exposure period. The RNA content of the muscle of the control fish showed a non-significant correlation (P = NS) with the exposure period. The RNA content of the exposed fish muscle showed a significant negative correlation ($r = -0.938$, $P \leq 0.05$) with the exposure period. The two-way analysis of variance ratio test based on Tables-3.17 and 3.18, pertaining to changes and per cent change in RNA content in brain, liver and muscle of exposed fish indicated the existence of a significant difference between rows and columns (Table XV and XVI).

Changes in protein content in control and exposed brain, liver and muscle tissues at different days of exposure and recovery has been presented in Figs. 3.54 to 3.59 and Tables 3.18 and 3.19. The protein content in brain tissue declined from 35.3 ± 3.1 to 29.1 ± 2.1 mg g^{-1} dry tissue after 28 days of exposure showing a maximum depletion of 17.4 per cent, when compared to the control value. (Tables 3.18 and 3.19 and Figs. 3.54 and 3.57). When the exposed fish was transferred to toxicant free medium for recovery studies, no recovery was marked. Rather depletion of protein content was marked. During recovery studies, the protein content declined from 35.3 ± 1.6 to 25.3 ± 2.1 mg g^{-1} dry tissue after 28 days of recovery (Table 3.18). The protein content decreased by 0.08 per cent on 7th day, 0.3 per cent on 14th day, by 11.8 per cent on 21st day and by 17.4 per cent on 28th day (Fig. 3.57). The protein content in liver tissue declined from 54.7 ± 2.3 to 31.2 ± 2.3 mg g^{-1} dry tissue after 28 days of exposure showing a maximum depletion of 42.9 per cent, when compared to the control value. (Tables 3.18 and 3.19 and Figs. 3.55 and 3.57). When the exposed fish was transferred to toxicant free medium for recovery studies, no recovery was marked on 14th day of recovery and partial recovery by 4.2 per cent was marked on 28th day of recovery (Table 3.19 and Fig. 3.57). Though depletion of protein content continued but the percent of decrease was less when compared to 28th day exposure period value. During recovery studies, the protein content declined

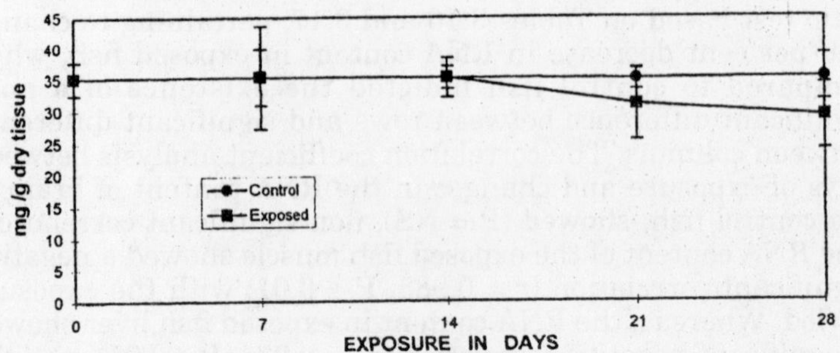

Fig. 3.54 Changes in protein content of brain of control and exposed fish at different exposure periods

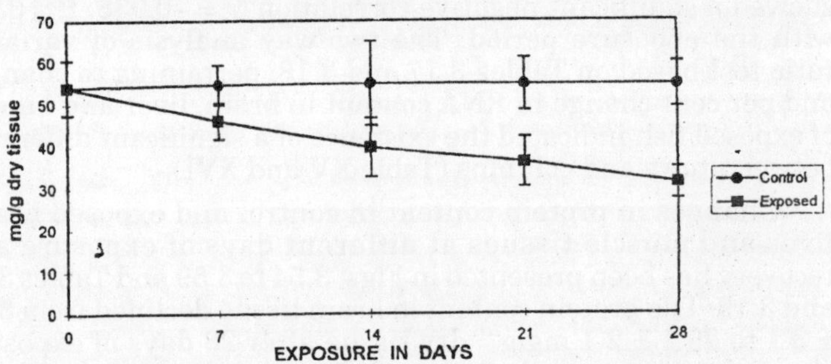

Fig. 3.55 Changes in protein content of liver of control and exposed fish at different exposure periods

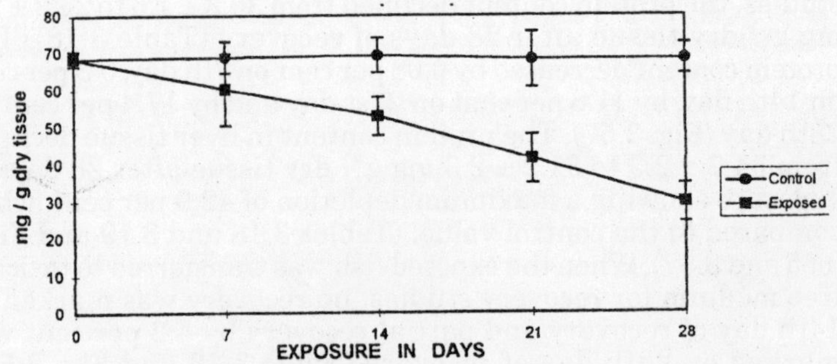

Fig. 3.56 Changes in protein content of muscle of control and exposed fish at different exposure periods

Table 3.18 Changes in Protein content (mg.g^{-1}. dry weight) in control and exposed fish brain, liver and muscle at different days of exposure and recovery. Data are the mean of 3 estimates ± standard deviation

Tissue	*Condition*	*Exposure in Days*					*Recovery in Days*	
		0	*7*	*14*	*21*	*28*	*14*	*28*
Brain	Control	35.2±2.2	35.4±2.3	35.3±2.2	35.1±2.2	35.3±3.1	35.2±2.1	35.3±1.6
	Exposed	35.2±2.2	35.4±2.5	35.3±2.8	31.0±2.1	29.1±2.1	27.1±1.8	25.3±2.1
Liver	Control	54.1±3.1	54.7±2.8	55.0±1.6	54.8±2.7	54.7±2.3	54.7±2.8	54.7±2.6
	Exposed	54.1±3.1	46.1±3.1	39.8±2.2	36.3±1.8	31.2±2.3	30.4±2.6	33.5±2.1
Muscle	Control	68.5±2.2	68.8±2.1	69.2±0.9	68.1±1.6	68.4±1.8	68.6±2.1	69.1±2.4
	Exposed	68.5±2.2	60.2±1.6	52.9±3.2	41.4±2.6	29.6±3.1	36.4±2.6	41.2±3.4

Table 3.19 Per cent change in Protein content in exposed fish brain, liver and muscle at different exposure and recovery. Values in parentheses indicate per cent recovery. (Data calculated from the mean of the samples) NR = No recovery

Tissue	*Exposure in Days*					*Recovery in Days*	
	0	*7*	*14*	*21*	*28*	*14*	*28*
Brain	—	–0.08	–0.03	–11.8	–17.4	–22.9 (NR)	–28.2 (NR)
Liver	—	–15.7	–27.5	–33.6	–42.9	–44.3 (NR)	–38.7 (4.2)
Muscle	—	–12.5	–23.6	–39.3	–56.6	–46.9 (9.6)	40.3 (16.2)

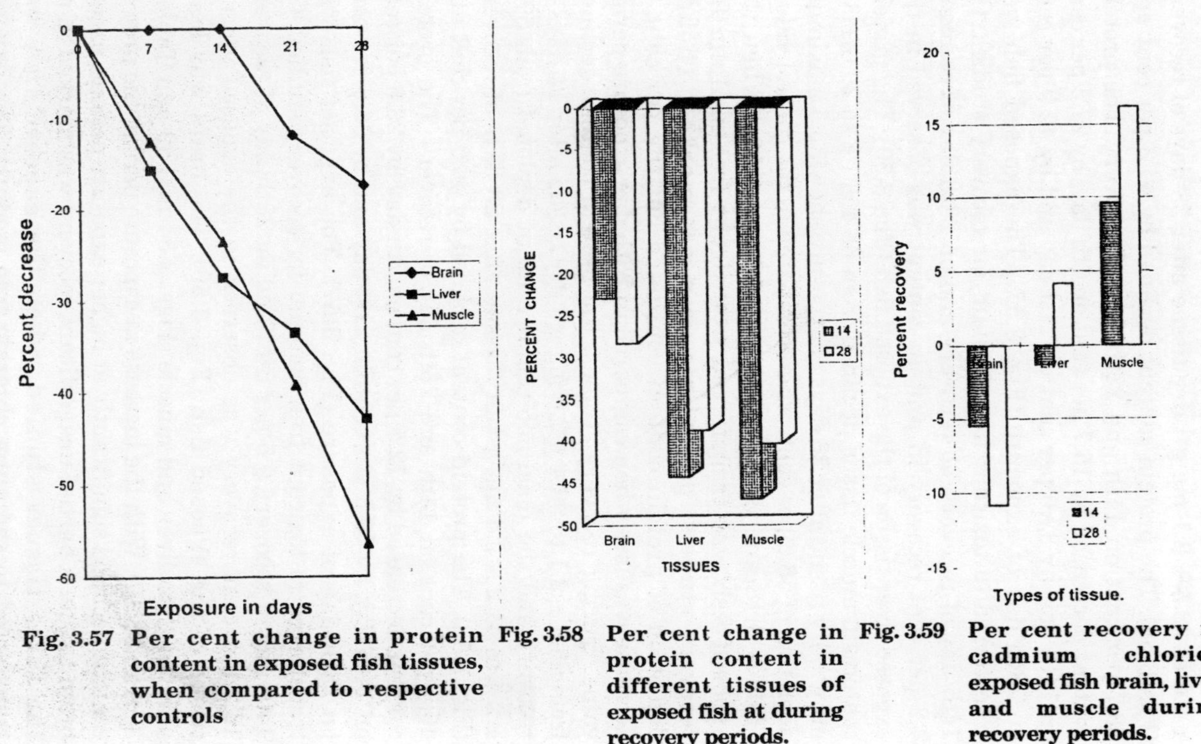

Fig. 3.57 Per cent change in protein content in exposed fish tissues, when compared to respective controls

Fig. 3.58 Per cent change in protein content in different tissues of exposed fish at during recovery periods.

Fig. 3.59 Per cent recovery in cadmium chloride exposed fish brain, liver and muscle during recovery periods.

from 54.7 ± 2.8 to 30.4 ± 2.6 mg g^{-1} dry tissue after 14 days of recovery and the macromolecular content depleted from 54.7 ± 2.6 to 33.5 ± 2.1 mg g^{-1} dry tissue after 28 days of recovery (Fig. 3.58). The protein content declined by 44.3 per cent and 38.7 per cent on 14th and 28th day of recovery. The protein content decreased by 15.7 per cent on 7th day, by 27.5 per cent on 14th day, by 33.6 per cent on 21st day and by 42.9 per cent on 28th day of exposure (Fig. 3.57). The exposed fish was transferred to toxicant free medium for recovery studies. On 14th day of recovery no recovery and on 28th day of recovery 4.2 per cent recovery in protein content was observed in the exposed liver tissue of the exposed fish (Fig. 3.59). The protein content in muscle tissue declined from 68.4 ± 1.8 to 29.6 ± 3.1 mg g^{-1} dry tissue after 28 days of exposure showing a maximum depletion of 56.6 per cent, when compared to the control value. (Tables 3.18 and 3.19 and Figs. 3.56 and 3.57). When the exposed fish was transferred to toxicant free medium for recovery studies, partial recovery was marked. Though depletion of protein content continued but the per cent of decrease was less when compared to 28th day exposure period value. During recovery studies, the protein content declined from 68.6 ± 2.1 to 36.4 ± 2.6 mg g^{-1} dry tissue after 14 days of recovery and the macromolecular content depleted from 69.1 ± 2.4 to 41.2 ± 3.4 mg g^{-1} dry tissue after 28 days of recovery (Fig. 3.58). The protein content declined by 46.9 per cent and 40.3 per cent on 14th and 28th day of recovery. The protein content decreased by 12.5 per cent on 7th day, by 23.6 per cent on 14th day, by 39.3 per cent on 21st day and by 56.6 per cent on 28th day of exposure (Fig. 3.57). The exposed fish was transferred to toxicant free medium for recovery studies. On 14th day of recovery 9.6 per cent and on 28th day of recovery 16.2 per cent recovery was observed in the exposed muscle tissue of the exposed fish (Fig. 3.59). The brain was least affected than liver and muscle (Figs. 3.54 to 3.59 and Tables-3.18 and 3.19). With the increase in exposure period, the protein content declined significantly at higher exposure periods, except brain tissue. A partial insignificant recovery was marked in all the three tissues studied, when the exposed fish was transferred to cadmium chloride free medium. The exposed brain showed significant depletion from the control value after

28 days of recovery. The protein content of exposed liver recovered by 4.2 per cent after 28 days of recovery. The protein content in exposed muscle, recovered by 16.2 per cent only, after 28 days of recovery. Hence, no significant variation was marked during recovery period. From the observations and from recovery studies, it is evident that cadmium chloride induces permanent damage, where 100 per cent recovery was not possible under experimental conditions. The slow recovery rate in the tissues indicate the direct effect of the toxicant on the biochemical metabolism of the fish affecting the protein synthesis and amino-acid synthesis by effecting at the transcription and translation stage. The correlation coefficient analysis between days of exposure versus the protein content of brain, muscle and liver of control fish indicted the existence of no correlation. The protein content of brain, liver and muscle of the exposed fish showed significant ($P \leq 0.05$), negative correlation (brain, $r = -0.988$; liver, $r = -0.972$; muscle, $r = -0.976$) with the exposure period. The two-way analysis of variance ratio test conducted based on Table-3.19, pertaining to per cent change in protein content of exposed fish tissues, indicated the existence of significant difference between in rows and columns (Table XVIII).

Changes in FAA content in brain, liver and muscle tissues of control and cadmium chloride exposed fishes at different days of exposure and recovery has been presented in Tables 3.20 and 3.21 and Figs. 3.60 to 3.66). The FAA content in brain tissue decreased from 178.4 ± 15.5 to 151.8 ± 8.5 μg g^{-1} dry tissue after 28 days of exposure showing a maximum decrease by 14.9 per cent, when compared to the control value. (Tables 3.20 and 3.21 and Figs. 3.60 and 3.64). When the exposed fish was transferred to toxicant free medium for recovery studies, partial recovery was marked. During recovery studies, the FAA content decreased from 177.6 ± 12.2 to 160.2 ± 12.4 μg g^{-1} dry tissue after 28 days of recovery (Figs. 3.63 and 3.65). The FAA content decreased by 0.1 per cent on 7th day, 3 per cent on 14th day, by 7.1 per cent on 21st day and by 14.9 per cent on 28th day of exposure (Fig. 3.64). The FAA content in liver tissue decreased from 184.5 ± 8.4 to 132.4 ± 5.8 μg g^{-1} dry tissue after 28 days of exposure showing a maximum decrease of 28.2 per

Table 3.20 Changes in free amino acid content ($\mu g.g^{-1}$. dry weight) in control and exposed fish at different days of exposure and recovery.(Data are the mean of 5 samples ± standard deviation)

Tissue	*Condition*	*Exposure in Days*					*Recovery in Days*	
		0	*7*	*14*	*21*	*28*	*14*	*28*
Brain	Control	178.4±3.2	177.6±9.5	176.5±12.5	178.2±13.6	178.4±15.5	176.5±13.7	177.6±12.2
	Exposed	178.4±3.2	177.4±9.4	171.2±10.6	165.4±12.4	151.8±8.5	156.4±8.9	160.2±12.4
Liver	Control	182.5±6.5	186.4±5.4	184.2±9.5	183.5±11.2	184.5±8.4	184.6±7.5	185.2±5.8
	Exposed	182.5±6.5	172.6±8.2	165.4±6.8	155.4±9.4	132.4±5.8	144.5±9.5	151.5±11.8
Muscle	Control	164.5±10.6	164.8±9.2	164.2±8.6	164.6±10.9	164.2±7.5	164.8±10.2	164.2±8.5
	Exposed	164.5±10.6	158.4±8.4	152.8±6.4	131.2±6.8	114.5±9.2	117.4±8.4	121.4±11.5

Table 3.21 Per cent change in free amino acid content in exposed *Tilapia* fish at different exposure and recovery periods. Values in parentheses indicate per cent recovery. (Data calculated from the mean of the samples) NR = No recovery

Tissue	*Exposure in Days*					*Recovery in Days*	
	0	*7*	*14*	*21*	*28*	*14*	*28*
Brain	0.0	–0.1	–3.0	–7.1	–14.9	–11.3 (3.6)	–9.7 (5.2)
Liver	0.0	–7.4	–10.2	–15.3	–28.2	–21.7 (6.5)	–18.1 (10.1)
Muscle	0.0	–3.8	–6.9	–20.2	–30.2	–28.7 (1.5)	–26.0 (4.2)

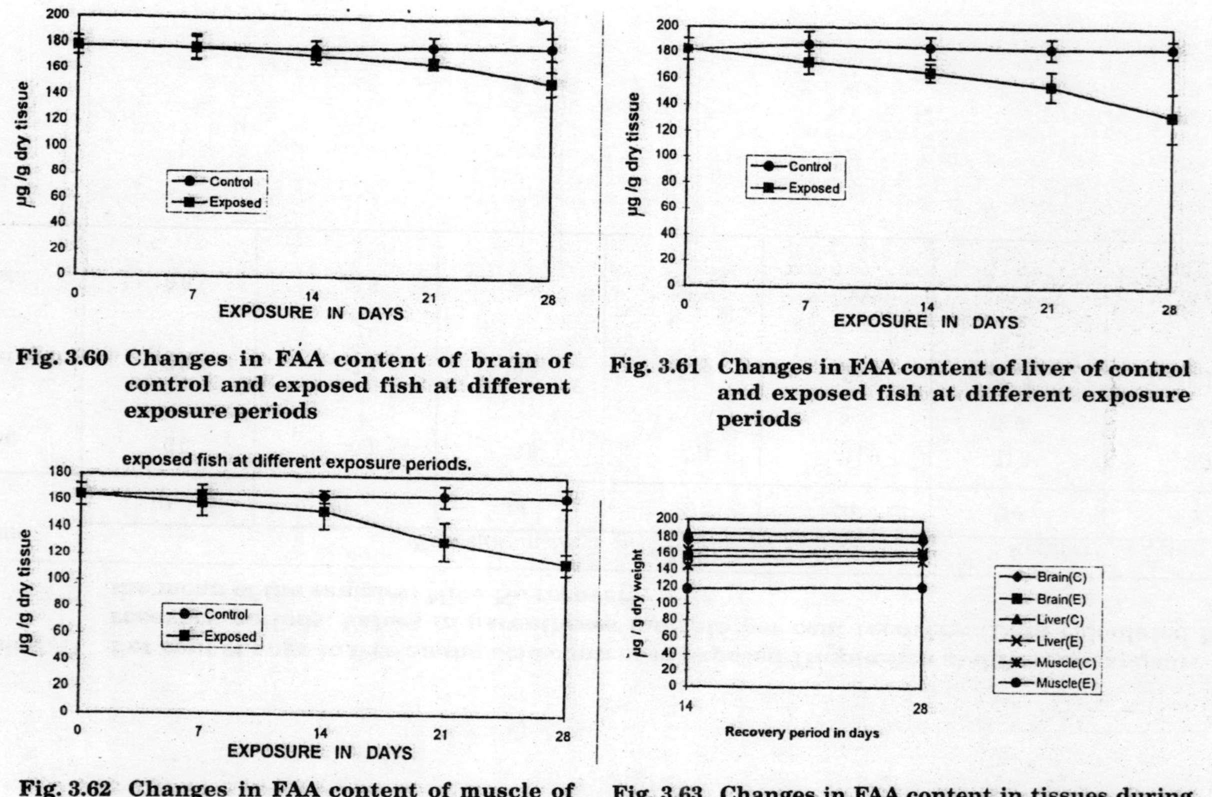

Fig. 3.60 Changes in FAA content of brain of control and exposed fish at different exposure periods

Fig. 3.61 Changes in FAA content of liver of control and exposed fish at different exposure periods

Fig. 3.62 Changes in FAA content of muscle of control and exposed fish at different

Fig. 3.63 Changes in FAA content in tissues during recovery periods

cent, when compared to the control value. (Tables 3.20 and 3.21 and Figs. 3.61 and 3.64). When the exposed fish was transferred to toxicant free medium for recovery studies, partial recovery was marked on 14th and 28th day of recovery (Table 3.21). Though decrease in FAA content continued but the per cent decrease was less when compared to 28th day exposure period value. During recovery studies, the FAA content decreased from 184.6 ± 7.5 to 144.5 ± 9.5 μg g^{-1} dry tissue after 14 days of recovery and the macromolecular content decreased from 185.2 ± 5.8 to 151.5 ± 11.8 μg g^{-1} dry tissue after 28 days of recovery (Figs. 3.63 and 3.65).The FAA content decreased by 21.7 per cent and 18.1 per cent on 14th and 28th day of recovery (Fig. 3.65). The FAA content decreased by 7.4 per cent on 7th day, by 10.2 per cent on 14th day, by 15.3 per cent on 21st day and by 28.2 per cent on 28th day of exposure (Fig. 3.64). The exposed fish was transferred to toxicant free medium for recovery studies. On 14th day of recovery partial recovery by 6.5 per cent and on 28th day of recovery 10.1 per cent recovery in FAA content was observed in the exposed liver tissue of the exposed fish (Fig. 3.66). The FAA content in muscle tissue decreased from 164.2 ± 7.5 to 114.5 ± 9.2 μg g^{-1} dry tissue after 28 days of exposure showing a maximum decrease by 30.2 per cent, when compared to the control value. (Tables 3.20 and 3.21 and Figs. 3.62 and 3.64). When the exposed fish was transferred to toxicant free medium for recovery studies, partial insignificant recovery was marked. Though decrease in FAA content continued but the per cent of decrease was less when compared to 28th day exposure period value. During recovery studies, the FAA content decreased from 164.8 ± 10.2 to 117.4 ± 8.4 μg g^{-1} dry tissue after 14 days of recovery and the maromolecular content decreased from 164.2 ± 8.5 to 121.4 ± 11.5 μg g^{-1} dry tissue after 28 days of recovery (Figs. 3.63 and 3.65). The FAA content declined by 28.7 per cent and 26 per cent on 14th and 28th day of recovery (Fig. 3.65). The FAA content decreased by 3.8 per cent on 7th day, by 6.9 per cent on 14th day, by 20.2 per cent on 21st day and by 30.2 per cent on 28th day of exposure (Fig. 3.64). The exposed fish was transferred to toxicant free medium for recovery studies. On 14th day of recovery 1.5 per cent and on 28th day of recovery

4.2 per cent recovery was observed in the exposed muscle tissue of the exposed fish (Fig. 3.66). The brain was least affected than liver and muscle (Figs. 3.60 to 3.66 and Tables-3.20 and 3.21). With the increase in exposure period, the FAA content decreased insignificantly at all exposure periods. A partial insignificant recovery was marked in all the three tissues studied, when the exposed fish was transferred to cadmium chloride free medium. The exposed brain showed no significant change from the control value after 28 days of recovery. The Brain FAA content recovered by 5.2 per cent. The FAA content of exposed liver recovered by 10.1 per cent after 28 days of recovery. The FAA content in exposed muscle, recovered by 4.2 per cent only, after 28 days of recovery. The FAA content significantly decreased with the increase in exposure period, showing an inverse relationship with the exposure period. At all exposure period, the FAA content decreased when compared to the control value. Muscle showed the highest percentage of decrease to the tune of 30.2 per cent on 28th day exposure period. Brain and liver showed around 14.9 per cent and 28.2 per cent decrease on 28 day of exposure, respectively. No significant recovery was marked in the fish tissues, when transferred to toxicant free medium. None of the exposed fish could recover to its pre-test level, showing the damage caused to the biologic system. The significant decrease in FAA content was probably due to proteolysis induced by the toxicant and consequent degradation of aminoacid. The correlation coefficient analysis between days of exposure and changes in the FAA content of the brain of the control fish showed non-significant correlation. The FAA content of the exposed fish brain showed a positive correlation ($r = -0.964$, $P \leq 0.05$) with the exposure period. The FAA content of the liver of control fish and the muscle of the control fish showed non-significant correlation with the exposure period. In contrast, non-significant negative correlations between days of exposure and FAA content of the brain, liver and muscle of exposed fish (brain, $r = -0.979$, $P \leq 0.05$; liver, $r = -0.966$, $P \leq 0.05$ and muscle, $r = -0.986$, $P \leq 0.05$) was marked. The statistical analysis conducted on the data of FAA content indicated that no doubt in all the tissues studied and at all exposure and

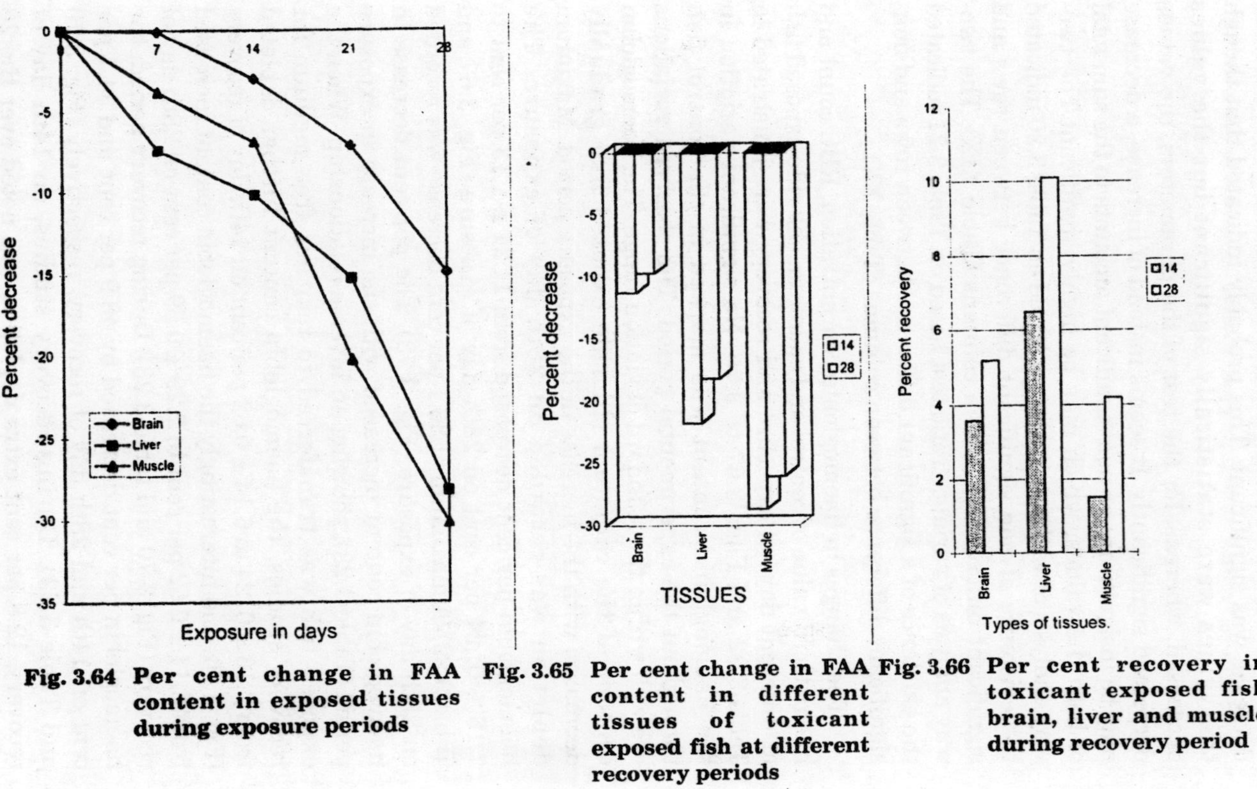

Fig. 3.64 Per cent change in FAA content in exposed tissues during exposure periods

Fig. 3.65 Per cent change in FAA content in different tissues of toxicant exposed fish at different recovery periods

Fig. 3.66 Per cent recovery in toxicant exposed fish brain, liver and muscle during recovery period

recovery periods, the macromolecular content decreased but the decrease was significant. This probably indicated that though the values were statistically significant but the values decreased, whereas, for the rest of the parameters, the values decresaed significantly. It seems instead of increase, a decrease may be insignificant or non-significant amounts to the sum total of both the values, which may be highly significant.The two-way analysis of variance ratio test based on Table 3.20 indicated the existence of non-significant difference between rows and significant difference between columns (Table XIX). The two-way analysis of variance ratio test based on Table 3.21 indicated the existence of a significant difference between rows and non-significant difference between columns (Table XX).

The changes in haemoglobin concentration, RBC count and haematocrit value of control and cadmium chloride exposed fish at different days of exposure and recovery were illustrated in Table-3.22 and Figs. 3.67 to 3.75. No significant variation in the haemoglobin content was marked in the control fish throughout the experimental period. The observed variations are well within the standard deviation range. The haemoglobin content of the cadmium chloride exposed fish gradually decreased with the increase in the exposure period. Maximum depletion was recorded on 28th day of exposure. The haemoglobin per cent decreased from 11.21 ± 1.13 per cent to 7.16 ± 0. 24 per cent on 28th day of exposure (Fig. 3.67 and Table-3.22). A maximum of 36.1 per cent decrease was recorded on 28th day of exposure (Fig. 3.73). The per cent decrease in haemoglobin content increased with the increase in exposure period (Table-3.23), showing an inverse relationship. When the exposed fish was transferred to toxicant free medium for recovery studies, the haemoglobin content further depleted from 7.16 ± 0. 24 to 6.14 ± 0.62 per cent on 14th day of recovery (Fig. 3.70) and interestingly the haemoglobin content increased from 6.14 ± 0.62 per cent to 7.29 ± 0.59 per cent on 28th day of recovery (Fig. 3.70 and table-3.23). During recovery period, the haemoglobin per cent decreased by 48.9 per cent and 34.7 per cent on 14th and 28th day of recovery, respectively (Fig. 3.70 and Table-3.23). During recovery studies, on 14th day of recovery, 12.8 per cent extra depletion was noted over the 28

Table 3.22 Changes in Haemoglobin, RBC content and Haematocrit values of control and exposed fish at different days of exposure and recovery. (Data are the mean of 5 samples ± standard deviation)

Tissue	*Condition*	*Exposure in Days*		*Recovery in Days*	
		14	*28*	*14*	*28*
Haemoglobin	Control	11.15 ± 0.85	11.21 ± 1.13	11.16 ± 0.92	11.18 ± 0.45
	Exposed	9.21 ± 0.26	7.16 ± 0.24	6.14 ± 0.62	7.29 ± 0.59
RBC count × 10^6 cell	Control	1.30 ± 0.11	1.31 ± 0.08	1.30 ± 0.06	1.32 ± 0.08
	Exposed	0.79 ± 0.04	0.63 ± 0.06	0.65 ± 0.09	0.71 ± 0.08
Haemotocrit (%)	Control	34.7 ± 0.6	34.4 ± 0.8	34.5 ± 0.9	34.5 ± 0.6
	Exposed	25.4 ± 0.5	24.8 ± 1.1	23.1 ± 0.5	22.1 ± 0.3

Table 3.23 Per cent change in Hb%, RBC count and Haematocrit value in exposed fish at different exposure and recovery. Values in parentheses indicate per cent recovery. (Data calculated from the mean of the samples)

Tissue	*Exposure in Days*		*Recovery in days*	
	14	*28*	*14*	*28*
Hb%	–19.9	–36.1	–48.9 (NR)	–34.7 (1.4)
RBC Count	–39.2	–51.9	–50.0 (1.9)	–46.2 (5.7)
Haematocrit (%)	–26.8	–27.9	–33.0 (NR)	–35.9 (NR)

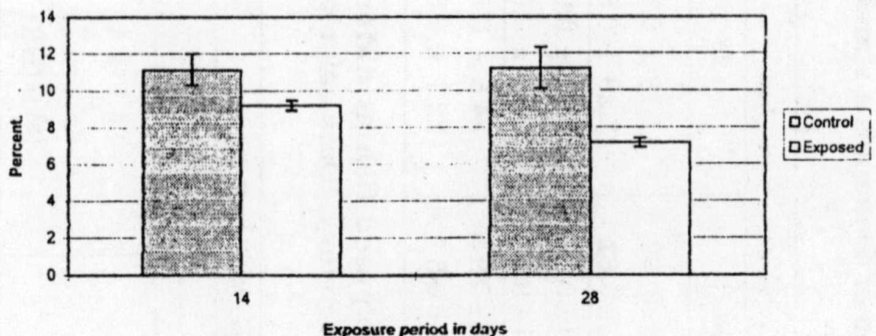

Fig. 3.67 Changes in haemoglobin content in control and exposed fishes at different exposure periods

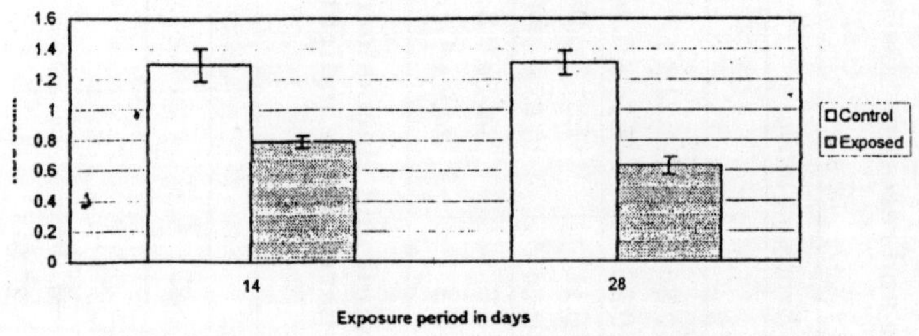

Fig. 3.68 Changes in RBC count in control and exposed fish during exposure periods

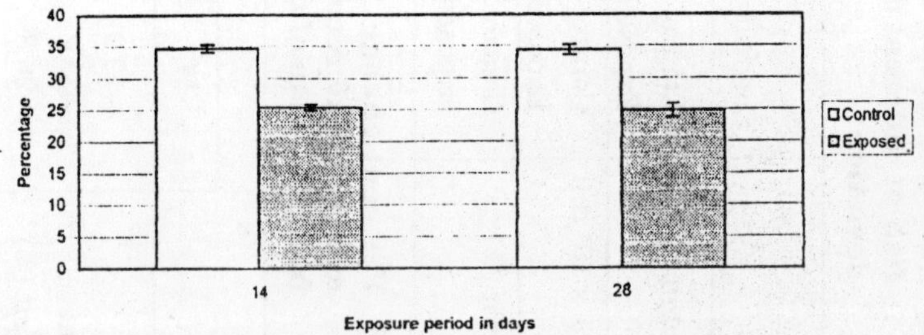

Fig. 3.69 Changes in Hct. value in control and exposed fish diring exposure

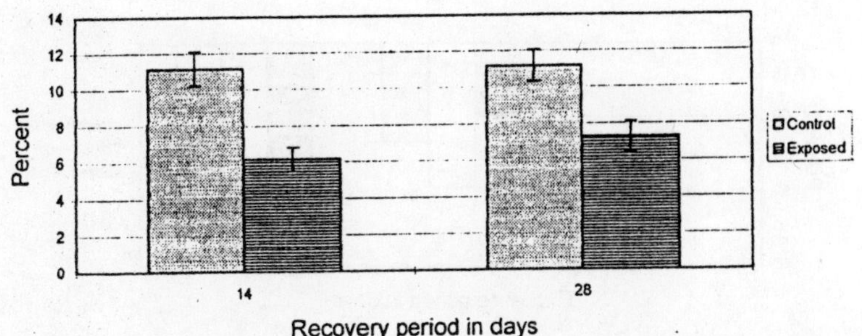

Fig. 3.70 Changes in haemoglobin content in control and exposed fish during recovery periods

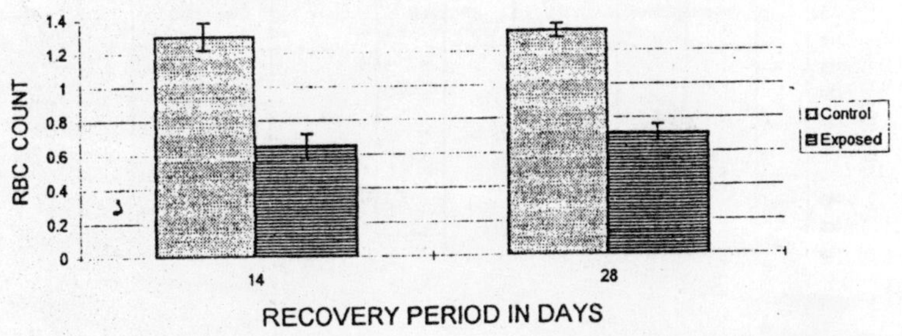

Fig. 3.71 Changes in RBC count in control and exposed fish during recovery periods

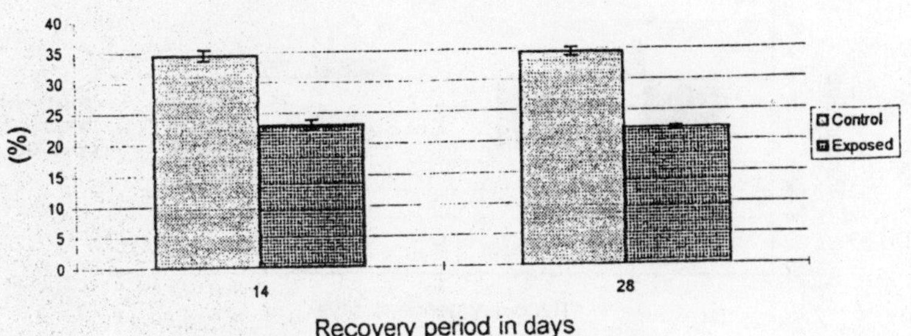

Fig. 3.72 Changes in haematocrit value in control and exposed fish during recovery periods

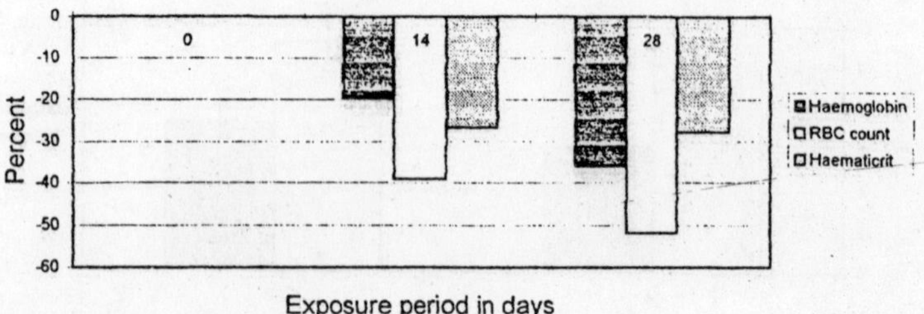

Fig. 3.73 Per cent change in blood parameters during exposure periods

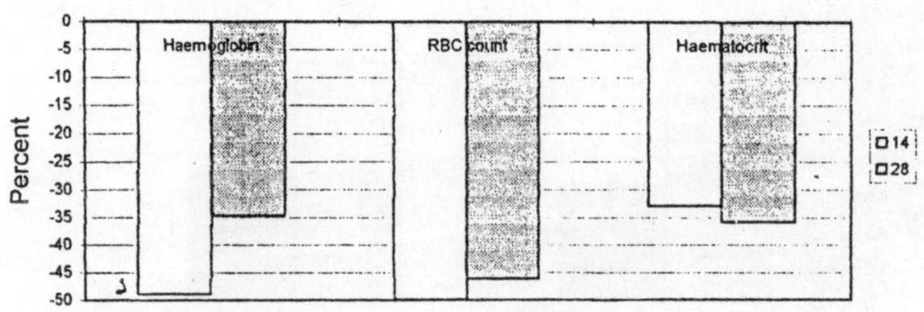

Fig. 3.74 Changes in blood parameters during recovery periods

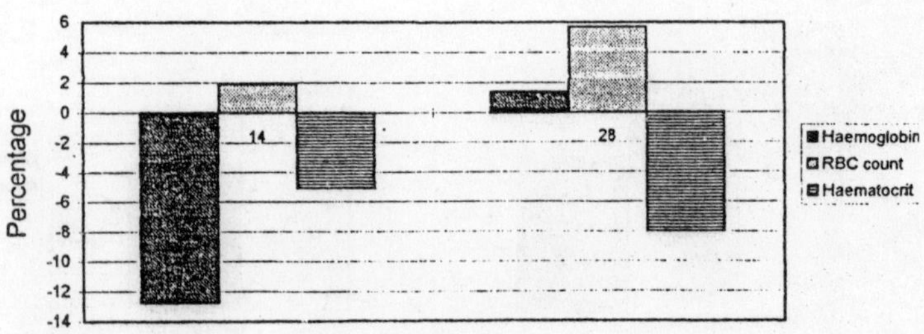

Fig. 3.75 Per cent recovery in blood parameters during recovery periods

days exposure value and this value was much less, when compared to the respective control value. However, on 28th day of recovery, 1.4 per cent recovery in haemoglobin content was observed (Fig. 3.75 and Table-3.23). The haemoglobin content decreased steadily with the increase in exposure period and the per cent decrease increased with the increase in exposure period. No correlation exists between the haemoglobin content of control fish and exposure period. However, a significant negative correlation was marked ($r = -0.964; p \leq 0.05$) between haemoglobin content and exposure period in the cadmium chloride exposed fish. The per cent decrease in haemoglobin content increased with the increase in exposure period showing a significant positive correlation ($r = 0.974; p \leq 0.05$).

The changes in RBC count of control and cadmium chloride exposed fish at different days of exposure and recovery were illustrated in Tables 3.22 and 3.23 and Figs. 3.68, 3.71 and from 3.73 to 3.75. No significant alteration in the RBC count was marked in the control fish throughout the experimental period. The observed variations are well within the standard deviation range. The RBC count of the cadmium chloride exposed fish gradually decreased with the increase in the exposure period. Maximum depletion was recorded on 28th day of exposure. The RBC count decreased from 1.31 ± 0.08 to $0.63 \pm 0.06 \times 10^6$ cells/mm^3 on 28th day of exposure (Fig. 3.68 and Table-3.22). A maximum of 51.9 per cent decrease was recorded on 28th day of exposure (Fig. 3.73). The per cent decrease in RBC count increased with the increase in exposure period (Table-3.23), showing an inverse relationship. When the exposed fish was transferred to cadmium chloride free medium for recovery studies, the RBC count increased from 0.63 ± 0.06 to 0.65 ± 0.09 per cent on 14th day of recovery (Fig. 3.71) and interestingly the RBC count increased from $0.63 + 0.06$ to $0.71 \pm 0.08 \times 10^6$ cells/mm^3 on 28th day of recovery (Fig. 3.71 and Table-3.23). During recovery period, the RBC count per cent decreased by 50 per cent and 46.2 per cent on 14th and 28th day of recovery, respectively (Fig. 3.74 and Table-3.23). During recovery studies, on 14th day of recovery, 1.9 per cent increase was noted over the 28 days exposure value and this value was much less, when compared to the respective control value. However, on 28th day of recovery, 5.7 per cent recovery in RBC count was observed

(Fig. 3.75 and Table-3.23). The RBC count decreased steadily with the increase in exposure period and the per cent decrease increased with the increase in exposure period. No correlation exists between the RBC count of control fish and exposure period. However, a significant negative correlation was marked ($r = -0.997; p \leq 0.001$) between RBC count and exposure period in the cadmium chloride exposed fish. The per cent decrease in RBC count increased with the increase in exposure period showing a significant positive correlation ($r = 0.996; p \leq 0.001$).

The changes in haematocrit value of control and cadmium chloride exposed fish at different days of exposure and recovery were illustrated in Tables-3.22 and 3.23 and Figs. 3.69 to 3.75. No significant alteration in the haematocrit value was marked in the control fish throughout the experimental period. The observed variations are well within the standard deviation range. The haematocrit value of the cadmium chloride exposed fish gradually decreased with the increase in the exposure period. Maximum depletion was recorded on 28th day of exposure. The haematocrit value decreased from 34.4 ± 0.8 per cent to 24.8 ± 1.1 per cent on 28th day of exposure (Fig. 3.69 and Table-3.22). A maximum of 27.9 per cent decrease was recorded on 28th day of exposure (Fig. 3.73). The per cent decrease in haematocrit value increased with the increase in exposure period (Table-3.23), showing an inverse relationship. When the exposed fish was transferred to cadmium chloride free medium for recovery studies, the haematocrit value further depleted from 24.8 ± 1.1 to 23.1 ± 0.5 per cent on 14th day of recovery (Fig. 3.72) and interestingly the haematocrit value decreased from 23.1 ± 0.5 per cent to 22.1 ± 0.3 per cent on 28th day of recovery (Fig. 3.72 and Table-3.22). During recovery period, the haematocrit per cent decreased by 33 per cent and 35.9 per cent on 14th and 28th day of recovery, respectively (Fig. 3.74 and Table-3.23). During recovery studies, on 14th day of recovery, 5.1 per cent extra depletion was noted over the 28 days exposure value and this value was much less, when compared to the respective control value. On 28th day of recovery, 8 per cent decrease in haematocrit value was observed (Fig. 3.75 and Table-3.23). The haematocrit value decreased steadily with the increase in exposure period and the per cent

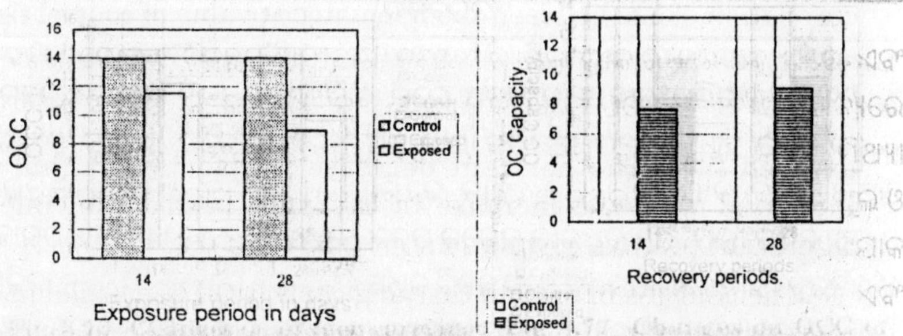

Fig. 3.76 Changes on oxygen carrying capacity of blood in control and exposed fish during exposure

Fig. 3.77 Changes on OCC of blood in control and exposed fish at different recovery periods

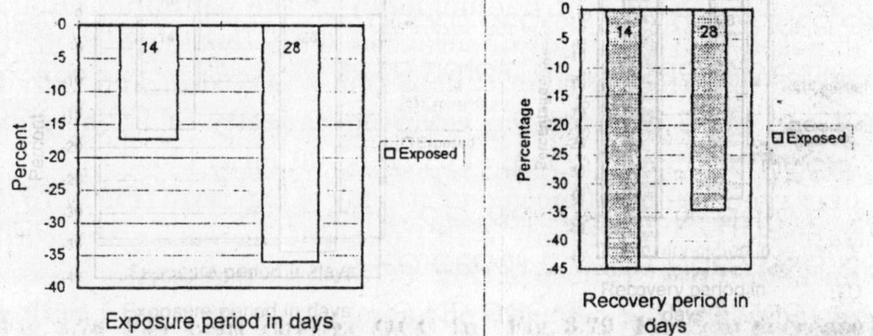

Fig. 3.78 Per cent change OCC in exposed fish blood, when compared to control

Fig. 3.79 Per cent decrease in OCC of blood of exposed fish during recovery

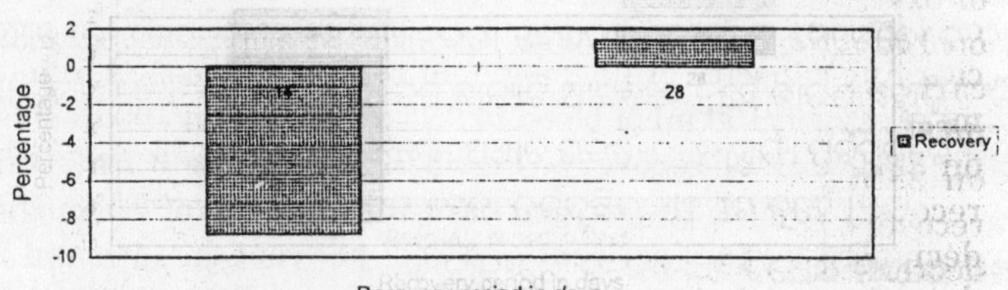

Fig. 3.80 Per cent recovery in OCC of blood of the exposed fish during recovery periods

decrease increased with the increase in exposure period. No correlation exists between the haematocrit value of control fish and exposure period. However, a significant negative correlation was marked ($r = -0.988$; $p \leq 0.05$) between haematocrit value and exposure period in the cadmium chloride exposed fish. The per cent decrease in haematocrit value increased with the increase in exposure period showing a significant positive correlation ($r = 0.984$; $p \leq 0.05$).

The changes in oxygen carrying capacity of haemoglobin of control and cadmium chloride exposed fish at different days of exposure and recovery were illustrated in Table-3.24 and Figs. 3.76 to 3.80. No significant alteration in the oxygen carrying capacity of haemoglobin was marked in the control fish throughout the experimental period. The observed variations are well within the standard deviation range. The oxygen carrying capacity of haemoglobin of the cadmium chloride exposed fish gradually decreased with the increase in the exposure period. Maximum depletion was recorded on 28th day of exposure. The oxygen carrying capacity of haemoglobin decreased from 14.01 ml of oxygen/100 ml of blood to 8.95 ml of oxygen/100 ml of blood on 28th day of exposure (Fig. 3.76 and Table-3.24). A maximum of 36.1 per cent decrease was recorded on 28th day of exposure (Fig. 3.78). The per cent decrease in oxygen carrying capacity of haemoglobin increased with the increase in exposure period (Table-3.24), showing an inverse relationship. When the exposed fish was transferred to cadmium chloride free medium for recovery studies, the oxygen carrying capacity of haemoglobin further depleted from 8.95 ml of oxygen/100ml of blood to 7.68 ml of oxygen/100ml of blood on 14th day of recovery (Fig. 3.77) and interestingly the oxygen carrying capacity of haemoglobin content increased from 8.95 ml of oxygen/100 ml of blood to 9.11 ml of oxygen/100ml of blood on 28th day of recovery (Fig. 3.77 and Table-3.24). During recovery period, the oxygen carrying capacity of haemoglobin decreased by 44.9 per cent and 34.7 per cent on 14th and 28th day of recovery, respectively (Fig. 3.79 and Table-3.24). During recovery studies, on 14th day of recovery, 8.8 per cent extra depletion was noted over the 28 day exposure value and this value was much less, when compared to the respective control

Table 3.24 Changes in Oxygen carrying capacity of haemoglobin in control and exposed fish at different exposure and recovery periods. (Data are the mean of 5 samples ± standard deviation)

Tissue		*Exposure in days*		*Recovery in days*	
	Condition	*14*	*28*	*14*	*28*
O.C.C.	Control	13.93	14.01	13.95	13.97
	Exposed	11.51	8.95	7.68	9.11
Per cent change	Exposed	–17.30	–36.10	–44.9	–34.7
Per cent recovery	Exposed			–8.8	1.40

O.C.C.= Oxygen Carrying Capacity

value. However, on 28th day of recovery, 1.4 per cent recovery in oxygen carrying capacity of haemoglobin was observed (Fig. 3.80 and Table-3.24). The oxygen carrying capacity of haemoglobin decreased steadily with the increase in exposure period and the per cent decrease increased with the increase in exposure period. No correlation exists between the oxygen carrying capacity of haemoglobin of control fish and exposure period. However, a significant negative correlation was marked ($r = -0.991$; $p \leq 0.01$) between oxygen carrying capacity of haemoglobin and exposure period in the cadmium chloride exposed fish. The per cent decrease in oxygen carrying capacity of haemoglobin increased with the increase in exposure period showing a significant positive correlation ($r = 0.995$; $p \leq 0.01$). The oxygen carrying capacity of haemoglobin values were calculated from the mean values of haemoglobin content, hence, the statistical values were alomost same and also the per cent decrease values were similar with the haemoglobin values. A strong similarity in the tendency of both the parameters were observed.

The changes in AChE activity in brain, liver and muscle of control and cadmium chloride exposed fish at different days of exposure and recovery and it's per cent changes were shown in Figs. 3.81 to 3.85. The brain tissue showed a maximum decrease by 58 per cent and the enzyme activity declined from 0.386 ± 0.052 to 0.162 ± 0.048 of µmole of ACh hydrolysed hr^{-1} mg^{-1} of tissue on 28th day of exposure (Fig. 3.81). When the exposed fish was transferred to toxicant free medium, the AChE activity declined from 0.385 ± 0.045 to 0.146 ± 0.035 of µmole of ACh hydrolysed hr^{-1} mg^{-1} of tissue on 14th day of recovery and from 0.382 ± 0.042 to 0.152 ± 0.025 of µmole of ACh hydrolysed hr^{-1} mg^{-1} of tissue on 28th day of recovery (Fig. 3.82). This enzyme activity decreased by 62 per cent on 14th day recovery and decreased by 60.2 per cent over the 28th day exposure value, after 28 days of recovery, indicating no significant recovery at all (Fig. 3.84). The per cent decrease increased with the increase in exposure period from 7th day to 28th day. Initially the per cent decrease was 16 per cent on 7th day, 31.4 per cent on 14th day, 54.1 per cent on 21st day and the highest of 58 per cent being on 28th day of exposure

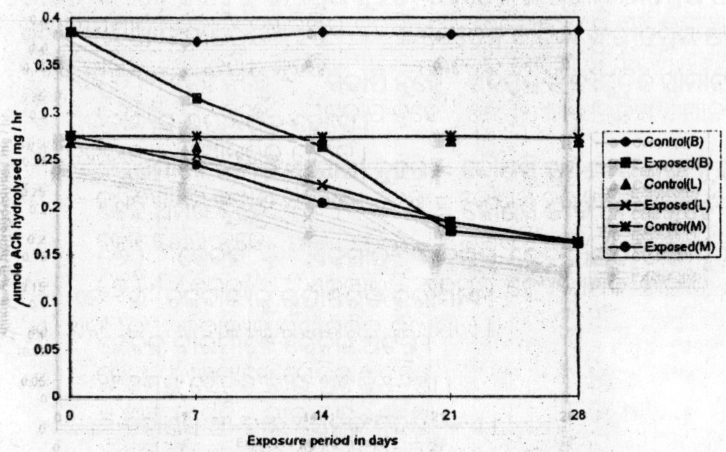

Fig. 3.81 Changes in the enzyme activity in different tissues during recovery period

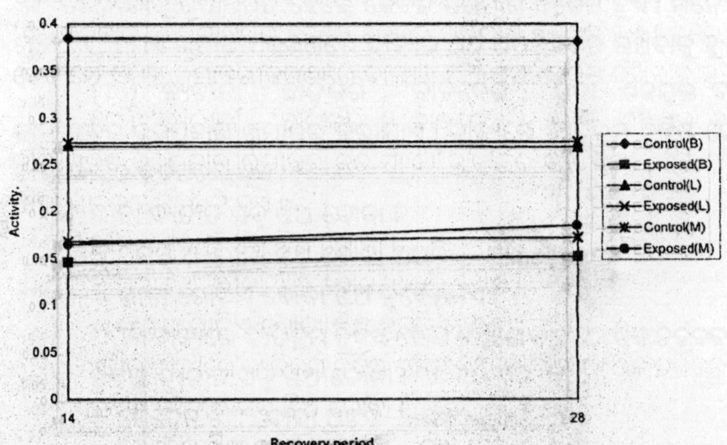

Fig. 3.82 Changes in the enzyme activity in different tissues during recovery period

Table 3.25 Changes in total AChE activity (μ moles of Ach hydrolysed mg^{-1} hr^{-1}) in control and Cadmium chloride exposed fish brain, liver and muscle at different days of exposure and recovery

Tissue	*Condition*	*Exposure in Days*					*Recovery in Days*	
		0	*7*	*14*	*21*	*28*	*14*	*28*
Brain	Control	0.385±0.065	0.375±0.041	0.385±0.062	0.382±0.065	0.386±0.052	0.385±0.045	0.382±0.042
	Exposed	0.385±0.065	0.315±0.045	0.264±0.042	0.175±0.035	0.162±0.048	0.146±0.035	0.152±0.025
Liver	Control	0.268±0.070	0.264±0.045	0.270±0.026	0.269±0.065	0.268±0.035	0.270±0.45	0.269±0.055
	Exposed	0.268±0.070	0.255±0.042	0.224±0.022	0.185±0.054	0.164±0.044	0.168±0.055	0.172±0.046
Muscle	Control	0.276±0.026	0.275±0.035	0.274±0.055	0.275±0.012	0.273±0.023	0.274±0.048	0.275±0.036
	Exposed	0.276±0.026	0.245±0.056	0.205±0.026	0.185±0.028	0.162±0.034	0.165±0.42	0.185±0.024

(Fig. 3.83). The per cent decrease increased significantly with the increase in exposure period in exposed fish exposed to cadmium chloride. The exposed fish brain enzyme activity could not recover even partly on 14th and 28th day of recovery showing permanent damage caused to the system (Fig. 3.85). The changes in total AChE activity in liver of control and cadmium chloride exposed fish at different days of exposure and recovery and it's per cent changes were shown in Figs. 3.81 and 3.82. The liver tissue showed a maximum decrease by 38.8 per cent and the enzyme activity declined from 0.268 + 0.035 to 0.164 + 0.044 of μmole of ACh hydrolysed hr^{-1} mg^{-1} of tissue on 28th day of exposure (Fig. 3.81). When the exposed fish was transferred to toxicant free medium, the AChE activity declined from 0.270 ± 0.045 to 0.168 ± 0.055 of μmole of ACh hydrolysed hr^{-1} mg^{-1} of tissue on 14th day of recovery and from 0.269 ± 0.055 to 0.172 ± 0.046 of μmole of ACh hydrolysed hr^{-1} mg^{-1} of tissue on 28th day of recovery (Fig. 3.82). This enzyme activity decreased by 37.7 per cent on 14th day recovery and decreased by 36 per cent over the 28th day exposure value, after 28 days of recovery, indicating partial insignificant recovery (Fig. 3.84). The per cent decrease increased with the increase in exposure period from 7th day to 28th day. Initially the per cent decrease was 3.4 per cent on 7th day, 17 per cent on 14th day, 31.2 per cent on 21st day and the highest of 38.8 per cent being on 28th day of exposure (Fig. 3.83). The per cent decrease increased significantly with the increase in exposure period in exposed fish exposed to cadmium chloride. The exposed fish liver enzyme activity could recover insignificantly by 1.1 per cent on 14th and 2.8 per cent recovery on 28th day of recovery showing drastic damage caused to the system (Fig. 3.85). The changes in AChE activity in muscle of control and cadmium chloride exposed fish at different days of exposure and recovery and it's per cent changes were shown in Figs. 3.81 to 3.85. The muscle tissue showed a maximum decrease by 32.7 per cent and the enzyme activity declined from 0.273 ± 0.023 to 0.162 ± 0.034 of μmole of ACh hydrolysed hr^{-1} mg^{-1} of tissue on 28th day of exposure (Fig. 3.81). When the exposed fish was transferred to toxicant free medium, the AChE activity declined from 0.274 ± 0.048 to 0.165 ± 0.042 of μmole of ACh hydrolysed hr^{-1} mg^{-1} of tissue on 14th day of recovery and from 0.275 ± 0.036 to 0.185

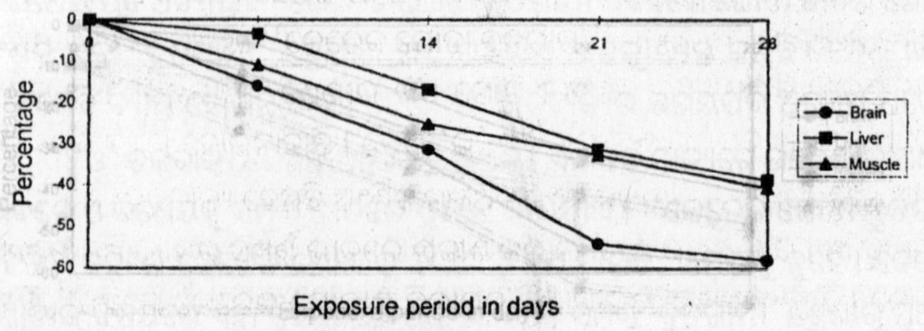

Fig. 3.83 Per cent decrease in AChE activity in the exposed fish, when compared to control fish tissue

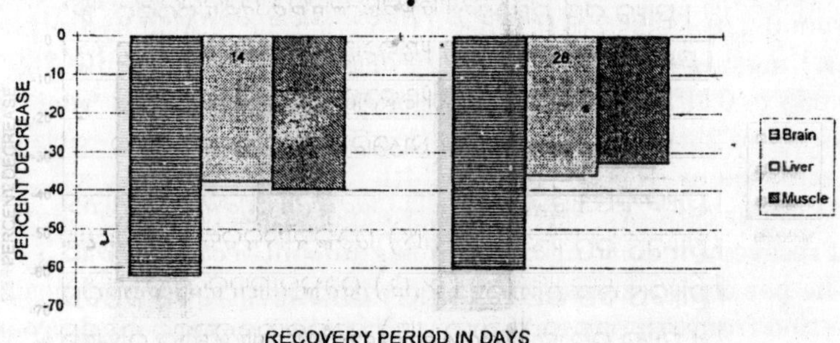

Fig. 3.84 Per cent decrease in AChE activity in brain, liver and muscle of Cadmium chloride exposed fish, when compared to control at different recovery periods

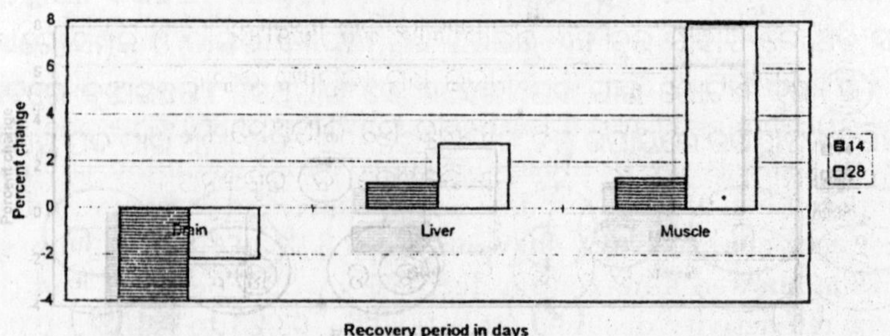

Fig. 3.85 Per cent recover in the enzyme activity during recovery period

± 0.024 of A μmole of ACh hydrolysed hr^{-1} mg^{-1} of tissue on 28th day of recovery (Fig. 3.82). This enzyme activity decreased by 39.7 per cent on 14th day recovery and decreased by 32.7 per cent over the 28th day exposure value, after 28 days of recovery, indicating partial recovery (Fig. 3.84). The per cent decrease increased with the increase in exposure period from 7th day to 28th day. Initially the per cent decrease was 10.9 per cent on 7th day, 25.1 per cent on 14th day, 32.7 per cent on 21st day and the highest of 40.6 per cent being on 28th day of exposure (Fig. 3.83). The per cent decrease increased significantly with the increase in exposure period in exposed fish exposed to cadmium chloride. The exposed fish muscle enzyme activity could recover only partly by 1.3 per cent on 14th and by 7.9 per cent on 28th day of recovery showing damage caused to the system (Fig. 3.85). Out of the three tissues studied, the exposed brain showed the highest damage than liver and muscle. The correlation coefficient analysis between days of exposure and AChE activity in control fish brain showed a positive but non-significant correlation, whereas, the exposed fish brain showed a significant negative correlation (r = –0.989, $P \leq 0.01$). The control set did not show any positive significant correlation (P = NS). The per cent change in the enzyme activity in the exposed fish brain when compared to control fish brain showed the existence of a negative significant correlation with the exposure period. The correlation coefficient analysis between days of exposure and the AChE activity of liver slices of the control fish did not show any significant correlation , whereas the exposed fish liver showed a negative and significant correlation (r = –0.987, $P \leq 0.01$) with the exposure period. The per cent change in AChE activity showed the existence of a negative, significant correlation (r = –0.984, $P \leq 0.01$) with the exposure period. The analysis of variance ratio test indicated the existence of significant difference between rows and non-significant difference between columns. The control muscle did not show any significant correlation between exposure period and enzyme activity. However, the muscle of the exposed fish showed negative and significant correlation (r = –0.985, $P \leq 0.05$) with the exposure period. The per cent change in the enzyme activity showed negative and significant correlation

Table 3.26 Per cent change in total AChE activity in exposed *Tilapia* fish brain, liver and muscle at different days of exposure and recovery, when compared to control tissues. Values in parentheses indicate per cent recovery

Tissue	*Exposure in Days*					*Recovery in Days*	
	0	*7*	*14*	*21*	*28*	*14*	*28*
Brain	0.0	–16.0	–31.4	–54.1	–58.0	–62.0 (NR)	–60.2 (NR)
Liver	0.0	–3.4	–17.0	–31.2	–38.8	–37.7 (1.1)	–36.0 (2.8)
Muscle	0.0	–10.9	–25.1	–32.7	–40.6	–39.7 (1.3)	–32.7 (7.9)

with the exposure period. The analysis of variance ratio test for muscle showed significant difference between rows and non-significant difference between columns. The exposed fishes were when transferred to cadmium chloride free medium, the enzyme activity showed recovery in liver and muscle tissues but the recovery was not statistically significant. Brain showed the highest damage and no recovery, liver showed the lowest recovery and muscle showed partial recovery after 28 days of recovery (Fig. 3.85).

The results obtained in this study are quite consistent and verified for its accuracy. Some of the data compared with the data obtained by Harichandan (2002) and interestingly many are reproduceable under laboratory experimental conditions. Some of the data showed wide variation and some data indicated new informations. In the present investigation, care was taken to study the eco-toxicological part of cadmium poisoning with greater accuracy. Harichandan (2002) studied on cadmium effects but correlated with the findings and residual accumulations with field data of Ballarpur Paper Mills. In the present investigation, only stress was given to pure experimental study on the same fish. The data obtained here fills the gap created by Harichandan (2002) and an effort was made to find out the causes of fish death during poisoning. Some of the informations given by Harichandan (2002) were not marked in the present investigation. The differences in both the studies might be due to experimental error or computational errors. In this study no significant variation in blood cell morphology was noted. The observed changes by Harichandan (2002) might be due to the defect and delay in processing of the red blood cells but the changes observed by the above author is not reproducable. Hence, we strongly conclude that no such morphometric change can be observed in short duration of exposure. By prolonged exposure of fish to cadmium salts, such type of symptoms can be marked, which we have not marked at present and we have not conducted any long term experiments with cadmium chloride as toxicant and fish as the experimental animal.

4
DISCUSSION

The mortality percentage for any fixed period increased with the increasing concentration of Cadmium chloride. There was an increase in mortality percentage with the increase in exposure period, also. The proportion of these animals that died in a fixed time increased with the increase in the toxicant concentration and the median tolerance limit value decreased with the exposure period (Hodson *et al.*, 1977; Das and Misra, 1982 and Panigrahi, 1984). The close response approach to assessment of pollutant toxicity involves several assumptions. The route of entry of the pesticide is generally agreed to be via the gills (Holden, 1962; Ferguson *et al.*, 1966) and thus enters directly into the circulatory system. This caused damage to tissues as a result of which there is depression in active metabolism (Macleod and Passah, 1973). Depression in active metabolism that directly reduced scope of activity was demonstrated by Fry (1957). Probably this has relevance with the impaired swimming ability, erratic movements, paralysis, anorexia and ataxia which were observed in all test fish at higher exposure periods. Initial disturbance was caused by the Cadmium chloride but latter on the fishes stabilised and performed normal activity. High percentage mortality of fish due to the action of Cadmium chloride might be due to the pathological changes, as Mathur (1969) pointed out that fish subjected to insecticides such as lindane, dieldrin, DDT and BHC die due to pathological disorders. Choudhury (1975) showed the organochloro insecticides were highly toxic to fish even at very low concentrations. Ray and David (1962) concluded that deficiency of dissolved oxygen concentration caused by decomposition of algae or bottom deposits was mostly the cause of the fish kills in ponds and impounded water. Inorganic ions can equally prc   fatal by limiting oxygen intake causing respiratory and circulatory failure influencing smooth osmotic exchange of gases caused by flocculation of iron or gill filaments. David *et al.*, (1976) showed that of the metals tested, silver and mercury were the most toxic *i.e.,* silver was 95 per cent toxic at 0.086 ppm and mercury at 0.150 ppm, while LC_{50} values were 0.033 ppm for silver and 0.089 ppm for mercury. During the experimental period temperature, hardness, time of exposure size of the test-fish and all such factors were monitored since the interference of one of these factors will alter the TLM values and MAC values. At present, the sub-lethal concentration selected for further study is 1.20 ppm of cadmium chloride for 28 days, where no death was recorded. Hence, with the recognition that all heavy metals are potentially lethal to fish even at relatively low concentrations. It is now a normal practice to test all new chemicals for their toxicity to fish. The LC_{50} and MAC values can be helpful to understand about the amount of heavy metal, cadmium that can be discharged into the environment by any industry, which discharges cadmium in the effluent or in any other waste discharged by the industry.

The rapid absorption of Cadmium chloride through the gill, skin and gastro-intestinal tract of fish was well evident in the present investigation. The toxicity of Cadmium chloride becomes more apparent in a very shorter period in aquatic animals. Panigrahi (1980) documented a detailed behavioural changes in relation to inorganic-mercury intoxication. Panigrahy (1984) reported the impact of MEMC on *Anabas scandens,* a fresh water fish and noted a substantial change in behaviour of the test fish. Although he had observed swelling of eyes and consequent blindness. Such type of symptom was not observed in Cadmium chloride exposed fish, probably such a symptom is unique in mercury exposure or contamination. Higgins (1974) and Macleod and Passah (1973) reported that loss of appetite, loss of weight, nervousness, dizziness, loss of equilibrium, erratic swimming and gradual onset of inactivity were the sub-clinical effects of inorganic mercury intoxication. Similar symptoms were marked in cadmium exposure here. These symptoms might be the regular symptoms of heavy metal exposure. Panigrahy (1984) also reported similar symptoms relating to a mercury based fungicide. Neurological damage in inorgano-mercury intoxicated fish relating to behavioural studies was also reported (Panigrahi 1980), and he opined that the damage was caused only by inorganic mercury. The observed depression in active metabolism in cadmium exposed fish were indicative of damage to nervous tissues, inhibition of enzymes or a vital system, was totally in agreement with Panigrahi (1980) and Panigrahy (1984). Fry (1957) demonstrated the depression in active metabolism directly reduced "scope for activity". This in turn, may result in decreased growth, impaired swimming ability with erratic outburst at times. Loss in weight due to starvation was noted by Larsen and Lewander (1973). But the loss due to starvation was very less. Panigrahi and Misra (1978, 1980) reported the loss of body weight due to mercury intoxication and confirmed that this loss in body weight was only due to mercury stress. In addition, exposed fish maintained their feeding habit only after a short span of time. Hence the weight loss cannot be correlated with starvation but can only be related with heavy metal intoxication. Whereas, the control fish showed increase in weight. The differences observed between control fish and exposed fish in terms of body weight is only due to the administration of Cadmium chloride in exposed aquarium.

Borg *et al.*, (1970) reported inappetance, muscular weakness, ataxia and loss of body weight as the main clinical symptoms of mercury poisoning. On autopsy, he found muscular atrophy, which can be correlated with the weight loss in the goshawks. Hanko *et al.*, (1970) reported loss of appetite, weakness of the extremities, excitation in the animal and loss of body weight due to mercury poisoning in chickens. A decline in liver somatic index and brain somatic index in exposed fish could be correlated with the degeneration of cells and decrease in other macromolecular variables. Concisely, at this stage it is not possible to establish the cause of loss in body weight and decrease in liver and brain somatic index, except a generalised comment on the behaviour of the exposed fish to heavy metal stress that the observed symptoms were most probably be due to cadmium intoxication. Bhatia *et al.*, (1973) reported that change in behaviour in test fish had some relationship with insecticide intoxication. Rath and Misra (1980) reported the change in behavioural activity of fish exposed to dichlorvos (DDVP) and confirmed the idea that the change in activity was related to pesticide intoxication, which is totally agreeable with our observation in this study of cadmium exposure. Acute lethal toxicity tests are usually done to assess the numerical value of toxicity and to compare potencies of toxicant. The mortality percentage for any fixed period increased with the increasing concentrations of the toxicant. An increase in mortality was observed with the increase in exposure period and with the increase in the concentrations of the toxicant. The proportion of test animals that died in a fixed time increased with the increase in the cadmium chloride concentration and the medium tolerance limit decreased with the exposure period (Hodson *et al.,* 1977; Das and Misra, 1982; Panigrahi, 1984; Samanta, 1989; Pattnaik, 2001; Misra, 2002 and Harichandan, 2002). The dose response approach to assessment of pollutant toxicity embodies several assumptions. Unless these are satisfied under the actual test conditions the inference that may be drawn from the resulting mortality data are questionable in any rigorous sense, although they may, of course provide usesful pragmatic informations (McCarty *et al.,* 1978 and Samant, 1989).

The route of entry of the toxicant is generally agreed to be via the gills (Holden, 1962; Ferguson *et al.,* 1966) and thus gets directly into the vascular system. This causes damage to tissues and as a result of which, there is depression in acvtive metabolism (Mac Leod and Pessah, 1973). Depression in active metabolism that directly reduced scope of activity was demonstrated by Fry (1957). Probably this has relevance with the impaired swimming ability, erratic movements etc. which were observed in all the test fish. High percentage mortality of fish due to action of the cadmium chloride might be due to the pathological changes, as Mathur (1969) pointed out that fish subjected to insecticide such as lindane, dieldrin, DDT and BHC die, due to pathological disorders. Samant(1989) showed that phenyl mercuric acetate was highly toxic to fish even at very low concentrations. Ray and David (1962) concluded that deficiency of dissolved oxygen concentration caused by decomposition of algae or bottom deposits was mostly the cause of fish kill in pond and impounded water. Inorganic ions can equally prove fatal by limiting oxygen intake causing respiratory and circulatory failure influencing smooth osmotic exchange of gases caused by flocculation of iron on gill filaments.The leached chemicals of the solid waste increased the turbidity of the water and transpirancy decreased significantly (Pattnaik, 2001). Which might have played an important role to decrease the dissolved oxygen present in the exposed aquarium (Pattnaik, 2001). In the present investigation, we have used cadmium chloride as the toxicant and this chemical in particular has no role to play to deplete the oxygen level in the aquatic environment. But the action of cadmium chloride on the gill filaments need attention. The effect of cadmium chloride on the functioning of the gill filaments in gaseous exchange and environmental chemical absorption and consequent translocation into the blood vascular system require a detailed study.

David *et al.,* (1976) showed that of the metal tested sliver and mercury were the most toxic *i.e.,* silver was 95 per cent toxic at 0.086 ppm and mercury at 0.150 while LD_{50} values were 0.333 ppm for silver and 0.089 ppm for mercury. During the experimental period temperature, hardness, time of exposure, size of the test fish and all such factors will alter the MAD values. Smaller fishes can tolerate lower concentrations. Bigger fishes can resist upto a concentration where all small fishes die. With the increase in exposure period toxic tests becomes more pronounced in small fishes,when compared to bigger fishes. Probaly the toxicity varies and corresponds to age of the fish. The solid waste of the chlor alkali industry contained mainly mercury as toxicant in different forms at different concentrations (Pattnaik,2001).

Cadmium was recognised many years ago to be a highly toxic element but it was not until comparatively recently that concern began to be expressed over the possible effects on human health on long term exposure to low concentrations of this element. The discovery that Cadmium pollution from a base metal mining and smelting complex could cause serious illness and possible death in a local community has led to widespread public anxiety (Kobayashi and Hagino, 1965). Although industrial operations are major sources of Cadmium, many countries now show concern that disposal of metal with sewage sludge on land may adversely affect the fertility of the soil and render plants a health hazard, if consumed by man and animals. Nevertheless, the increasing awareness of the political hazards of Cadmium contamination should not obscure the fact that Cadmium is present in natural ecosystems and an ubiquitous element in all living organisms. For the environmental impact of Cadmium to be assessed, major steps in the biogeo-chemical pathway must be outlined and gaps in our knowledge identified for future research undertakings. The concern over the public health implications of cadmium pollution has resulted in a considerable amount of research being carried out by regional and national laboratories and field stations throughout the world. The most notable aspects of the geochemistry of Cadmium with regard to its rock-soil-plant-animal relationships is its low concentrations in the Earth's crust. Consequently, soil and plant contents of this element are generally low except where soils are formed on rocks with anomalously high concentrations of the metal, such as black shales of where pollution has occured. Plants and animals are unlikely to have evolved mechanisms to cope with relatively high concentrations of Cadmium, since these rarely occur in nature. However, with the increasing production of Cadmium, pollution will assume a greater significance for soil plant animal pathways. Cadmium has an estimated crustal abundance of between 0.15 $\mu g.g^{-1}$ (Weast, 1969) and 0.2 $\mu g.^{-1}$ (Fleischer *et al.,* 1974) and thus occurs in sixty seventh position in an order of relative abundance (Aylett, 1973). The estimated mean Cadmium concentration in igneous rocks is O_2 $\mu g.g^{-1}$.With a range of 0.01-1.6 $\mu g.g^{-1}$ Cadmium, but very few values of over 0.5 $\mu g.g^{-1}$ are found (Fleischer *et al.,* 1974). These low contents of Cadmium in igneous rocks accounts for its low crustal abundance. With the exception of ore bodies, trace elements occur as impurities in primary minerals, which form igneous rocks. They are substituted for one of the major ions in the crustal of a mineral without significantaly attening the internal structure. This "isomorphous substitution" requires the potential replacing ion and the major ion to be replaced to have similar ionic radii (Wittin ± 15%). Similar charges unless other substitutions occur to maintain electrically neutrality, and similar electronegativities or ionisation potentials (Siegel,1974). Cadmium has the same valency and similar ionic radius as Calcium, but dose not commonly substitute for Calcium in minerals such as the plagioclase(Anorthite)or in secondary Calcium-containing minerals such as Calcite. This is probably due to Cadmium's higher electronegativity in comparison with that of Calcium (1.0) which implies that Cadmium has a greater tedency to form covalent bonds, whereas those formed by Calcium are predominantly ionic (Krausk opf, 1967). Therefore, since Cadmium is unable to substitute easily for a common constitutent of primary minerals of concentration in igneous rocks is low. The main minerals which have been found to contain small but significant amounts of Cadmium are buiotite and riebeckite. Waketa and Schmitt (1970) found concentrations of upto 4.8 $\mu g.g^{-1}$ .Cadmium in the biotite of biotite granite from Nigeria and Holmen (1976) quotes values upto 5.8 $\mu g.g^{-1}$ cadmium for reibeckite. Some substitution of Cadmium for sodium could have occured in reibeckite due to their similar ionic radii although their valencies and electro-negativities are different.

Heavy metal contamination caused by either natural processes or by human activities is one of the most serious eco-toxicological problems (Reedy and Prasad, 1990). Since, plants function as the principal entry point of heavy metals into the food chain leading to animals and man (Rauser, 1990), the agricultural use of Cadmium containing fertilisers and of Cu as a fungicide is of major concern. Whereas, it is well established fact that Cadmium is more toxic to man and other mammals than Cupper, the differential toxicity of these two heavy metal for plants is not clear (Galli *et al.*, 1996). The use of phosphate fertilisers will invariably increase at least to a slight extent, the Cadmium concentration in all soils used for commercial agriculture as long as the accumulation exceeds the amount removed by crops harvested and leached from the plough layer (Alloway, 1990 and Singh, 1994). Application of Cadmium containing fertilisers may not appreciably increase the plant cadmium concentration at present, but low annual application may result in elevated cadmium concentrations in the cultivated layer, especially where high Cadmium fertilisers are used. Some of the Cadmium added to soils will invariably be removed by the crop or by leaching with the former playing a more important role. The amounts of cadmium removed by the crop depend on the crop species or variety grown, the Cadmium concentration of the fertiliser used, the prevailing soil conditions and the magnitude of yields. Cadmium removal through leaching is generally of less importance than through crop removal, although reliable values are still missing (Jeng and Singh,1995). Knight and McGrath (1995) reported specifically that heavy metal accumulation in soil due to application of sewage sludge was found to reduce the number and genetic diversity of *Rhizobium leguminosarum* biovar trifolii. There was growing concern that the soil microbial community may not be adequately protected from the effects of metals in soils receiving sewage sludge. The main sources of Cadmium in streams are effluents from industries such as electroplating, paints, paper, plastic, battery and zinc mining and refining. Because of its high toxicity, most countries include Cadmium among the "Priority pollutants" requiring suitable treatment prior discharge into the environmnent (Puranik *et al.,* 1995). The United States Environmental Protection Agency limits Cadmium levels in drinking water to 0.001 mg^{-1}. In India, the prmissible concentration of Cadmium in the industrial effluents discharged into inland surface waters is 0.1 $mg.l^{-1}$. At present a variety of physico-chemical processes are employed to treat Cadmium containing effluents. These processes, however prove expensive when situations involving high volume and low metal concentration (typically less than 50 mg^{-1}) are encountered (Puranik *et al.,* 1995). Various microorganisms are known to absorb metals from dilute solutions and concentrate them several fold by the process of biosorption. The use of dead cell mass in metal sorption can be of great interest because of the large variety and low cost of these biological materials. Heavy metals ions in small quantities are required for various physiological process and the normal functions of cells in plants and animals. Elevated levels of such metal ions are generally toxic and cause major damage to cells. In addition to the utilisation of metal ions as essential elements, adjustment of intracellular levels of free ions by binding to macromolecules or other mechanisms is indispensable if cells are to protect themselves against excessive metal ions or changes in levels of such ions in the environment. (Webb, 1987; Bremner and Beattie, 1990 and Mehra and Winge, 1991). Two different classes of cytoplasmic molecules that participate in binding of metal ions and thus, in resistance to metal ions have been identified in various plant and animal cells (Inouhe *et al.,* 1996). Animal cells produce heavy metal binding protections known as metallothioneins (Kagi and Kojima, 1987). Both types molecules are rich in cysteine residues as metal-binding sites but they are very different from each other in that the former are synthesised via an m-RNA transcript, while the latter are generated from GSH by PC synthase (Scheller *et al.,* 1987, Grill *et al.,* 1989). Inouhe *et al.,* (1996) opined that it was important to determine, why such different systems became established and are exploited by plant and animal cells. Both MT and PC have been identified in several species of yeast and other fungi.

Cadmium is toxic to most living organisms. It occurrs as part of different types of rocks, sedimentation sludges, coals and mineral oils in minerals, Cadmium (Cd) is frequently associated with zinc. It's world wide presence and considerable industrial use has given size to an increase in its content in trophic food chains, which contribute mainly to human exposure. Oral absorption is relatively low and is influenced by the solubility of the compound, type of diet, and individual nutritrional state. Interest in Cadmium contamination began after the outbreak of *"itai-itai"* diseases in Japan. Evaluation of cadmium contamination has been carried out in all the countries of the European Economic community and it has been estimated that in Spain emissions to the atmosphere and water are respectively 6.89 and 3.79 per cent of total emissions in the European Economic Communities (EEC). When critical body concentration is reached, renal malfunction and damages are produced, proteinuria being the first sign, with increased urinary excretion of low molecular weight proteins such as B_2-microglobulin, Lysozyme, resinal binding proteins and immunoglobulin chains (Elinder *et al.,* 1985). After exposure, the kidney is the organ which contains the highest concentrations of cadmium and retains it longest. Moreover studies carried out in humans not occupationally exposed to cadmium reveal that 50 per cent body burden is found in the Kidneys (Kjellstrom, 1979). In the present investigation the control fish brain, liver, muscle, kidney and gill did not show any accumulation of cadmium indicating absence of any background cadmium and also indicated that the control system was uncontaminated. It was observed that the exposed fish liver accumulated the highest amount of cadmium when compared to exposed fish brain, and muscle.

In recent years, much research has focussed on determining factors contributing to the level of exposure and degree of accmulation of cadmium in renal cortex (Spicket and Lazner, 1979; Blanusa *et al.*, 1985, Scott *et al.*, 1987). Cadmium in the renal cortex increases with age, reaching a maximum between 40-50 years (Elinder,1985). Heavy metals in soil occurs in various forms, each possessing different mobilities and phyto-availabilities (Alloway/1990; Kuo *et al.*, 1983; and Tuin and Tels, 1990). Areas near industrial establishments may be enriched by metals via aerial deposition in particulate form. These particulately may come from varied sources such as autom 'ile emission , combustion of fossil fuel (Particibly coal), smelting and refining of metal ores and other. Because, these particulates arose from varying thermal conditions and matrices, they come in various forms *i.e.,* chloride, sulfate, carbonates, oxides etc. Three different stages of Cadmium stress are reported to interact with the uptake and movement or water in plants. The first short term stage occurs within a few hours of exposure with primary effects on root metabolism and growth, an indirect effect was a stomatal opening generated by the increase of the leaf osmotic potential of the leaves. The second occurs after 24-48hrs from Cadmium treatment. In this stage, Cadmium acted directly on the guard cells and severe root growth inhibition limits water uptake causing a decrease in RWC of the leaves and stomate closure (Leita *et al.,* 1995). In the third stage there was a general metabolic breakdown with loss of turgor and hydropassive stomatal closure, at very high cadmium supply or prolonged exposure time(Leita *et al.,* 1995). Cadmium is one of the most toxic metals occurring in nature. There is ample evidence in the literature that this metal is highly toxic to all living organisms (Yannai and Berdicevsky, 1995). In humans, chronic exposure to Cadmium causes, severe damage to the kidneys and it has been linked to enhanced ageing processes, as well as cancer (Jentsch *et al.,* 1993). Due to its many industrial uses such as an electroplating plants, dyestuffs industry and metallurgy and mining industries, this metal, cadmium has become widely employed and is now a major threat to man's environment. Numerous studies have demonstrated that the organic derivatives of metals are by far more toxic than their inorganic ions (Iverson and Brinckman, 1978). Further, the organic derivatives of heavy metals possess a much higher capability for absorption and accumulation in animal bodies than the inorganic ions(Venugopal and Luckey, 1978; Nakajima and Sakagnchi, 1986; Gadd, 1990). Little information is available on the formation of organic derivatives of Cadmium by environmental process. There were no findings in the literature of any direct evidence of such a process, except for a suggestion that a volatile cadmium compound, formed by a certain strain of *Pseudomonas,* may have been methylcadmium (Summers and Silver, 1978).

Commercial plastics use heavy metals in their formulation (Bode, 1992; Wagner *et al.,* 1992). Heavy metals are added to plastics for a number of reasons, namely as: stabilisers, plasticisers, antioxidants, colourants and fire retardants (Bode, 1992 and Wagner *et al.,* 1992). Cadmium is widely used as a colourant and plasticiser (Tamaddon and Hogland, 1993; Bergback *et al.,* 1994) and is often used in per cent amounts in PVC. Bode (1992) reports that they found Cd at levels upto 4 per cent in PVC. Other metals used in high concentrations in plastics formulations include Sb, Hg, Pb, Zn, Cr and Cu (Bode, 1992). Biesinger *et al.,* (1982) reported loss of mercury by volatilisation and adsorption which has not often been reported by investigators and hence suggested that mercury concentrations given in the literature should be considered less than those reported., unless test solution measurements were included. Mercury loss from the water in renewed static tests occurred by both biological activity and physical effects (adsorption and volatilisation), while some loss also occurred in flow through systems, concentrations remained fairly stable throughout the test period, because the test solution was not changed during the entire period of experimentation. No report was available to indicate volatilisation of cadmium from environmental samples. The cadmium compounds remain static, the only probability of decrease in the cadmium concentration might be either due to absorption by plants and animals or by way of cadmium reacting with environmental chemicals forming complexes, rendering the metal/chemical inactive or non-functional.

The rapid absorption of (inorganic and organic) mercury and cadmium through the gill, skin and gastro-intestinal tract of fish is well evident (Gibilin and Massaro, 1973, Panigrahi, 1984; Samant, 1989 and Harichandan, 2002). The toxicity of mercury and cadmium becomes apparent in a shorter period in aquatic animals. Panigrahi (1980) documented a detail behavioural changes in relation to inorganic mercury intoxication. Panigrahi (1984) reported the impact of MEMC on *Anabas scandens,* freshwater fish and noted substantial changes in behaviour of the test fish. Harichandan (2002) reported the toxicity and effect of cadmium on fresh water fish and opined that the metal cadmium is deadly toxic. In the present investigation, swelling of eyes were not marked. Later on reddening of eyes were marked. This might be due to the toxicant, Cadmium chloride. Swelling of eyes and reddening of eye can be attributable to mercury poisoning (Panigrahi, 1980) and consequent early blindness, migh be due to the combined effect of the chemicals present in the leachate of the solid waste (Pattnaik, 2001). Higgins (1974); Mac Leod and Pessah (1973); Panigrahi (1980); Samant (1989) and Harichandan (2002) reported that loss of appetite, loss of weight, nervousness, dizziness, loss of equilibrium, erratic swimming and gradual onset of inactivitity were the subclinical effects of inorganic and organic mercury intoxication. Identical observations were not marked here in *Tilapia* fish exposed to cadmium choride. Panigrahi (1984) also reported similar symptoms relating to a mercury based fungicide. Mac Leod and Pessah (1973) and Panigrahi (1980) reported neurological damage caused by mercury on fish, basing on the behavioural studies. In the present investigation, peculiar symptoms were marked. The cadmium chloride exposed fish showed initial symptoms like mercury poisoning but later on the exposed fish became over excited and periodic outbursts in irratic swimming was noted, ultimately the excited fish died of suffocation. When the excited fishes were heavily oxygenated and kept in undisturbed water survived. The movement of the fish slowed down and became sluggish (Harichandan, 2002). The exposed fishes showed high level of sensitivity. Any type of external stimuli like a fish of light, some one coming closer to the aquarium, any type of movement even any sound. Under the influence of any stimulus, the sluggish fish instantly starts vigorous movement and many a times colloid with the glass of the aquarium frequently and showed circular movements. After one or two minutes, the movements slow down and the fish becomes senseless, ventillation rate almost stops (Harichandan, 2002). If heavily oxygenated, the fish survives otherwise the exposed fish dies. During this later period of slowing down the movement, the colour of the fish becomes black due to dispersion of melanin pigment. This black colour disappears, when the system was heavily oxygenated. At times, the shocked fish automatically comes back to normal, and the black colour disappears. This type of self recovery was only in 30 per cent of the cases (Harichandan, 2002). Heavy oxygenation can help to around 65 per cent fishes to survive but the rest of the excited fish die instantly and never recover from the shock.The black colour persists for some time and after death the black colour again disappears (Harichandan, 2002). In cadmium exposed fish lesions develope on the fins and later the skin erodes and the bones were clearly visible and becomes naked and shedding of fins were noted in few exposed fish towards later period of exposure or at higher exposure period (Harichandan, 2002). This seems to be an important symptom in cadmium exposure, which was not marked in mercury or pesticide exposure.

Body weight of the control fish increased by 3.96 per cent after 28 days and by 7.86 per cent after 56 days of exposure. Whereas, the body weight of the exposed fish gradually decreased during the exposure period and a maximum of 6.17 per cent decrease was observed after 28 days of exposure, when compared to control fish. Control fish did not show any signs of toxicity (Harichandan, 2002). No recovery in body weight was marked, when the exposed fish was transferred to toxicant free normal medium. Rather further depletion upto 8.92 per cent over the 28 days exposure value was marked, on 28th day of recovery. Recovery studies clearly indicated that transferring the cadmium chloride exposed fish to normal water medium has no effect (Harichandan, 2002). Rather higher depletion in body weight was marked. The body weight showed a linear increase showing the existence of significant positive correlation with the exposure period in the control set. Whereas, a significant negative correlation was observed between the exposure period and body weight. With the increase in exposure period, the body weight significantly declined. Autopsy studies revealed that the liver and brain of exposed fish were congested and tender. The brain somatic index initially increased from 1.13 to 1.22 after 7days of exposure.Than, the BSI decreased gradually with the increase in exposure period. On 28th day of exposure, the BSI decreased from 1.12 to 0.87 (Harichandan, 2002). After 28 days of exposure to cadmium chloride, the exposed fish was transferred to toxicant free medium for recovery studies. The BSI further decreased from 0.87 to 0.72 on 14th day of recovery. Interestingly, on 28th day of recovery, the BSI increased to 1.09 but the value was less than the control value (Harichandan, 2002). The Hepato Somatic Index (HSI) remained almost at the same level in the control fish throughout the experimental period. The HSI gradually and significantly decreased with the increase in exposure period. The value depleted from 2.37 to 0.67 on 28th day of exposure. Partial recovery from 0.67 to 1.09 on 14 day and to 1.31 on 28 day of recovery was noted, when compared to control value. A consistent Kidney Somatic Index was recorded in the control fish in the entire period of experimentation (Harichandan, 2002). Interestingly and unlike BSI and HSI, the KSI value in the exposed fish when compared to control fish, increased with the increase in exposure period. The KSI value increased from 0.25 to 0.42 on 21st day of exposure and on 28th day of exposure the KSI value decreased from 0.25 to 0.31. The exposed fish was transferred to toxicant free medium for recovery studies (Harichandan, 2002). No recovery was noted.We find strong similarity in the trend of change in body weight with the reports of Harichandan (2002), but in the present case, our data is more accurate as we have taken individual species in seaprate containers, so that the per cent change in weight becomes more logistic.

In the preliminary study the animals showed all regular features of cadmium poisoning; such as excitation, irritation and restlessness. Towards the end of the experimental period *i.e.* prior to death the locomotion of fish almost ceased and remain suspended vertically in the water medium, indicated loss of equilibrium. In addition, periodic and erratic paralytic movements were observed in exposed fish. Samant (1989) reported an identical trend in mercury poisoning but in the present investigation the observed changes were more significant due to cadmium poisoning. The early signs of poisoning were probably due to the effect of chemical cadmium on fish. The body of the exposed fishes did not show semi U or V bendings either in the earlier period or towards later period of exposure, like mercury poisoning as reported by Panigrahi(1980) and Samanta (1989). Control fish remained clinically healthy, throughout the experimental period.

The observed depression in active metabolism in cadmium chloride exposed fish are indicative of damage to nervous tissues, inhibition of enzymes or vital system was totally in agreement with Mac Leod and Pessah (1973); Panigrahi (1980) Panigrahi (1984) and Misra (2002). Fry (1957) demonstrated that depression in active metablism directly reduce "scope for activity". This in turn may result in decreased growth, impaired swimming ability with erratic outbrust at times. It is possible that even a small reduction in the normal active metabolic rate may be indicative of stress in the animals (MacLeod and Pessah, 1973). Loss in weight due to starvation was noted by Larson and Lewander (1973). But the loss due to starvation was dry-less. Panigrahi and Misra (1978, 1980) reported the loss of body weight due to mercury intoxication and confirmed that this loss in body weight was only due to mercury stress. In addition, exposed fish maintained their feeding habit only after a short span of time. Hence the weight loss can not be correlated with starvation but can be related with the solid waste intoxication. A significant correlation exists between body weight and days of the exposure.

Blindness and exophthalmia in fish were presumably caused by the effects of mercury on the brain and optic nerves. Magos *et al.,* (1985) reported very little difference in the neurotoxicities of methylmercury and ethylmercury when effects on the dorsal root ganglia or coordination disorders were compared, an increase in mercury content of the brain is potentially hazardous. Brain tissue should therefore be carefully examined for carcinogenic or histo-pathological signs. Gopalkrishnan (1961) reported the different stages of eye infection, the second stage of infection of eye being the reddening of the eye ball and whitening of the cornea. Similar eye infection was observed with a prior swelling of the eyes. This is probably be due to the destruction of brain cells and nerve cells which causes loss in consistency in the whole tissues. Yamamura *et al.,* (1987) reported no change in body weight in short term exposure in both control and MMC exposed rats. However, a decrease in body weight was reported after 8 weeks Me Hg-exposed rats. Stevenson *et al.,* (1977) reported no change in body weight gain between control and lead exposed rats upto 8 weeks exposure. Growth has often been used to assess the effect of toxicants on fish (Bulkema *et al.,* 1982). However, biochemical changes during toxicosis should precede reductions in growth because growth is the culmination of many biochemical processes, and physiological and biochemical effects are the underlying cause of measurable whole organism effects (Mehrle and Mayer, 1980). A decline in liver somatic index and brain somatic index in exposed fish could be correlated with degeneration of cells and decrease in other biochemical variables. Stone *et al.,* (1977) reported no significant effect on body weight or size of kidneys, liver as related to body weight in lead exposed Japanese Quail. Concisely, at this stage it is not possible to establish the cause of blindness, loss in body weight and decrease in liver and brain somatic index, except a generalised comment on the behaviour of the exposed fish to stress that the observed symptoms were most probably be due to the leached chemicals of the solid waste. Bhatia *et al.,* (1973) reported that changes in behaviour in test fish had some relationship with insecticide intoxication. Rath and Misra (1980) reported the change in behaviour activity of exposed fish to dichlorovous (DDVP) and confirmed the idea that the change in activity was related to pesticide intoxication, which is totally agreable with our observation in this study. Panigrahi (1980), Panigrahi (1984) Pattnaik (2001) and Misra (2002) reported similar decline in parameters. However, in this present piece of investigation, the extent of damage was probably more acute and prnounced, might be due to the effect of the chemical.

In pollution monitoring programmes, efforts have been directed towards obtaining information on the body burdens of common or commercially important species (Micallef and Tylor, 1990). Besides studies of biaccumulation, the physiological responses of the animals must also be followed since the whole body response is critical to an animal's survival (Goldberg *et al.,* 1978 and Micallef and Tyler, 1990). The effect of inorganic mercury and organic mercury on the whole animal oxygen uptake the respiratory metabolism was as expected and presented earlier by Panigrahi (1980) and Samant (1989). A high concentration toxicant inhibition of metabolism, was almost complete. Oxygen consumption. decreased with the increase in exposure period. An inverse correlation reported between oxygen consumption and exposure period (Pattnaik, 2001). Similar inverse relationship of oxygen consumption is noticed with the concentration of the mercury in the leachate in the medium. The ventilation rates of the exposed *Tilapia* fish increased significantly when compared to control fish was reported by Pattnaik (2001). In the present investigation an initial increase in ventillation rate followed by drastic decrease in ventillation rate was observed. The increase or decrease in ventillation rate is an indicator of poisoning and at times , this indicator can indicate the status of the aquatic environments. In this study, unlike the previoous authors working on different types of toxicants/pollutants indicated that the ventillation rate of the exposed fish increased. The increase in ventillation rate was correlated with the high rate of pumping of water through the gills/operculum to absorb more amount dissolved oxygen. High rate of pumping of water becomes essential only when a body deficiet for oxygen was felt by the exposed organism. This *Tilapia* fish has bimodal system of gaseous exchange. In deficient condition, this fish can engulf air staraight and make up the oxygen deficiency of the body. Hence, for this type of fish or any fish with bimodal gaseous exchange system can avoid pumping more amount of contaminated water to avoid stress. Hence, in the present investigation, an initial rise in ventillation can be attributable to over excitation and instant coming in touch with a pollutant. Later, the fish could breath from air straight by engulfing the air and trapping the oxygen present in the air. With the increase in exposure period the whole animal oxygen uptake of *Tilapia* decreased significantly. Regression coefficient are all negative confirming the increase in inhibition at higher concentrations and also with the exposure period. A depression in the filtration rates of bivalves has been shown to take place place following exposure to a variety of metal ions other than mercury (Abel, 1976; Watling and Watling, 1982; Ward, 1982; Howell *et al.,* 1984 and Grace and Gainey, 1989). The results for the effects of mercury and cadmium on the filtration rates showed that mercury and cadmium repidly decreased the filtration rate in musseles (Micallef and Tyler, 1990). Panigrahi(1980) reported that with the increase in pollutant the whole animal oxygen uptake and respiratory metabolism declined sharply both in *in vitro* and *in vivo*. Rath and Mislira (1979) reported a striking decline in whole animal oxygen uptake and respiratory metabolism declined sharply both *in vitro* and *in vivo*. Rath and Mishra (1979) reported a striking decline in whole animal oxygen uptake and respiratory metabolism when exposed to dichlorvos an organo-phosphours compound. Panigrahi (1984) reported an identical data showing agreement with the findings of Panigrahi (1980). Incidentally the observation of this study tallied with the findings of Panigrahi (1984) and of Rath and Mishra (1979). Rath and Misra (1980) suggested an inverse relationship in active metabolism and pollutant concentration. The decline in whole body oxygen uptake can be attributable to several factors. Some important points are: *First*, due to coagulation of mucus with the gill lamellae induced by the toxicant (Pattnaik, 2001), *Second*, due to degeneration of epithelial cells, from gill lamellae by the toxicant (Misra,2002), *Third*, disruption of gases exchanges at gills due to differential erythrocyte behaviour (Panigrahi, 1980) and haemolysis induced by mercury, *Fourth*, loss of appetite and ataxia due to merecury intoxication etc. The idea is being well supported by Panigrahi (1980), Panigrahi, (1984) and Samant, (1989). Residual mercury concentration was probably responsible for the decline in oxygen uptake by the exposed fish when compared to control fish (Pattnaik, 2001). At this stage, it is very difficult to assess the excact cause of the decrease in the parameters. However, the role of cadmium can never be ignored at this stage of discussion. Fang and Fallin (1974) have shown in tissue slices incubated with these alkyl mercurials that the decomposition of ethylmercury was more noticable than other mercurials. Dorn (1974) reported the alteration of ionic distribution and osmoregulatory activity of the animal (Passow, *et al.*, 1961) and accounted for the increased respiratory rate in Congeria. Fox *et al.*, (1975) reported that inorganic mercury has no effect on the oxygen consumption by the brain tissue slices upto 0.5 mM concentration of mercury nitrate in contrast to organic mercury. Organo mercurials inhibit the CO_2 production at lower concentrations even (Fox *et al.*, 1975) in brain slices of guinea pig. Panigrahi (1980) reported an intial increase in oxygen consumption at lower concentration in liver, brain and muscle slices and gill tissues, and suggested that this was probably due to the fact that at much lower concentrations mercury stimulated an increase in oxygen consumption and also revealed that such a generalisation in this stage would at best be prematured. In the present investigation, it was observed that all three tissues studied did not show any stimulation of oxygen uptake/CO_2 release at lower periods of exposure and at lower concentrations. No stimulatory effect was noticed in cadmium chloride exposure to fish, in contrast to mercury exposure, where stimulation of tissue slices led to increase in respiration rate of the exposed fish tissue slices, when compared to control fish tissue slices. The stimulation induced by mercury was well established by Panigrahi (1980), Panigrahi *et al.*, (1996) and Pattnaik (2001). In the present investigation no stimulation was marked under any circumstances. Hence, this heavy metal cadmium is different from mercury in the action pattern. Panigrahi (1984) reported a similar trend in freshwater fishes when exposed to mercury based fungicide. In contrast, the observation of this study reveals no such increase at lower concentration of the toxicant.

However, a decline in active metabolism which related to respiratory metabolism was marked with the increase in exposure period and toxicant concentration. This observation totally agree with the findings of Rath and Misra (1981) and Samant (1989) and does not coincide with the trend of Panigrahi (1984). The difference may be due to the fact that at much lower concentration mercury induces an increase in oxygen consumption (Panigrahi, 1980), whereas, in the present study cadmium induced decrease in oxygen consumption.

The gill surface of the fresh water teleosts in intimate contact with the water are particulary susceptible to aquatic contaminants, and changes in respiratory metablism (Schaumburg *et al.,* 1967). Since the respiratory and circulatory systems are intimately connected, any significant changes in one system would reflect in the other. The gills are the primary site for the active absorption and respiratory exchange of gases. Because of the insufficiency of low solubility, the gills in obtaining the required oxygen for survival, low solubility of oxygen and increased toxicity of water, large amount of water must be passed over the gills to meet the oxygen demands of the fish (O'Conner and Fromm, 1975). At the first introduction of the toxic chemical to the aquatic systems, the ventilation rate increased over the control value. When the fish slowely acclimatised to the concentration of the toxicant and increased in the toxicant residual concentration in different organs of the fish like-brain, liver, muscle, gill, the physiological activity decreased with the intial increase in ventilation rate followed by decrease in ventillation rate. With prolonged exposure to a particular concentration, the fish ultimately faces death due to high accumulation of the toxicant inside the body tissue. The ventilation rate increased probably because the body demand for oxygen increased. More amount of water was probably pumped by the opercular movement, to make up the oxygen demand by the body. Lunn *et al.,* (1976) reported the increased respiration rates and decreased heart rates in fish exposed to DDT in rainbow trout. Brown and Newell (1972) reported a 50 per cent depression in respiration rate of the whole animal by copper. Vernberg and Vernberg (1972) reported a decrease in respiration rate with the exposure of fiddler crabs, *Uca pugilator* by inorganic mercury ($HgCl_2$). Macinnes and Thurberg (1973) found that silver depressed whole animal oxygen consumption in the mud snail, *Nassarius obsoletus.* Dorn(1974) reported the alteration of ionic distribution and osmo-regulatory activity of the animal (Passow *et al.,* 1961) and accounted for the increased respiratory rate in *Congeria.* The decline in exposed gill respiration can be correlated with the residual mercury concentration. The gill filaments coagulate with the mucus forming a coating over the gill epithelial layed, which restrict and reduce the area of gaseous exchanges. The gill of the fish is most important, because gill is the only site of O_2 absorption (Panigrahi, 1980; and Rath and Misra, 1980). Due to the decrease in the area of gaseous exchanges, the body demand for oxygen increases significantly (Rath and Misra, 1980a).As a result, increase in ventilation rate was seen in the exposed fish (Harichandan, 2002).

The interpretation of metal induced changes in respiration is complicated by the fact that such alterations differs from metal to metal, from speies to species and from one experimental condition to another (Thurberg *et al.,* 1974 and Panigrahi, 1980). Presence of mercury in the environment has received considerable attention. The rate of accumulation of mercury is dependent on the type of species (Matsunga, 1978) and its metabolism (Norstrom *et al.,* 1976 and Cutshall *et al.,* 1978). Food and feeding habits are also the factor affecting mercury concentration (Greig *et al.,* 1975). The same author also reported mercury content to vary with species. This variation may be assigned to the feeding habit. The rate of cadmium uptake from water by *Tilapia* fish was quite rapid in all tissues (Harichandan, 2002),as reported earlier but in the present experiment such a feature was not marked.

Considerable literatures are available regarding the accumulation of Hg in liver, gill, muscle and brain. *Tilapia* fish could accumulate a higher concentration of mercury in gills, when compared to other tissues like liver, brain and muscle. This is possibly due to the fact that *Tilapia* fish totally depends on the gills for gaseous exchange. The patten and distribution of mercury in different tissues of the fish reported by Gibilin and Massaro, 1973; Me Kim *et al.,* 1976; Hannerz, 1968, Panigrahi (1980), Panigrahi (1984) and Samant (1989) are quite agreeable with our findings. The brain of *Tilapia* fish was found to accumulate mercury slowly than gill and liver and the excretion of mercury was at a much slower rate than other tissues (Pattnaik, 2001). However, further higher accumulation instead of excretion was found in brain. Similar phenomenon has been reported by Gibilin and Massaro (1973) in rainbow trout, Takeda *et al.,* (1968) in rat, Syzuki *et al.,* (1963) in mouse and Swensson and Ulfvarson (1968) in birds and Hannerz (1968) in other species of fish. This is possibly due to the retarding effect of blood brain barrier to a certain degree. A similar phenomenon was marked in the present investigation of cadmium poisoning. In recovery studies, the increase in cadmium concentration in brain of the fish can be explained well, which agrees with the findings of Harichandan, (2002). The route of entry of cadmium to brain is mostly by blood vascular system. The fish was transferred to cadmium free medium but cadmium concentration in blood, liver, gill and muscle helps to build higher concentations of cadmium in brain (Harichandan, 2002). Similar findings were reported by Panigrahi (1980), Panigrahi (1984); Harichandan, (2002). and Samant (1989) in inorganic and organic mercury intoxication. The excretion rate of cadmium in brain is very very slow, as it lacks any special mechanism of excretion (Samant, 1989). Mercury in fish muscle builds upto such an extent that this becomes dangerous for consumption by humans. Larman *et al.,* (1976) reported that, by removing the fish from contaminated areas and placing them in uncontaminated environments do not reduce the cadmium concentration but rather get diluted due to the growth of the fish. The data indicate that the rate of elimination of cadmium is slow. The percentage of elimination from gill is higher when compared to other tissues, might be due to easy transport and elimination. The percentage of elimination from gill is higher than the other tissues. It is possible that inorganic cadmium biotransformed to methylcadmium/methyl mercury (Omata *et al.,* 1980) and phenyl mercury, also distrubs cellular activities at the site of its accumulation in these tissues, although qualitative and quantitative differences in the toxicity bertween these compounds remain to be elucidated (Harichandan, 2002).

Swensson and Ulfvarson (1968) calculated values for half retention times which will increase as length of the exposure period was increased, since there is a relatively rapid excretion of mercury shortly after administration, when the rate of uptake exceeds the rate of excretion, mercury accumulates in the tissues. Gills come in direct contact with the exposure medium which accumulates more than brain and liver. The elimination rate of liver is faster than brain and muscle. The rate of accumulation is directly proportional to the period of exposure to the toxicant. The rate of elimination is proportional to the recovery period (Harichandan, 2002) as was observed in the present investigation.

All the types of test conducted, revealed that with the increase in exposure period different parameters decreased significantly. With the increase in exposure period the residual cadmium accumulation showed an increasing trend. Hence, it can be suggested that cadmium enriches in the tissues with the increases in exposure period and consequent decrease in parameters (Variables) were probably only due to cadmium absorbed from the environment, which in turn comes from the waste of the Paper industry, in the exoposed aquaria, when compared to control. Accumulation of inorganic mercury in the tissue of animals exposed to methyl mercury compounds (Neville and Berlin, 1974; Magos and Butler,1976 and Evans *et al.,* 1977) suggests the existence of bio transformation mechanism *in vivo* resulting in a release of inorganic mercury/ cadmium by cleavage of carbon-mercury and carbon-cadmium bond (Norseth and Clarkson, 1970). There is a considerable risk of accumulation of methylmercury in the tissues of fish and mammals (Yamamura *et al.,* 1987) by prolonged exposure to inorganic mercury and methylmercury compounds. Reports that mercury reacts with complex biomolecules (Panigrahi, 1980; Shaw, 1987 and Sahu, 1987) in different organs of the animals and forms complexes, and attachment of the compounds to different specific membrane structure (Panigrahi', 1980 and Panigrahi,1984) and other organelles of the tissues, explains the retention of mercury in the tissues for a longer period, instead of being excreted. A similar interpretation can be made here in the present investigation pertaining to cadmium retention, accumulation, excretion in the tissues of the cadmium chloride exposed fishes (Harichandan, 2002).

The changes in total ATPase activity in brain, liver and muscle of control and cadmium chloride exposed fish at different days of exposure and recovery and it's per cent changes were shown in Figs. 3.34 to 3.40 (Harichandan, 2002). The brain tissue showed a maximum decrease by 44.42 per cent. This enzyme activity decreased by 49.14 per cent on 14th day recovery and decreased by 36.69 per cent over the 28th day exposure value, after 28 days of recovery, indicating a partial recovery. The exposed fish brain enzyme activity could recover partly by 7.73 per cent on 28th day of recovery (Harichandan, 2002). No recovery in the brain enzyme activity was marked on 14 days of recovery, rather further depletion in the enzyme activity was noted. The changes in total ATPase activity in liver of control and cadmium chloride exposed fish at different days of exposure and recovery and it's per cent changes were shown in Figs. 3.35 and 3.38. The liver tissue showed a maximum decrease by 69.19 per cent (Harichandan, 2002). The changes in total activity in muscle of control and cadmium chloride exposed fish at different days of exposure and recovery and it's per cent changes were reported (Harichandan, 2002). The exposed fish muscle enzyme activity could recover partly by 18.59 per cent and 29.95 per cent on 14th and 28th day of recovery. The correlation coefficient analysis between days of exposure and Na^+, K^+, Mg^{++} dependent ATPase activity in control fish brain showed a positive but non-significant correlation, whereas, the exposed fish brain showed a significant negative correlation (Harichandan, 2002). The control set showed positive but insignificant correlation. The per cent change in the enzyme activity in the exposed fish brain when compared to control fish brain showed the existence of a negative significant correlation with the exposure period (Harichandan, 2002). Hinton *et al.,* (1973)reported that mercury in fish tissue causes enzyme alteration even at very low concentration. Upon continued exposure toxicity leads finally to structural alterations (Hossain and Dutta, 1986). The maintainance of certain concentration gradient in different tissue as a matter of fact depends on the integrity of the ATPase activity. ATPase is specifically required for the transport of ions against concentration gradient as well as across the membrane. Yagi *et al.,* (1976) reported the existence of a strong inter relationship between ATPase activity and Na^+, K^+ , Ca^{++} and Mg^{++} content of the tissues (Harichandan, 2002). ATPase is specifically required for the transport of ions against concentration gradation and across membranes. Ahuja and Subrahmanyam (1978) concluded that ATPase plays a central role in synaptic transmission and nerve impulses generation.The decrease in brain ATPase activity may be due to over excitation of the fish to the stress. Ahuja and Subrahamanyam(1978). Subrahamanyam (1978) reported, decrease in brain Na^+ , K^+ ATPase activity in the trained rats may be due to their nervous over excitation during training. A drastic depletion in this enzyme activity in liver, gill and muscle was observed in the exposed fish. Panigrahi (1984) reported a similar trend in mercury based fungicide exposed fishes. The data of this investigation coincides with the findings of Rath and Misra(1980) in difrerent vital organs of a freshwater fish exposed to dichlorovos. Since liver is the active site of all metabolisms, depletion in ATPase activity in the liver caused diminishing of enzymes activity at 10 mg/kg and 20 mg/kg MMC in rats. The same author reported a slight activation of the enzymes activity with an injection of Hg.Verma *et al.,* (1978)reported depression in ATPase activity by chronic Chlordance intoxication in freshwater fishes and suggestged that the mechanism of the action of the pesticides on ATPase system may be due to the uncoupling of oxidative phosphorylation which cuses a depeletion in the phosphorylation product -ATP. Panigrahi(1980) also showed similar trend as suggested by Verma *et al.,* (1978). Panigrahi (1980)noted that the reduction in available free phosphate would be directly proportional to the reduction of total ATP produced. Panigrahi (1980) that a signficant difference in the response of the ATPase activity to inorganic mercury was observed between *in vivo* and *in vitro*. In the exposed fish a gradual decrease of total ATPase activity with the exposure period was marked in all the tissues. In contrast, in *in vitro* studies, mercury contained in the solid waste at low concentrations stimulates total ATPase activity. However, on further increase in solid waste concentration, the total ATPase activity decrease significantly. Stimulation occurs at low concentration of the stress (Harichandan, 2002) and the fish behaviour was more erratic. The extreme behaviour of the exposed fish, exposed to cadmium containing waste, now can be correlated with the enzyme activity (Harichandan, 2002). There exists a strong correlation among the ions concentration in the tissue, ATPase activity, AChE activity and metabolic rate (Panigrahi,1980; Webb,1966 and Harichandan, 2002) with the behaviour of the fish. Any change in the above said parameters due to the toxicant, will change the behaviour of the fish directly or indirectly. The present investigation strongly indicates that the enzyme activities are related to residual cadmium concentration in the tissues.We can conclude here that probably the causative agent for all such observed changes in this study is the cadmium present in the aquarium and similar results and interpretation can be expected in case of the waste of the paper industry, which contains cadmium alongwith other chemicals. The waste of the industry is a complex mixture of many chemicals. When we take the effluent of the industry as a whole, the observed effects might be either due to the synergistic or antagonistic effect of the combined chemicals on the organism (Harichandan, 2002). The decrease in activity of the cadmium exposed fish, the decrease in oxygen uptake by the exposed fish, the decrease in tissue slices respiration, the lethargic movement by the cadmium exposed fish may be well correlated to the decrease in ATPase activity. At lower concentrations, there appears to be sufficient evidence from these studies to indicate that ATPase inhibition was probably the site of attack of cadmium in fish tissues. A significant depression of ATPase activity was observed with the excessive absorption of cadmium (Harichandan, 2002). The decrease in total ATPase activity in gill of the exposed fishes lead to the decrease in ion exchange and also, in addition, gaseous exchange. The depeletion in total ATPase activity with the exposure period in brain, liver, muscle and gill caused the depression in the activity of the fish was most probably due to cadmium present in the medium. The neurotoxic action of mercurial compounds and cadmium compounds as reported earlier may be due to a secondary response of the fish to the stress(Panigrahi, 1980). It may be quite possible that mercury/ cadmium and metabolities in the tissues, combinyl responsible for the observed for the observed toxic action of cadmium. Further more, Yagi *et al.,* (1976) correlated the decrease in Na^+, K^+, Mg^{++} content in different tissues of PCB poisoned rate with Na^+, K^+, Mg^{++} dependent ATPase activity. Similarly a strong correlation was observed between Na^+, K^+, Mg^{++} content of different tissues with the Na^+, K^+, Mg^+ depependent ATPase activity in respective tissues. A direct positive correlation exists between the minerals and the activity of total ATPase. The fact that there is no clear parallel between ATPase inhibition and per cent mortality, deserves attention. Desaiah *et al.* (1975) suggested that such a case is possible due to detoxifying mechanism operating *in vivo* preventing development of a graded dosage inhibition type of response even though such graded response has been resported *in vitro*. But in contrast, in our recovery experiments no significant recovery of total ATPase activity in brain, liver, and muscle was noticed. Hence, the hypothesis that detoxifying mechanism decrease the dosage inhibition type of response, was not agreeable, as no significant recovery was noticed in the fishes (Harichandan, 2002). The amount of recovery may be mostly due to the excretion of cadmium from the body (Harichandan, 2002). The cation exchangbe system has direct relation with the ATPase enzyme activity. The activity of this paprticular enzyme depends on several factors such as concentration of substracte (ATP), products (inorganic phosphate, ADP) and metal accelerators (Harichandan, 2002). Hence, any sort of change in one of these above mentioned factors would lead to the inhibition of enzyme activity or it might be due to the resultant of all the above factors. The decrease in Na^+-ATPase, K^+-ATPase and Mg^{++}-ATPase might be due to the distrubance of Na^+, K^+ and Mg^{++} ion concentration in different tissues of the fish (Samant, 1989; Pattnaik, 2001; Misra, 2002 and Harichandan, 2002). The response of ATPase to inorganic and organic mercury vaired from fish to fish, tissue to tissue and also within the same tissue (Pattnaik, 2001). The toxicant causes permanent damage to cell and other vital systems. Due to decline in enzyme activity the metabolic activity declined significantly. The decline in enzymatic activity, periodic failure of nerve impulse generation, depletion in metabolic activity can be correlated to toxicant toxicity which gets reflected in the behaviour of the organism in the form of impaired swimming, periodic outbrust, imbalance, ataxia, inappetence, inthargicity etc. Although quantifying these effects and changes, will be a very difficult task in the present set up of conditions, still then an approximation can be made from the structural and behavioural changes (Harichandan, 2002). The change in behaviour in exposed organisms was always compared with that of control organisms. Both the sets were kept under identical conditions and the only difference being the exposed set gets the pollutant stress. So the difference in both the sets might be due to the toxicant stress. In both and control and exposed *Tilapia* fish, a great variation in total ATPase was marked among brain ,liver, and muscle tissues (Harichandan, 2002). It has been observed that at very low concentrations of the toxicant no activation of the enzyme activity was marked in all the three types of tissues as observed by Samant (1989).This was probably due to the total effect of the toxicant acted as a whole to produce such a higher toxic effect. Panigrahi (1984) reported reduction in Na^{+},K^{+} Mg^{++} and Ca^{++} ion concentration in brain, liver muscle and gill tissues of MEMC exposed fish, when compared to control fish. These ion are very important because they control the permeability of the cell membrane. Yamane and Davidson (1961) and Katz (1963) have found that the Hg(II) ions are bound predominantly to the pyrimnidine and purine bases in pure DNA, preference being shown in AT-base pair-(Yamane and Davidson, 1961; Wong *et al.*, 1965 and Davidson *et al.*, (1965) eventhough a reaction with phosphate group cannot be excluded. Neuro-transmission in animals were controlled by these metallic ions. The change in ion concent ratio leads to disruption of neurotransmission. The present findings totally agree with the findings of Panigrahi (1984), Samant (1989); Pattnaik (2001) and Harichandan, 2002).

The sodium ion content declined in brain, liver, muscle and kidney after 28 days of exposure showing maximum decrease by 26.84 per cent, 36.99 per cent, 41.68 per cent and 44.68 per cent in brain, liver, muscle and kidney tissues, respectively (Harichandan, 2002). The kidney showed the highest per cent decrease, when compared to muscle, liver and brain tissues of the exposed fish. The potassium ion content declined in brain, liver, muscle and kidney of the exposed fish showed 29.18 per cent, 38.69 per cent, 47.91 per cent and 33.83 per cent decrease in potassium ion content, when compared to the control value, where muscle was highly affected showing the maximum depletion. Decrease in potassium ion content in brain, liver, muscle and kidney of exposed fish, compared to the control fish, was marked. Significant variation was marked in the calcium ion content in different tissues of the exposed fish, when compared to control fish tissues (Harichandan, 2002). Maximum depletion by 65.14 per cent in kidney tissue, 34.04 per cent in muscle tissues, 10.42 per cent in liver tissue and least depletion by 9.98 per cent in brain tissues of the exposed fish, when compared to control fish tissues were recorded (Harichandan, 2002). Maximum depletion in magnesium ion by 63.78 per cent in kidney tissue, 59.14 per cent in liver tissues, 54.14 per cent in muscle tissue and least depletion by 51.71 per cent in brain tissues of the exposed fish, when compared to control fish tissue was recorded. Out of the four ions studied in the exposed fish tissues, significant decrease was recorded in sodium ion and calcium ion content and highly significant differences were observed in potassium ion and magnesium ion content in all the tissues studied. Out of the four tissues studied the kidney and liver was the most affected than the least affected was brain for some ion and for the rest of the ions the muscle was least affected. Significant differences in ion content of different tissues of the exposed, when compared to control fish clearly indicate the nature of the toxicant and effects caused by the toxicant ($CdCl_2$) on the nervous tissue, synaptic transmission, nerve impulse generation, ionic balance and membrane transport system of the exposed fish (Harichandan, 2002).

In the fishes a declining trend in minerals has been noticed. The probable decrease as predicted by Yagi *et al.*, (1976) may be impairment in intestinal absorption of these minerals. Due to decrease in these minerals the ionic regulation of different tissues decreased (Prossor, 1973). Hurkat and Mathur (1976) reported that these minerals are highly essential for the maintenance of osmatic fragility and mechanical resistance of blood cells and proper function of all types of tissues. Reports that Ca^{++} plays a vital role in blood coagulation can be correlated to the fact that the pollutant induces decline in ion content of the exposed fish. The existence of activator ions of alkali metal series for alkaline earth met al series were highly essential for the activity of most of the enzymes which required ions for their optimum action, as a result of which the decrease in ion concent rations in different to issues were likely to influence any of the biological functions of the enzymes. Mercury, acting as a protein denaturant, binds to membranes, altering ionic distribution and osmoregulatory activity of the animal(Passow *et al.,* 1961). Prossor (1973) reported that the decrease in the concentration of minerals tend to decrease the ionic regulations of the different tissues and also added that the depletion in Na^{+} and K^{+} level tends to decrease in the active membrane transport. No significant variation in case of exposed liver and brain was marked when compared to control fish, so far as Ca^{++} studies are taken into account. However, a significant depletion in Ca^{++} content was observed in gill tissues. It is feasible that the requirement of calcium in liver and brain tissues increased in cadmium intoxicated fishes and the decrease of calcium content of gills did not promote a homeostatic adaptation as inferred by Yagi *et al.,* (1976); Harichandan, (2002). and Samant (1989). Hence, mercury plays an important role in the regulation system of calcium metabolism.

These ions play a vital role in the circulatory system of the animals. The plasms ion concentration plays a significant role in different metabolism. Any change in ion concentration will definitely reflect in the metabolic activity and physiological activity of the organism. Dawson (1979) reprted significant decrease in different haematological parameters with the decrease in plasma calcium and increase in plasma sodium of winter flounder exposed to mercury. Panigrahi and Misra(1979) reported changes in blood morphology in mercury exoposed fishes. The same author correlated the finger like projections, beak like proliferations and vacuolisation in the erythrocytes of mercury exposed fish with that of change in ion concentrations and drastic depletion in different enzymes activities. Similar decline in enzyme activities and disturbance in ion concent ratios were marked in solid waste exposed fish. Hence, it can be concluded that the changes in different enzymes activities and ion concentrations were related to nervous over excitation, which leads to impaired swimming and erratic movements of the exposed fish. The decline in Na^+, K^+ and Mg^{++}concentration in gill tissues indicates the depression in gaseous exchange in the exposed fish.

The existence of a close quantitative relationship between RNA content and protein synthesis was pointed out by Caldwell *et al.*, (1950) in cultures of microorganisms Priece (1952) showed the existence of an excellent correlation between the synthesis of RNA and the synthesis of proteins. Gale and Folkes (1953) showed the synthesis of proteins in the presence of glucose and amino acids and also pointed out that if purines and purines and pyrimidines were added to the said medium, nucleic acids were synthesised. The same authors also pointed out that in absence of aminoacids in the medium, instead of nucleic acids synthesis, the presence of purine and pyrimidines will enhance protein synthesis. Mansy and Tobias (1975) reported that mercurials can react with uracil, uridine, or thymidine in three different ways: coordination to a carbonyl oxygen of the neutral legand, electrophillic attack on the ring with displacement of a protein and formation of a mercury-carbon bond, and electrophilic attack with displacement of a protein and formation of a mercury nitrogen bond. Toxicant induced stimulation of nucleic acid and protein content indicated an acceleration of cellular metabolism and growth (Steel and Johannesson,1975; Peters, 1977; Love, 1980 and Harichandan, 2002) that might be responsible for the observed stimulation of juvenile growth. Toxicant effect on macromolecular content is often due to an indirect action on nucleic acid and protein synthesis, since a toxicant that interfers with energy yielding reactions is directly an inhibitor of the synthesis of RNA, DNA and protein (Holbrook, 1980 and Barren and Adelman, 1984).

Yamane and Davidson (1961) and Katz (1963) have found that the Hg (II) ions are bound predominantly to the pyrimidine and purine bases in pure DNA, preference being shown to AT-base pair (Wang *et al.*, 1965 and Davidson *et al.*, 1965) even though reaction with phosphate group cannot be excluded. Mercury, acting as a protein denaturant, binds to membranes, altering ionic distribution and osmoregulatory activity of the animal (Passow *et al.*, 1961). The inhibition of ATP production might effect the transport of ions across the cell membranes. But Deseiah *et al.*, 1975) reported a possible direct involvement of microsomal Na^+, K^+, ATPase in the transfer of substance across the cell membranes (Harichandan, 2002).

The changes in AChE activity in brain, liver and muscle of control and cadmium chloride exposed fish at different days of exposure and recovery and it's per cent changes were recorded and interesting results were obtained. The present results agrees with the findings of Harichandan, (2002). The differences in the data pattern are mostly either due to biological error or biological diversity. The brain tissue showed a maximum decrease by 58.5 per cent in AChE activity in cadmium chloride exposed fish. When the exposed fish was transferred to toxicant free medium, the AChE activity declined by 61.5 per cent on 14th day recovery and decreased by 58.3 per cent over the 28th day exposure value, after 28 days of recovery, indicating no significant recovery at all (Harichandan, 2002).

The observation indicated that with the increase in exposure period the DNA, RNA and protein content decreased significantly. Free amino acid content indicated a negative correlation with exposure period. The data are totally in agreement with the findings of Panigrahi(1984) and Harichandan (2002). Liver being the active site of all metabolic functions, it plays a crucial role in bio transformation of toxic agents (Bruin, 1976). The phenomenon of heavy metal induced stimulation of the incorporation of thymidine into tissue DNA is not unique to lead and has been reported in the case of kidney obtained from folic acid treated rats. Of particular interest is nuclear pyknosis in view of mercury binding to nuclcid acids (Valle and Ulmedr, 1972) and reported DNA damage induced by mercury (Cantoni *et al.*, 1982). If sub cellular structures are the actual site of toxic action of mercury it would lend credence to our hypothesis proposed earlier (Sharma *et al.*, 1981 and Sharma, 1987) that mercury toxicity is at least partly due to its combination with co enzyme A and resultant interference in CoA functions, the co enzyme A exists in free and ester forms in every tissue in different intracellular compartments

(Robishaw and Neely, 1985 and Sharma *et al.*, 1988). The decrease in DNA content in liver, brain and muscle tissue was most probably due to loss of cells. The decline in brain DNA content may also be due to decreased glial cell number as a consequence of toxicity. The decrease in RNA content in liver, brain and muscle of exposed fish was most probably due to an increased RNA breakdown Ahuja and Subrahmanyam (1978) reported a decline in RNA content in the brain cells due to nervous over excitation induced by prolonged training. A striking decrease in protein content was observed in treated fish exposed to leached chemicals of the solid waste when compared to control fish. The decrease in free amino acid content may be due to decrease in peptidase activity or might be due to proteolysis or might be due to inhibition in amino acid synthesis as consequence of toxicant poisoning. Since structural RNA constitutes more than 80 per cent of the total RNA content (Ahuja and Subrahmanyam, 1978) the decline in RNA content could be most probably due to decrease in structural RNA, which will not reflect the change in protein content. Chao *et al.*, (1984) have studied the effect of MMC, EMC, dimethyl mercury, PMA, p-HMB, p-HMBS, $HgCl_2$,$HgSO_4$, $Hg(ClO_4)_2$ on He La cell viability and DNA and RNA synthesis in intact cells and in isolated nuclei. The same author reported occurrence of significant change in the composition of the RNA synthesis even with compounds which did not actually stimulate the α-amanitin β-sensitive synthesis, such as phenyl mercuric acetate and $HgCl_2$ and even where both types of synthesis were inhibited, as with $Hg(ClO_4)_2$ and $Hg_2(ClO_4)_4$.

In the present investigation DNA, RNA, Protein and free-amino acid content decreased with the increase in exposure period in cadmium chloride exposed fish tissues, when compared to control fish tissues (Harichandan, 2002).

Haematological studies in fishes is a promising tool for investigating physiological stress and related diseases in fish. The haemoglobin percentage decreased with the increase in exposure period and also a drastic depletion in the number of red blood cells was noticed with the increasing exposure period. When transferred to cadmium free oxygen saturated water, the fish recovered only partly showing a permanent damage. The decrease in red blood cells is probably due to: (1) reduction of erythrocyte life span due to metal poisoning. Cadmium effects the osmotic resistance and mechanical fragility of the red blood cells. Reports of Vincent and Blackburn (1958) and Joyce *et al.*, (1959) on the defect in membrane permeability such as to derange the normal monovalent cation exchange, are clearly evident; (2) a significant depression of (Na^+, K^+)ATPase is associated with excessive absorption of cadmium and mercury (Singerman and Catalina, 1969). The decrease in red blood cells may be related to the destructive or suppressive effects of erythrogenic tissues, which is expressed in a failure in red blood cell production (de Bruin, 1976). The decrease in red blood cells content is probably due to injury to peripheral red cells or a defect in erythropoiesis. Reports of Webb (1966), Johansson-Sjobeck *et al.*, (1975) and Panigrahi and Mishra, (1978) suggests that the decrease in red blood cells is due to haemolysis. Haemolysis causes haemolytic anaemia. The anemias associated with chronic or acute poisoning by certain heavy metal are by no means entirely accountable to direct detrimental action upon the red cells membrane. Cadmium and mercury causes haemolysis by interacting with legands, constituents of the erythrocyte lipoprotein membrane, as the protein-SH group located in the membrane is the most favoured centre of attack. Other legands including hydroxyl, phosphate and ammonia grouping may ako precipitate complex formations with the metal ion. Such interactions while altering the permeability characteristic of the membrane, invariably results in derangement of the cation exchange function of red cell (de Bruin, 1976). The decrease in viability of red blood cells gives rise to accelerated destruction of the erythrocyte. Fish haemoglobins are unstable tending to form a variety of derivatives which lead to alterations in electroophoretic pattern (Yamanaka *et al.,* 1965). With the exposure, the blood oxygen carring capacity decreased which plays a central role in oxygen demand and subsequent oxygen consumption by the fish (Houston *et al.,* 1976 a, b). A remarkable increase in haematocrit value upto an exposure period of 21 days and then a depletion in haematocrit value on further exposure was noticed by Panigrahi (1980). Larason and Lewander (1973), reported no significant change in the haematocrit values of the European eel, after 145 days of starvation. Hence the increase in haematocrit values observed in the exposed fish cannot be attributable as the effect of starvation but probably due to the poisoning by mercury and cadmium (Panigrahi, 1980 and Harichandan (2002). The rise in haematocrit value was probably due to swelling of erythrocytes. The swelling of the erythrocyte was probably due to change in osmotic resistance induced by the mercury (Panigrahi, 1980). In the present investigation, it was observed that the exposed red blood cells were comparatively larger than the control red blood cells (Harichandan, 2002). The enlargement of exposed red blood cells was probably due to cadmium poisoning. Under reduced oxygen tension, swelling of red cell has been reported to take place, but is reversible in O_2 equilibrated condition (Sovio and Nyholm, 1974). Instead of steady rise drastic depletion of haematocrit value was noticed, which further confirms the idea that the swelling of erythrocytes is not due to reduced oxygen tension but due to change in osmotic balance, which was induced by the stress, mercury (Panigrahi, 1980). The decrease in haematocrit value after exposure is mostly due to hemolysis(Harichandan, 2002). The decrease in haematocrit value is due to shrinkage of the blood cells (Sovio and Nyholm, 1974). The present result agrees with the findings of Harichandan, (2002). The haematocrit value also decreased when treated with PCB reported by Johansson-Sjobeck *et al.,* (1975) and Westman *et al.,* (1975). No significant difference with regard to haematological parameters was marked in Cadmium exposed fish although a very significant difference was found in Hg. exposed fish by Calabrese *et al.,* (1975) in the winter flounder, *Pseudopleuronectes americanus.* Interactions of several pollutants and or natural factors can also alter the characters or degree of a pollutant effects (Thurberg *et al.,* 1974 and Gray *et al.,* 1974 and Harichandan, 2002). Dubale (1963) concluded that air breathing fishes, particularly teleosts, possessed a higher oxygen holding capacity then the non migratory water breathing fishes. Lenfant and Johansen (1972) have also shown that there is a tendency for haemoglobin concentration to be higher in those fishes which get their oxygen from air. Ramaswamy and Gopalkrishna Reddy (1978) reported higher haemoglobin concentration and higher oxygen holding capacity in *Anabas scandens*. *Anabas* showed a higher haemoglobin concentration and higher oxygen holding capacity than *Tilapia* fish, as reported by Panigrahi (1980) and Panigrahi and Misra (1978, 1979, 1980). The *in vivo* oxygen haemoglobin equilibrium is often remarkably sensitive to the metabolic needs of the animal (Riggs, 1970). Krogh and Leitch (1919) reported the higher oxygen capacity in air breathing fishes to reflect the degree of oxygen deficiency of the ambient medium. Air breathing fishes could tolerate oxygen deficient ambient conditions. This, probably correlates to the higher tolerance capacity to mercuric nitrate by *Anabas* fish then *Tilapia* fish (Panigrahi, 1980).

Results from the previous investigation by Panigrahi and Misra (1980) and Harichandan (2002). had shown a remarkable increase in haematocrit value upto an exposure period of 21 days when exposed to mercurial compounds and then a depletion in haematocrit value on further exposure to mercury was noticed. The rise in haematocrit value was due to swelling of erythrocytes. The swelling of the red blood cell was probably due to change in the osmotic pressure induced by mercury (Panigrahi and Misra, 1980). As reported earlier (Sovio and Nyholm, 1974) swelling of red cells used to take place under reduce O_2 tension but the trend was reversible in O_2 equilibrated conditions. The decrease in haematocrit value was due to shrinkage of the red blood cells as reported by Sovio and Nyholm (1974) seemed improbable (Panigrahi, 1980). In the present investigation, we found enlargement of red blood cells of the cadmium exposed fishes. But this increase in red blood cell size did not increase the haematocrit value or packed cell volume. Drastic depletion in haeomoglobin concentration, RBC count and haematocrit value in the cadmium chloride exposed fish might indicate destruction of red blood cells. At higher exposure periods vacuolisation of red blood cell was marked. At higher exposure period, erythrocyte membrane disintigrated and finally disappearance of erythrocyte membrane was marked in the cadmium chloride exposed fishes. After disappearance of the red blood cell membrane, the insignificant shrinkage and later total destruction red blood cell was marked. The above observations were caused by the toxicant, Cadmium chloride. Earlier reports showed that mercury affected the osmotic resistance and mechanical fragility of the red blood cells (de Bruin, 1976), which confirmed the findings of Levander *et al.,* (1977) and also the findings relating to freeshwater telcost, *Anabas scandens* by Panigrahi (1980). However, reports pertaining to molecular level studies on these red cell shape changes and small finger like proliferations are scanty. Sheetz and Singer (1976) suggested that the asymmetrically lipid composition of the red cells membrane bilayer could account for the stomatocytic and echinocytic transformations by concentrations of cations in the inner half of the bilayer and of anions in the outer half respectively. Olson (1972) reported vacuolisation of red blood cells after exposure for periods 4 and 8 weeks to 0.03 μg of Hg. 1^{-1} administered as methyl mercuric chloride.

The eco-toxicological assessment of toxic chemicals depend on two basic items of information. First, the environmental available concentrations of the chemical which occur as a result of discharge and distribution in the natural environment and secondly, the toxicological properties of the chemical at that concentration and its possible impact on the biota including humans. Different methods and procedures are used to draw all the available eco-toxicological informations together to arrive at an assessment. The basic requirements for such procedures are the pattern of use of chemicals; their disposal and release; physico-chemical characteristics; degradation and bioaccumulation; and biological factors such as growth inhibition, toxicity testing etc. Thus, the ecotoxicology of chemicals is an important aspect of environmental management and the management of pollution. In nature, plants and animals experience extensive damage due to different types of industrial effluents and wastes etc. The infected and contaminated fingerlings spread the disease when grown in field conditions. Thus, to avoid decline in fish productions, pesticides are applied to fish culture ponds. Hence, the aquatic ecosystems in general and ponds in particular increases substantial amount of toxicant within a notable period of time making it dangerous for human health, when wastes enter nutritional cycle through contaminated fish intentionally or due to carelessness (Koronowski, 1973).

The excessive loading of cadmium and other heavy metals in recent years tend to contaminate the environment. Controversy has centred around both the mode of action of toxicants in affecting plant and animal metabolism and the extent of its toxicity resulting from penetration into the biologic system. Towards last part of the present century the agricultural contamination of cadmium and its entry through food chain, have not only drawn the attention of the scientists of all over the world, but also a lot of research work in this Line have already been undertaken. Many countries have enacted their legislation to restrict the use of pesticide, mercury and cadmium both in industry and in agricultural sectors (Harichandan, 2002). Here it can be stressed that, before introduction of any chemical proper scientific scrutiny, from all possible aspects is essential, so the reckless handling of the chemical, cannot cause any residual toxicity problem in future. Secondly, sound knowledge on chemical behaviour and toxicity will be very much essential prior to introduction of the chemicals either through irrigation or natural entry through leaching or by way of discharge from any industry. Most of the results of different parameters were found to be statistically significant, it does mean that, the trend or changes observed in the present piece of work are to be taken into confidence. However, many interferences and predictions raised during discussion, provides gaps or fields unexplored yet. In this piece of investigation, though we felt to a link a gap but after completion of this piece, we find many questions remain unanswered. In this piece of investigation, we tried to find out the effects of Cadmium chloride, a heavy metal of importance, on the physiology of fish, effect on the macromolecules controlling the biochemical metabolism, impact on the haematology of fish and most important is the residual estimation of cadmium in different tissues of the exposed fish, which can provide pragmatic informations along with the data and interpretations of Harichandan (2002).

From the results obtained in present study and the reports of Harichandan (2002), it is clearly evident that, Cadmium chloride, which is now well known for its interference in biochemical metabolism, becomes toxic when used in lower and moderate concentrations. Many similarities exist in biological process among all forms of life, and investigative effects of this nature are not only important to plants, fish and wildlife, but to all life forms, including man. However, as long as these chemicals are thrown into the environment without proper check, this type of effects will always be there. Safe disposal of these wastes and possible decontamination of the contaminated areas, can protect both the target and non-target organisms. Due to careless handling of chemicals, unplanned disposal of wastes, future and fate of the waste chemicals in the environment, non-adoption of safty measures, non-maintenance of ecological balance, non-selection of pollution reducing plantation, will significantly harm the man made agricultural ecosystem in particular and the ECOSYSTEM in general. Due to heavy and constant discharge of these waste chemicals without following the directions given by Center and State Pollution Control Boards, Department of Environment, many a times, failure of the crop and depletion in fish production was marked. This failure was always attributed and pointed towards the other factors but not to man made problems. The heavy metal pollution was not a big problem for a pretty long time in India. But the recent awareness and environmental impact assessment programmes conducted by different Pollution Control Boards, Department of Environment and Forests of both State and Centre, environmental monitoring and status reports forced every one to think about the environment and its protection.

5

SUMMARY AND CONCLUSION

The present study was designed to study of effects of Cadmium chloride on a fresh water fish, *Tilapia mossambica,* Peters and its ecological implications.

1. Fishes were exposed to graded series of concentrations of cadmium chloride for acute toxicity studies. The MAC value deduced was 1.05 mg l^{-1} of cadmium chloride in 50 liters of water for 30 days. A safety concentration of 1.00 mg l^{-1} of Cadmium chloride was selected for this study.
2. The LC_{10}, LC_{50}, LC_{90}, LC_{100}, determined for *Tilapia* fish was found to be 1.20, 1.85,2.75 and 3.5 mg l^{-1} respectively after 30 days of exposure.
3. Exposed fishes appeared lethargic when compared to the control fish. Inappetence and ataxia was observed in the exposed fish.
4. Exposed fishes showed erratic movements, loss of equilibrium, gradual onset of inactivity etc. when compared to the control fish.
5. Restlessness and circular movement of fish were noted.
6. Bleeding of gills and disintegration of fins were noted.
7. Heavy oxygenation helped the exposed fishes to survive, otherwise the effected fishes died.
8. The body weight of the exposed fish decreased significantly, when compared to the control fish, where a significant increase by 10.88 per cent in body weight was marked. In the exposed fish 5.52 per cent decrease in body weight was marked.
9. When the exposed fish was transferred to toxicant free medium, partial recovery by 1.84 per cent was noted.

10. The BSI, and HSI significantly declined in the $CdCl_2$ exposed fish when compared to the control fish. A maximum of 52.9 per cent decrease was noted in BSI of $CdCl_2$ exposed fish, where 9.2 per cent recovery was noted after 28 days of recovery. The HSI decreased by 40.7 per cent after 28 days of exposure and no recovery was noted after 28 days of recovery indicating damage to liver of the exposed fish.
11. No significant recovery was marked in body weight, HSI, and BSI, when the exposed fish was transferred to toxicant free medium. The exposed fish could not recover to its pre-test activity.
12. The whole body oxygen uptake significantly depleted by 67.2 per cent in the exposed fishes, when compared to control fishes. When the exposed fish was transferred to toxicant free medium, 19.0 per cent recovery in the parameter was noted.
13. The ventilation rate decreased significantly by 45.1 per cent on 28 days of exposure. Increase in ventilation rate was not marked. A significant recovery by 34 per cent was noted in the exposed fish during recovery period.
14. The tissue slice respiration studies of brain, liver and muscle tissues in exposed fish, when compared to control fish, indicated toxic effects of cadmium chloride. The liver tissue was more affected than the muscle and brain tissue. Brain tissue was least affected during 28 days of exposure. Maximum recovery was noted in the muscle tissue and no recovery was noted in the brain tissue.
15. The experimental residual cadmium accumulation in different tissues were studied at different exposure and recovery period. The brain, liver, and muscle of the exposed fish accumulated 0.33,12.3 and 0.51 mg of cadmium/gm tissue after 28 days of exposure, respectively.
16. With the increase in exposure period the residual cadmium concentration increased in different tissues studied. The rate of excretion was also faster. The exposed fish probably required more time to excrete the accumulated cadmium.

17. Significant depletion of total ATPase activity in the cadmium chloride exposed fish tissues, when compared to control fish tissues was marked. The exposed fish muscle tissue was highly affected, where 76.1 per cent depletion in the activity was marked. The exposed brain tissue was least affected. The per cent decrease depleted during recovery period. During recovery period, the muscle of the exposed fish recovered by 28.5 per cent, liver tissue by 20.0 per cent and the brain tissue by 7.8 per cent, when compared to 28 days exposure value. This depletion in the enzyme activity affected the movements of ions across the membrane and severely affected the energy metabolism.
18. Drastic depletion in sodium, potassium, calcium and magnesium ion content in the cadmium chloride exposed fish tissues was marked when compared to the control fish. In case of sodium ion the liver was highly affected. For potassium ion, the liver of the exposed fish was highly affected, for calcium ion the muscle of the exposed fish was most affected and for magnesium ion, the brain tissues were affected. The liver was worst affected than muscle and brain. The brain tissue of the exposed fish was least affected.
19. Least difference was noted in the brain DNA content and maximum difference was noted in liver and muscle DNA content of the exposed fish, when compared to control. No recovery was marked in the exposed brain tissue, rather further depletion in DNA content was marked. An insignificant recovery by 11.4 per cent was noted in the exposed liver. Maximum recovery (11.7%) was marked in the exposed fish muscle.
20. Significant change in RNA content was noted in muscle and liver of exposed fish, when compared to control fish. Least difference was noted in the exposed brain tissue, when compared to control. No recovery in RNA content was noted in the exposed brain tissue, rather the per cent decrease increased during recovery period. Partial recovery by 5.1 per cent and 9.2 per cent was observed in the fish liver and muscle tissues during recovery period.

21. The protein content of the brain, liver and muscle of the $CdCl_2$ exposed fish depleted significantly, when compared to the tissues of control fish. Maximum depletion in protein content was noted in muscle than liver and than brain. No recovery was noted in the exposed brain tissue. Liver tissue recovered by 4.2 per cent and the muscle of the exposed fish recovered by 16.2 per cent, when compared to 28 days exposure value. The exposed fish could not recover to its pre-test level. The drastic decrease in protein content in the exposed fish was probably due to proteolysis in the exposed fish, caused by cadmium chloride.
22. Significant decrease in FAA content in the exposed fish brain, liver and muscle when compared to control fish tissue was due to proteolysis and subsequent disintegration of amino-acids after breakdown of proteins. The decrease in FAA content might be due to non-synthesis of amino acids and disruption in the synthesis of amino acids in the exposed fish. This might be a probability, because simultaneously all the four macromolecules decreased in the exposed fish tissues. $CdCl_2$ caused this disruption.
23. Maximum depletion in FAA content was noted in muscle tissue than liver and least decrease was noted in the brain tissue. Highest insignificant recovery was noted in liver tissue than brain and muscle. It seems muscle tissue of the exposed fish was highly affected.
24. Significant decrease in haemoglobin content was noted in the exposed fish, when compared to control fish during exposure period. A maximum of 19.9 per cent and 36.1 per cent depletion was noted on 14 days and 28 days of exposure. During recovery the haemoglobin content further depleted on 14 days of recovery. But on 28 days of recovery, 1.4 per cent recovery was noted, which was not significant.
25. The RBC count significantly declined by 51.9 per cent on 28 days of exposure, when compared to control fish. When the cadmium chloride exposed fish was transferred to toxicant free medium, 1.9 per cent recovery was observed on 14 days of recovery. On 28 days of recovery, 5.7 per cent recovery was marked.

26. The haematocrit value decreased in the cadmium chloride exposed fish, when compared to control fish. A maximum of 27.9 per cent depletion was noted on 28 days of exposure. When the exposed fish was transferred to toxicant free medium, no recovery was observed. Rather further decrease in the parameter was marked indicating damage to the blood vascular system.
27. The oxygen carrying capacity of the blood declined significantly and a maximum of 36.1 per cent decrease in OCC of blood was observed. When the exposed fish was transferred to toxicant free medium, no recovery was marked on 14 days of recovery and 1.4 per cent recovery was noted after 28days of recovery. The exposed fish could not recover to the status of the control fish. This indicated the damage caused to the fish within a period of 28 days.
28. The AChE activity significantly declined in the exposed fish tissues. The enzyme activity significantly declined by 58 per cent in the exposed brain tissue, 38.8 per cent decrease in liver tissue and 40.6 per cent decrease in muscle tissue of the exposed fish, when compared to control fish. When the exposed fishes were transferred to toxicant free medium no recovery was noted in the exposed fish brain tissue. Partial insignificant recovery was marked in the muscle and liver tissue of the exposed fish.
29. No recovery was marked in the exposed fish either by behavioural change or in respiratory physiology, when the exposed fish was transferred to toxicant free medium. This indicates the drastic effect of the toxicant on the organism. The main causative agent, which affects the exposed fish was the heavy metal, Cadmium chloride. With the increase in exposure period, the parameters decreased significantly showing an inverse relationship. This also indicated the toxic nature of the toxicant, Cadmium chloride .
30. All the statistical tests conducted to analyse the data indicated only the acute toxic nature of the toxicant, Cadmium chloride causing permanent non-recoverable damage.

31. The decrease in the parameters can be correlated to the residual accumulation of cadmium in the tissues. Otherwise, it can be stated that the changes caused in the exposed fish was only due to the heavy metal cadmium.
32. From the extent of damage caused to the exposed system, it can be inferred that cadmium is a slow poison unlike mercury that causes drastic effects.

 The variation in toxicity was only due to the concentration of the toxicant. This build up/ accumulation of the toxicant in the fish body may increase the body burden of the human system by contaminated fish consumption, may lead to another significant incident, like many other incidents related to cadmium pollution. The *"itai itai"* disease is caused by cadmium. Time is not far away, when such an incident may happen in places where significant amount of cadmium is available in the environment.

BIBLIOGRAPHY

A.P.H.A. (1974): American Public Health Association : Standard Methods for the Examination of Water and Wastes. Environmental Protection Agency, U. S.A.

Ahmad, F. E. Hart, R. W. and Lewis, N. J. (1977): Pesticide Induced DNA Damage and Its Repair in Cultured Human Cells. Mut. Res., 42:161.

Akagi, H., M. Fujita and Y. Sakagami (1972): I. Eiseikagaku, 18 : 309.

Alloway, B.J., Tills, A.R and Morgan, H. (1984) : The Speciation and Availability of Cadmium and Lead in Polluted Soil. In: Trace Substances and Environmental Health, XVIII. Ed. D.D. Hemphill, pp-187-201. University of Missouri, Columbia, USA.

Alloway, B.J. (1990): (Ed): Heavy Metals in Soils. John Wiley and Sons. Inc., New York. pp. 100-124.

Anderson, J.R. (1978): In "Pesticide Microbiology" (eds. I.R. Hilland and S.J.L. Wright), Academic Press, London, p. 313.

Annonymous (1989): Special Short Course Training on Seed Testing. Seed Testing Laboratory, Bhubaneswar. Directorate of Agriculture and Food Production.

Ashton, F.M. and A.S. Crafts (1973): "Modes of Action of Herbicides", John Wiley and Sons, New York.

Baeuford, W., J. Barber and A. R. Barringer (1977): Physiol. Plant., 39:261.

Baicu, T. And T. Diaconu (1972): An Inst. Cercet. Prot. Plant., 10: 381.

Bakir, F., S. F. Damluji, L. Amin-Zaki, M. Murtadha, A. Khalidi, N. Y. Al-rawi, S. Tikrite, H. I. Dhahir, T. W. Clarkson, J. C. Smith and P. A. Daherly, (1973): Science, 181: 230.

Baker. R.R and Proctor, C.J. (1990): The Origin and Properties of Environmental Tobacco Smoke. Environ. Int., 16:231245.

Banerjee, A. and A. S. Mukherji (1980): Indian Journal of Exp. Biol., 18 : 438.

Barcelo. J. and Poschenrieder, C. (1990): Plant Water Relations as Affected by Heavy Metals Stress: A Review. J. of Plant Nutrition, 13(1):1-37.

Bariaud, A. and Mestre, J.C. (1984): Heavy Metal Tolerance in a Cadmium Resistant Population of *Euglena gracilis,* Bull.Environ. Contam,. Toxicol., 32:597-601.

Barron, M.G. and I.R. Adelman (1984): Nucleic Acid, Protein Content, and Growth of Larval Fish Sublethally Exposed to Various Toxicants. Can. J.Fish. Aquat.Sci. 41:141.

Barthel, W. F.; Hawthorne, J. C.; Ford, J. H.; Bolton, G. C.; McDowell, L. L.; Cressinger E. H. and Parsons, D. A. (1969): Pesticide Monitoring J., 3, 8.

Baszynski, T.; Wajda, L.; Krol, M.; Wolinska. D.; Krupa. Z. and Tukendorf, A.(1980): Photosynthetic Activities of Cadmium-treated Tomato Plants. Physiol.Plantarum, 364-365.

Bateman, G. L. (1975): Ann. Appl. Biol. 79(3): 307.

Bebiauno, M. J. and Langston,W.J. (1992): Metallothionein Induction in *Littorina littorea* (Mollusca: Prosobranchia) on Exposure to Cadmium. J. of the Mar. Biol. tesn. of the U.K., 72:329-342.

Bebianno, M. J.; Serafirm, MAP. and Rita, M.F. (1994): Involvement of Metallothionein in the Cadmium in the Calm, *Ruditapes decuesata.* Bull:Environ.Contam.Toxicol, 53:726-732.

Benson, W. R. (1969): The Chemistry of Pesticides. Ann. New York Acad.Sci., 160.

Berg, G.G. and E.F.Miles (1979): Chem. Biol.lnt. 27:199.

Bergback, B.: Anderberg. S. and Lohm, U. (1994): Accumulated Environmental Impact: The Case of Cadmium in Sweden. Sci. Total Environ., 145:13-28.

Bertilsson, L. and Hs. Y. Neujahr (1971): Methylation of Mercury Compounds by Methylcobalamin. Biochemistry 10 : 2805.

Bhattacharya, M.H; Whelton, B.D.; Stern, P.H and Petuson, D.P. (1988): Cadmium Accelerates Bone Loss in Ovariectomised Mice and Fetal Rat Limb Bones in Culture. Proc.Natl.Acad.Sci., (USA), 89: 8761-8765.

Billen, G., C. Joiris and R. Wollast (1974): Bacterial Methylmercury Mineralising Activity in River Sediments. Water Res., 8 : 219.

Bingham, F.T.; Page.A.L and Strong, J.E. (1980): Yield and Cadmium Content of Rice Grain in Relation to Addition Rates of Cadmium, Copper, Nickle, and Zinc with Sewage Sludge and Liming. Soil Sci.,130:32-38.

Bishop, P. L. and E. J. Kirsch (1972): Biological Generation of Methylmercury in Anaerobic Pond Sediment. Eng. Bull. Purdue Univ. Sr. I, 14-1, pt. 2, 628.

Bishnoi, N.R., Sheoran, I.S., and Singh, R.: (1993): Influence of Cadmium and Nickel on Photosynthesis and Water Relations in Wheat Leaves of Different Insertion Level. Photosynthetica, 28:473-479.

Bishnoi, N.R.; Sheoran, I.S. and Singh, R. (1993): Effect of Cadmium and Nickel on Mobilisation of Food Reserves and Activities of Hydrolytic Enzymes in Germinating Pigeon Pea Seeds. Biol. Plant., 35:583-589.

Bisogni, J. J. and A. W. Lawrence (1973): Kinetics of Microbially Mediated Methylation of Mercury in Aerobic and Anaerobic Aquatic Environments. Tech. Rep. No. 63, Cornell Univ. Water Resources and Mar. Sci. Cent., Ithaca, N. Y.

Blanusa, M.; Kralj, Z.; Bunarevic, A. (1985): Interaction of Cadmium, Zinc-and Copper in Relation to Smoking Habit, Age and Histopathological Findings in Humans Kidney Cortex. Arch. Toxicol., 58:115-117.

Blom. A., Harder, W. and Matin, A. (1992): Unique and Overlapping Pollutant Stress Proteins of *E.coli.,* Appl.Environ.Microbiol., 58:331-334.

Bode, P. (1992): The Use of INAA for the Determination of Trace Elements, in Particular Cadmium in Plastics in Relation to Enforcement of Pollution Standards. J. Radiational & Nuclear Chem., 167:361-367.

Boddi, B.; Oravecz, A.R.; and Lehoczki, E. (1995): Effect of Cadmium on Organisation and Photoreduction of Protochlorophyllide in Dark Grown Leaves and Etioplast Inner Membrane Preparations of Wheat. Photosynthetica, 31(3):411-420.

Bouveng, H.O. (1967): Oikos, Supplement-9.

Bova, G. L. and V. Khis (1981): ZERAVEOPAZ., 24(3): 256

Braumemer, G.W.; Gerth, J. and Hermus, U. (1986): Heavy Metal Species, Mobility and Availability in Soils. Zeitschr.Pflanh. Bodenkd., 49:328-398.

Bremner, I. and Beattie, J.H. (1990): Metallothionein and the Trace Minerals. Ann. Rev. Nutr., 10:63-83.

Brooks, K. N. and D. B. Thorud (1971): Anti-transpirant Effects on Transpiration and Physiology of Tamarisk. Water Resour. Res., 7 (3): 499.

Brosset, C. (1981): The Mercury Cycle. Water, Air, Soil Pollution, 16:253.

Brubaker, P.E., G. W. Laicer and R. Klein (1971): The Effects of Methylmercury on Protein Synthesis in Rat Liver. Biochem. Biophys. Res. Commum., 44, 1552.

Bruin, A.De. (1976): Nucleic Acid Metabolism. In : Biochemical Toxicity of Environmental Agents. Ed. Bruin, A. De, pp. 605-655. Elsevier/ North Holland Biomedical Press, The Netherlands.

Bryan, S. E., A.L. Guy and K. J. Hardy (1974): Biochemistry, 13 : 313.

Buchet, J.P.; Lauwerys, R.; Roels, H.; Bernard A; Bruaul, P.; Claeys, F.; Ducoffre, G.; DePlaen, P.; Staessen, J.; Amerg, A.; Lijnen, P.; Thijs L; Rondia. D.; Sartor, F.; Saint Remy, A. and Nick, L(1990): Renal Effect of Cadmium Body Burden of the General Population. Lancet 336:699-702.

Bulow, F.J. (1970): RNA-DNA Ratio as Indicator of Recent Growth Rate of Fish. J. Fish. Res. Bd. Canada, 27: 2343.

Butler, G. C. (1978): Principles of Ecotoxicology Scope-12, John Wiley and Sons Chisester, New York, Brisbane, pp. 350.

Byford, W. J. (1971): Ann. Appl. Biol., 69 (3): 245.

Byford, W. J. (1971): Ann. Appl. Biol., 79 (2): 221.

Caldwell, P. C., E.L. Mackor and C. Hinshelwood (1950). J. Chem. Soc., 31:51.

Camerlynck, R. and Velghe, G. (1983): Criteria for Evaluation of the Influence of Trace Elements on Plants. In Essential and Non-Essential Trce Elements in the System Soil-water-plant. Ed.A. Cottenie pp. 58-75. Lab. Anal. Agrochem. State Univ. Ghent, IWONL, Brussels, Belgium.

Carlson, R.W.; Bazzas, F.A. and Rolfe,G.L.(1975): The Effect of Heavy Metals on Plants. 2. Net Photosynthesis and Transpiration of Whole Corn and Sunflower Plants Treated with Lead, Cadmium, Nickel and Thallium. Environ. Res., 10:113-120.

Carson, Rachel (1962): Silent Spring. Boston, Houghton Mifflin.

Carrillo Gonzalez, L.J.R.; Laird, R.J., R.J. and Cajuste, L(Jr.) 1996: Adsorption of Lead and Cadmium by Some Volcanic Ash Soils. J. Environ. Sci. Health. A. 31(2):339-354.

Chao, E.S.E., and G. D. Frenkel (1983): Studies on the Mechanism of the Stimulation of Polymerase II, Catalysed RNA Synthesis by Mercury Compounds. The J. Biol. Chemistry, 258:9861.

Chao, E. S. E., J. F. Gierthy and G. D. Frenkel (1984): A Comparative Study of the Effects of Mercury Compounds on Cell Viability and Nucleic Acid Synthesis in HeLa Cells. Biochemical Pharmacology, 33:1941.

Chawla, G., P. M. Viswanathan and S. Devi (1986): Effect of Linear Alkylbenzene Sulfon[illegible] on Scenedesmus Quardicauda in Culture.

Chlopecka, A. (1996): Formsx of Cd, Cu, Pb and Zn in Soil and Tfieir Uptake by Cereal Crops, When Applied Jointed as Carbonates. Water, Air and Soil Pollution, 87:297-309.

Choudhury, M.; Bailey, L.D. and Grant, C.A. (1994): Effect Zinc on Cadmium Concentration in the Tissue of Durum Wheat. Can. J. Plant. Sci, 74:549-552.

Chrisman, R. W., S. Mansy, H. J. Peresie, A. Randle, T. A. Berg and R. S. Tobias (1977): Bioinor. Chem., 17:245.

Chushury, M.; Bailey, LD.; Grant, C.A. and Leisle, D. (1995): Effect of Zn on the Concentration of Cd and Zn in Plant Tissue of Two Durum Wheat Lines. Can. J. Plant Sci.,75:445-448.

Cieslinski, G.; Mercik, S. and Neilsen, G.H. (1994): Effect of Soil Appliction of Cadmium Contaminated Lime on Soil Cadmium Distribution and Cadmium Concentration in Strawberry Leaves and Fruit. J. Plant Nutr. 17:1095-1110.

Cieslinski, G., Neilsen, G.H.; and Hogus, E.J. (1996): Effect of Soil Cadmium Application and pH on Growth and Cadmium Accumulation in Roots Lẹves and Fruit of Strawberry Plants (Fragaria Xananassa Duch). Plant and Soil., 180:267-276.

Clijsters, H. and Van Assche, F. (1985): Inhibition of Photosynthesis by Heavy Metals. Photosynthe. Res., 7:31-40.

Conway, H.L. (1978): Sorption of Arsenic and Cadmium and Their Effect on Growth, Micronutrient Utilisation and Photosynthetic Pigment Composition of *Asterionella formosa.* J. Fish. Res. Bd. Can., 35:286-294.

Cossa, D. (1976): Sorption of Cadmium by a Population of the Diatom *Phaeodactylum Tricornutum* in Culture. Mar. Biol., 34:163-167.

Crafts, A. S. (1964): "Herbicide Behaviour in the Plant". In L. J. Audus (Ed.), The Physiology and Biochemistry of Herbicides. Academic Press. London, p.75.

Cunningham, LM.; Collins, F.W. and Hutchison,T.C. (1975): Physiological and Biochemical Aspects of Cadmium Toxicity in Soyabean. l. Toxicity Symptoms and Autoradiographic Distribution of Cadmium in Roots, Stem and Leaves. In Symposium Proceedings of the International Conference on Heavy Metals in the Environment. pp. 97-120,Toronoto, Canada.

Cutlor, J.M. amd Rains, D.W. (1974): Characterisation of Cadmium Uptake by Plant Tissue. Plant Physiol., 54:64-71.

Cuvin-Aralar, M. L. A. and R. W. Furness (1988): Uptake and Elimination of Inorganic Mercury and Selenium by Minnows, *Phoxinus Phoxinus.* Aquat. Toxicol., 13:205.

Czuba, M. and D. C. Mortimer (1982): Can. J. Bot., 60(5): 657.

Das Gupta, B. And S. Mukherji (1982): Z. Pflanzen Physiol., 82:95.

Davenport, D. C. (1967): Effects of Chemical Anti-transpirants on Transpiration and Growth of Grass. J. of Expt. Bot., 18(55), 332.

Davies, A. G. (1976): J. Mar. Biol. Assoc., 56:39.

De Filippis, L. F. and C. K. Pallaghy (1976 a): Z. Pflanzen-physiol. Bd., 78:197.

De Filippis, L. F. and C. K. Pallaghy (1976 b): The Effect of Sub-lethal Concentrations of Mercury and Zinc on Chlorella II. Photosynthesis and Pigment Composition. Z. Pflanzen-physiol. Bd., 78:314.

De Filippis, L F. and C. K. Pallaghy (1976 c): Z. Pflanzen-physiol. Bd., 78:323.

De Filippis, LF. (1979): The Effect of Heavy Metal Compounds on the Permeability of *Chlorella* Cells. Z. Pflanzenphysiol., 92:39-49.

De, A. K., A. K. Sen, D. P. Modak and S. Jana (1985): Studies of Toxic Effects of Hg(ll) on *Pistia Stratiotes.* Water, Air and Soil Pollution, 24:351.

De, P. K.(1939): Proc. R. Soc. B., 127:121.

Debnath, R. and S. Mukherji (1982): Biologia Plantarum (PRAHA), 24(6):423.

DeKnecht, J.A.; Koevoets, P.LM.; Verkleij, J.A.C. and Ernst, W.H.O.(1992): Evidence Against a Role for Phytochelations in Naturally Selected Increased Cadmium Tolerance in Silence Vulgaris (Moench) Garcke. New Phytol., 122:681-688.

Delhaize, E.; Jackson, P.J.; Luj'an, LD.; Robinson, N.J. (1989): Poly (γ-glutamylcysteinyl Glycine Synthesis in *Datura Innoxia* and Binding with Cadmium. Plant Physiol., 89:700-706.

De Noyelles, F. Jr.; Knoechel, R.; Reinke, D.; Treanor, D, and Altenhoffer, C.(1980): 3 Continuous Culturing of Natural Phgytoplankton Communities in the Experimental Lakes, Area: Effects of Enclosure *In Situ* Incubation, Light, Phosphorus and Cadmium. Can. J. Fish. Aquat. Sci. 37:424-433.

Dodge, A. D. (1975): Sci. Prog., 62:447.

Donovan, T. J. And A. D. Day (1969): Some Effects of High Salinity on Germination and Emergence of Barley *(Hordeum Vulgare,* L.emand Lati). Agron. J., 61:236.

Dove, W. F. and T. Yamane (1960): Biochem. Biophys. Res. Commun., 3:608.

Du, S. H. and Z. J. Yu (1987): The Interaction of Hg and Se in Plants In : Proceedings of Symposium, Heavy Metals in Environmental,

Vol. 2, S. E. Lindberg and T. C. Hutchinson (Ed.), New Orlieans, p. 347-349.

Dudka. S. and Chlopecka, A., (1990): Water, Air, and Soil Poll., 51:153.

Durham, W. I. (1963): Ann. N. Y. Scao. Sci., 160,183.

Edwards, C. A. (1973): Persistent Pesticides in the Environment. C. R. C. Press, Cleveland Ohio.

Eichhorn, G. L. (1973): In 'Inorganic Biochemistry' G. L. Eichhorn, Ed., Elsevier, Amsterdam, 2:1191.

Environmental and Experimental Botany, 26:39.

Elinder, C.G.; Edling, C.; Lindberg, E., Kagedas, B and Vesterberg, O. (1985): B_2. Microglobulinuria Among Workers Previously Exposed to Cadmium: Follow-up and Dose Response Analyses. Am. J. lnd. Med., 8:553-564.

Elinder. C.G. and Jaruip, L. (1996): Cadmium Exposure and Health Risks,: Recent Findings. Ambio, 25(5): 185.

Eto, M. (1974): Organophosphorus Insecticides. CRC Press, Cleveland, Ohio, USA, p. 192.

Ferreira, R., E. Ben-Zoi, T. Yamane, J.Vasilevskis and N. Davidson (1961): In 'Advances in the Chemistry of the Coordination Compounds'. S. Kirschner, Ed., Macmillan, New York. p.457.

Ferretti, M.; Ghisi, R.; Merlo, L, Dalla Vecchia, F., Passera, C. (1993): Effect of Cadmium on Photosynthesis and Enzymes of Photosynthetic Sulphate and Jiitrate Assimilation Pathways in Maize (Zea mays L.) Photosynthetica, 29:49-54.

Fimereite, N. (1970): Mercury Use in Canada and Their Possible Hazardous Source of Mercury Contamination. Environ. Pollut., 1:119.

Finlayson, D. G. and H. R. Mac Carthy (1973): Pesticide Residues in Plants". In C. A. Edwards (Ed.), Environmental Pollution by Pesticides, Plenum Press, London, p.57.

Fiskesjo, G. (1979): V. 79-84. Hereditas., 90(1): 103.

Fletcher, W. W. (1974): The Pest War, Blackwell Oxford, p-36.

Florijn. P.J. and Van Beusichemn,M.L(1993): Uptake and Distributiuon of Cadmium in Maize Inbred Lines. Plant and Soil.,150:25-32.

Fodor, E.; Erdei, L. Szabo-Nagy, A. (1994): The Effect of Cadmium Stress on the Plasma Membrane of Wheat Root. Biol. Plant., 36 (Suppl): 362.

Fodor, F., Sarvari,e.; Lang, F.; F.; Szigeti, Z. and Csch, E. (1996): Effect of Pb and Cd on Cuccumber Depending on the Fe Complex in the Culture Solution. J. Plant Physiol., 148:434-439.

Forstner, U. and Wittamann, G.T.W. (1983): Metal Pollution in the Aquatic Environments. Springer-Verlag, New York.

Fox, J. H., K. Patel-Mandlik and M. M. Cohen (1975): Comparative Effects of Organic and Inorganic Mercury on Brain Slice Respiration and Metabolism. J. Neurochemistry, 24:757.

Foy, C.D.; Charey, R.L. and White, M.C. (1978): The Physiology of Metal Toxicity in Plants. Annu. Rev. Plant Physiol., 29:511-566.

Frenkel, G. D. and K. Randies (1982): Specific Stimulation of a-Amanitin-sensitive RNA Synthesis in Isolated HeLa Nuclie by Methyl Mercury. J. Biol. Chem., 257:6275.

Frenkel, G. D., R. Cain and E.S.E. Chao (1985): Exposure of DNA to Methyl Mercury Results in an Increase in the Rate of Its Transpiration by RNA Polymerase-II. Biochemical and Biophysical Research Communications, 127:849.

Fuehring, H. D. (1973): Effect of Anti-transpirants on Yield and Grain Sorghum under Limit Irrigation. Agron. J., 65:348.

Fuehring, H. D. and M. D. Finkner (1983): Effect of Folicote Anti-transpirant Application on Field Grain Yield of Moisture-Stressed Corn. Agron. J., 75:579.

Furukawa, K. and K. Tonomura (1972): Agric. Biol. Chem., 36:2441.

Furukawa, K., T. Suzuki and K. Tonomura (1969): Agric. Biol. Chem., 33:128.

Gadd, G. M. and A. J. Griffith (1978): Microbial Ecol., 4:303.

Gadd, G.M. (1990): Heavy Metal Accumulation by Bacteria and Other Microorganisms. Experientia, 46:834-839.

Galli, U.; Meier, M.; and Brunold, C. (1993): Effects of Cadmium on Non-mycorrhzal and Mycorrhizal Norway Spruce Seedlings (Piecea abies (L.) Karst.) and Its Ectomycorrhizal Fungues, Laccaria Lacata (Scop.ex Fr.) Bk. and Br.: Suilphate Reduction, Thiols and Distribution of the Heavy Metal. New Phytol., 125:837-843.

Galli, U.; Schuepp, H. and Brunold, C. (1996): Thiols in Cadmium and Copper Treated Maize (Zea mays, L). Planta, 198:139-143.

Geener, H. and J. R. Jeener (1952): Exptl. Cell Res., 3:675.

Geike, F. (1977): J. Plant Diseases and Protection, 84:84.

Geirid Fiskesjo (1979): Hereditas 91:961. In Proceedings of Symposium, Heavy Metals in the Environment, Vol. 2. S. E. Lindberg and T. C. Hutchinson (Ed.), New Orleans.

Gekeler, W.; Grill, E.; Winnacker, E.L. and Zenk, M.H. (1988): Algae Sequester Heavy Metis via Synthesis of Phytochelatin Complexes. Arch. Microbial, 150:197-202.

GESAMP, IMCO/FAO/UNESCO/WMO/IAEA/UN (1977): Joint Group of Experts on the Scientific Aspets of Marine Pollution (GESAMP), Impact of Oil on the Marine Environment, Rep. Study No. 6, Food and Agriculture Organisation, Rome.

Gessler, U. And L. Bass (1960): Z. Ges. Exp. Med., 133:18.

Giessel-Nielsen, G. (1973): Uptake and Distribution of Added Selenite and Selenate by Barley and Red Clover as Influenced by Sulphur. J. Sci. Food Agri., 24:649.

Gil, J.; Moral, R.; Gomez,l.; Navarro-Pedreno, J. and Mataix, J. (1995): Effect of Cadmium on Physiological and Nutritional Aspects of Tomato Plant. I. Chlorophyll (A and B) and Carotenoids. Fresenieus Envir. Bull., 4:430-435.

Gillberg, B. O. (1971): Arch. Mikrobiol., 75:203.

Godbold, D. L., A. Hutterman (1985): Environmental Pollution (Ser. A). Ecological and Biological., 38:375.

Godbold, D. L., W. J. Horet, J. C. Collins, D. A. Thurman and H. Marchener (1984): J. Plant. Physiol., 116:59.

Godbold, D.L. and Kettner, C. (1991): Lead Influences Root Growth and Mineral Nutrition of *Picea abies* Seedlings. J. Plant Physiol., 139:95-99.

Godocikova, J.; Polek, B. and Kliment, V. (1993): Influence of Metal Pre-treatment on the Acute Toxicity of Cadmium in the Larvae of *Galleria Mellonella.* Biologia, Bratislava,48:637-641.

Goldberg, E. D. (1978): In : Advances in Oceanography, Joint Oceanographic Assembly (Edited by H. Charmoch and G. Deacon), Scotland, 49.

Goldberg, E. D. (Ed) (1976): The Health of the Oceans, UNESCO Press.

Granger, R. L. and L. J. Edgerton (1966): Proc. Amer. Soc. Hort. Sci., 88:48.

Grazybowska. T. (1974): Herba Pol., 20 (2): 192.

Greger, M.; Johansson, M.; Stihl, A. and Hamza, K., (1993): Foliar Uptake of Cadmium by Pea *(Pisum Sativum)* and Sugar but *(Beta Vulgaris).* Physiol. Plant., 88:563-570.

Greville, G. D. and A. S. Mildvan (1962): Biochem. Biophys. Acta., 16:284.

Grill, E.; Winnalker, E. L. and Zenk, M.H. (1985): Phytochelatins: The Principal Heavy Metal Complexing Peptides of Higher Plants. Science, 230:674-676.

Grill, E.; Winnacker, E.L.; and Zenk, M.H. (1987): Phytochelatins, A Class of Heavy Metal Binding Peptides from Plants, are

Functionally Analogours to Metallothioneins. Proc. Natl. Acad. Sci., USA, 84:439-443.

Grill, E.; Loftler's.; Winnacker, E. Land Zenk, M.H. (1989): Phytochelatins-the Heavy Metals Binding Peptides of Plants are Synthethesized from Glutethione by a Specific γ-glutanyl Cysteine Dipeptidyl Transpeptidase (Phytochelatin Synthase). Proc. Natl. Acad. Sci. USA, 86:6838-6842.

Grose, E.C.; Richards, J.H.; Jaskot, R.H.; Menache, M.G.; Graham, J.A. and Dauterman, W.C. (1987): A Comparative Study of the Effects of Cadmium Chloride and Cadmium Oxide: Pulmonary Response. J. Toxicol. Environ. Health, 21:219-232.

Gruenwedel, D. W. and M. K. Cruikshank (1979): Biochem. Pharmacol. 28:651.

Gruenwedel, D. W. and N. Davidson (1966): J. Mol. Biol., 21:129.

Guerin. M.R. Higgins. C.E. and Jenkins, R.A. (1987): Measurement of Enmvironmental Emissions from Tobacco Combustion: Sidestream Cigarette Smoke Literature Review. Atoms.Environ., 21:291-297.

Gupta, S.K. and Chen, K.Y. (1975): Environ. Lett, 10:129.

Hageman. R.H.R.H. and Reed, A.J. (1980): Nitrate Reducrtase Activity from Higher Plants. Methods of Enzymol., 69:270-276.

Hamdy, M. K. and O. R. Noyes (1975): Formation of Methylmercury by Bacteria. Appl. Microbiol., 30:424.

Hamilton, G. and A. Ruthvein (1967): Journal of Science of Food and Agriculture, 18 (12): 558.

Hamner, C. L and H. B. Tukey (1944): Weed Sci., 100:154.

Haney, A. and L. L Richard (1973): Environ. Pollut., 5 (4): 305.

Hannan, P. J. and C. Patouillet (1972): Effects of Pollutants on Growth of Algae. Reports of Naval Res. Lab. Progress, p. 1-8.

Hanumann, H. G. (1987): Protoplasma, 136 (1): 37.

Harding, J. P. C. and B. A. Whitton (1977): Brit. Phycol. J., 12:17.

Hardyman. R.T. and Jacoby, B .(1984): Absortion and Translocation of Cd in Bush Beans *(Phaseolus Vulgaris)*. Physiol. Plantarum, 61:670-674.

Haois, R. C., D. B. White and R. B. Mac Farlane (1970): Mercury Compounds Reduce Photosynthesis of Plankton. Science, 170:736.

Hart, G. E., J. D. Schultz and G. B. Cottharp (1969): Water Resources Res., 5:407.

Hartley, G. S. and T. F. West (1969): Chemicals for Pest Control. Pergamon Press, Oxford, p. 248.

Hasset, J. J., J. E. Miller and D. E. Koeppe (1976): Environ. Pollut., 11:297.

Hemingway *et. al.* (1961): Nature, London, 192:993.

Henderson, G. R., W. Huang and A. Askari (1979): Biochem. Pharmacol., 28:429.

Herbert, D., P. J. Phipps and R. E. Strange (1971): Chemical Analysis of Microbial Cells. In : Methods of Microbiology, pp. 210-340. (Eds. J. R. Morris and D. W. Ribbons), Academic Press, N. Y., London.

Hill, C. H. (1974): Reversal of Selenium Toxicity in Chicks by Mercury, Copper and Admium. J. Natr., 104:593.

Holbrook, D. J. Jr. (1980): Effects of Toxicants on Nucleic Acid and Protein Metabolism. p. 261-284. In : E. Hodgson and F. E. Guthrie (ed.) Introduction to Biochemical Toxicology, Elsevier, New York.

Huang, C.Y.; Bazzaz, F.A.; Vanderhoef, LA (1974): The Inhibition of Soyabean Metabolism by Cadmium and Lead. Plant Physiol, 54:122-124.

Huckabee, J. W., S. D. Francisco, S. A. Janzena and J. Solmon (1983): Environ. Pollut., Ser. A., 30:211.

Huising, D. And D. M. Kline (1972): Phytopathology, 62:766.

Hutton, M. (1982): Cadmium in the European: A Prospective Assessment of Sources, Human Exposure and Environmental Impact. Monitoring and Assessment. Research Centre. Tech. Rep. 26. University of London, London, England.

Inagaki, T. (1940): J. Biochem. (Tokyo), 32:57.

Inouhe, M.; Mitsumure, M.; Tohoyama, H.; Joho, M. and Murayama, T. (1991): Contribution of Cell Wall and Metal Binding Peptides to Cadmium and Cu Tolerance in Suspension Cultured Cells of Tomato. Bot. Mag. Tokyo, 104:217-229.

Inouhe. M.; Ninomiya. S.; Tohoyana. H.; Joho. M.; and Murayama, T. (1994): Different Characteristics of Roots in the Cadmium Tolerance and Cadmium Binding Complex Formation Between Mono and Dicotyledonous Plants. J. Plant. Res. 107:201-207.

lnouhe, M.; Sumiyoshi, M.; Tohoyama, H.; and Joho, M. (1996): Resistance to Cadmium Ions and Formation of a Cadmium-binding Complex in Various Wild Type of Yeasts. Plant Cell Physiol., 37 (3): 341-346.

Iverson. W. and Brinckman, F.F. (1978): Microbial Metabolism of Heavy Metals. In Water Pollution Microbiology (R. Mitchell, Ed.) Vol. 2. pp. 201-232, Wily, New York.

Jackim, E. (1974): Enzyme Responses to Metals in Fish. In : Pollution and Physiology of Marine Organisms. Ed. F. J. Vernberg and W. B. Vernberg, Academic Press, London, p. 59.

Jackson. A.P. and Alloway, B.J. (1992): The Transfer of Cadmium from Agricultural Soils to the Human Food Chain. ln: Adriano, D.C. (Ed.) Biogeochemistry of Trace Metals, Lewis Publishers, London, pp. 109-158.

Jackson, P.J.; Delhaize, E. and Kuske, C.R. (1992): Biosynthesis of Metabolic Roles of Cadystins (γ-EC)n G and Their Precursons in Datura Innoxia. Plant Soil. 146:281-289.

Jann, R. C., R. D. Amen (1977): What is Germination ? In : a. A. Khan, Ed, The Physiology and Biohcemistry of Seed Dormancy and Germination. North-Holland, Amsterdam, p. 7-28.

Jeng, A.S. and Singh, B.R. (1995): Cadmium Status of Soils and Plants from a Long Term Fertility Experiment in Southeast Norway. Plant and soil, 175:67-74.

Jensen, S. and A. Jernelov (1969): Biological Methylation of Mercury in Aquatic Organisms. Nature, Lond., 223:453.

Jentsch, S. Schobert, C.; Reins, H.A. and Jungman(1993): Resistance to Cadmium Mediated by Ubiquitin-dependent Proteolysios. Nature, 361:369-371.

Jernelov, A. and A. L. Martin (1975): Ann. Rev. Micriobiol., 29:61.

Johnels, A. G., T. Westermark, (1969): In : Chemical Fallout (Eds. M. W. Miller and G. Berg) Charles Thomas Publishers, Springfield, Illinois, pp. 221.

John, M.K.; Van Laerhoven. C. and Chuah, H.H. (1992): Factors Affecting Plant Uptake and Phytotoxicity of Cadmium Added to Soil. Environ. Sci. Technol., 6:1005-1009.

Jonasson, I. R. (1970): Mercury in the Natural Environment : A Review of Work. Geological Survey of Canada Paper, 70.

Jonasson, I. R. and R. W. Boyle (1971): Geochemistry of Mercury. Geological Surv. of Canada. Paper Presented at the Royal Society of Canada Symposium, Ottawa, p. 5-21.

Kabata-pendias, A. and Pendias, H. (1992): Trace Elements in Soils and Plants. Second Edition. CRC Press inc. Boca Raton, FL, USA. pp. 365.

Kagi. J.H.R. and Kojioma, Y. (1987): Chemistry and Biochemistry of Metallothionein. ln: Metallothionein-II. Experimentia Supplementum Vol. 52. Ed. by Kagi. J.H.R. and Kojima, Y. pp. 25-61. Birkhauser Verlag, Basel.

Kahn. S. and Kahn, N.N. (1983): Influence of Lead and Cadmium on the Growth and Nutrient Concentration of Tomato (Lycopersicum Esculentum) and Egg Plant (*Solanum Melongena).* Plant and Soil, 74:387-394.

Kashyap, A. K. and S. L. Gupta (1981): Acta Botanica Indica, 9:265.

Kastori, R.; Popovic. M.; Gasic, O.; Petrovic, N.; Stajner, D. (1993): Effect of Iron on Nitrogen Metabolism and Anti-oxidant Enzymes. Zemljiste Biljka, 42:177-184.

Katz, S. And V. Santilli (1962): Biochem. Biophys. Acta., 55:621.

Kelly. M.G. and Whitton, B.A. (1989): Interspecific Different in Zinc, Cadmium and Pb Accumulation by Freshwater Algae and Bryophytes. Hydrobiologia, 175,1-11.

Kidley, W. P., L. J. Dizikes and J. M. Wood (1977): Biomethylaion of Toxic Elements in the Environment. Science, 197:329.

Kiekens, L. (1983): Adsorption, Desorption and Distribution of Trace Elements in Soils as a Function of Some Soil Parameters. In Essential and Non-essential Trace Elements in the System-soil-water-plant. Ed. A. Cottenie, pp. 23-45, Lab. Anal. Agrochem. State Univ., Gbent. lWONL, Brussels, Belgium.

Killey, W. W. and L. B. Bradley (1956): J. Biol. Chem., 218:653.

Kim, C. M. (1958): Physiol. Plant., 17:441.

Kimamura, M. and S. Kotoh (1972): Biochem. Biophys. Acta., 283:178.

Kimura, Y. and V. L. Miller (1964): The Degradation of Organomercury Fungicides in Soil. Journal of Agricultural and Food Chemistry, 12:253.

Kitamura, S. and K. Sumino (1972): Japanese Journal of Hygiene, 27:123.

Kjellstrom, T. (1979): Exposure and Accumulation of Cadmium in Populations from Japan. The United States and Sweden. Environ. Health Perspect, 28:169-197.

Knight. B. and McGrath, S.P. (1995): A Method to Buffer the Concentrations of Free Zinc and Cadmium Ions Using a Cation Exchange Resin in Bacterial Toxicity Studies. Env. Toxicol. and Chemistry, 14 (12): 2033-2039.

Koronowski, K. (1973): Mitt. Biol. Bundesanst. Land Forstwirtsch Berling-Dahlem. 153:1-21.

Kosmider, St (1964): Gewerbehyg, 21:60.

Kuboi, T.; Noguchi, A.; and Yazaki, J. (1986): Family Dependent Cadmium Accumulation Characteristics in Higher Plants. Plant Soil, 92:405-415.

Kuboi, T.: Noguchi, A. and Yazaki, J.H. (1987): Relationship Between Tolerance and Accumulation Characteristics of Cadmium in Higher Plants. Plants Soil, 104:275-280.

Kummerova. M. and Brandejsova, R. (1994): Project Tocoen. The Fate of Selected Pollentants on the Environmnent. Part XIX. The

Phytotoxicity of Organic and Inorganic Pollutants Cadmium. The Effect of Cadmium on the Growth of Germinating Maize Plants. Toxicological and Environmental Chemistry, 42:115-122.

Landner, L. (1971): Biochemical Model for the Biological Methylation of Mercury Suggested from Methylation Studies *in vivo* with *Neurospora* crassa. Nature (London), 230:452.

Landsberger. S. and Wu, D. (1995): The Impact of Heavy Metals from Environmental Tobacco Smoke on Indoor Air Quality as Determined by Compton Suppression Neutron Activation Analysis. The Science of the Total Environment, 173 /174:323:337.

Leborans, G.F. and Novillo, a. (1995): The Effects of Cadmium on the Successional Stages of Freshwater Protozoa Community. Ecotoxicology and Environmnental Safety, 31:29-36.

Ledoux, L. (1953): Biochim. Biophys. Acta., 11:517.

Lee, J.J.; Hutner, S.S. and Boveem, E.C. (1985): An Illustrated Guide to the Protozoa. Society of Protozoologists. Lawrence, KS.

Lee, Y. P. and T. Takahasi (1966): An Improved Colorimetric Determination of Amino Acids with the Use of Ninhydrin, Anal, Biochem., 14:71.

Legator, M. (1977): Mut. Res., 43:459.

Leita, L; Marchiol, L.; Martin, M., Peressotti, a.; Delle Vedove. G. and Zerbi, G. (1995): Transpiration Dynamnics in Cadmium Treated Soyabean (*Glycine max* L.) Plants. J. Agronomy and Crop Science, 175:153-156.

Leland, H. V., S. N. Luoma and J. M. Fielden (1979): J. Wat. Pollut. Contr. Fed., 51:1592.

Levitt, J. (1972): Response of Plants to Environmental Stresses. Academic Press, Inc. N. Y.

Lindberg. S. and Wingstrand, G. (1985): Mechanism for Cd^{2+} Inhibition of (K^+ + Mg^+) ATPase Activity and K^+ ($86Rb^+$) Uptake in Roots of Sugar Beet *(Beta vulgaris)* Physiol. Plant., 63:181-186.

Lindberg, S. E. (1987): Lead Mercury, Cadmium and Arsenic in the Environment, In : T. C. Hutchinson and K. M. Meema (Eds.), J. Wiley and Sons, N. Y., Ch.8.

Lipsey, A. (1978): Environmental Pollut., 8(2):149.

Lodenius, M. and E. Tulisalo (1984): Environmental Mercury Contamination Around a Chlor-alkali Plant. Bull. Environ. Contam. Toxico., 32:439.

Loganathan, P.; Hedley, M.J.; Gregg, P.E.H.; and Currie, L.D. (1977): Effect of Phosphate Fertiliser Type on the Accumulation and Plant

Availability of Cadmium in Grssland Soils. Nutrient Cycling in Agroecosystem, 47:169-178.

Lopez Artiluez, M. Camean, a.; Gonzalez, G. and Repetto, M. (1995): Cadmium Concentrations in Human Renal Cortex Tissue (Necropsies). Bull. Environ. Contam. Toxicol, 54:841-847.

Lorenz, H. (1979): Ecotoxicology Environmental Safety, 31:47.

Love, R. M. (1980): The Chemical Biology of Fishes. Vol. 2, Academic Press, New York, p. 943.

Lowry, O. H., D. J. Rosebrough, A. L. Farr and R. J. Randal (1951): Protein Measurement with the Folin Phenol Reagent. J. Biol. Chem., 193:265.

Madsen, N. B. (1963): In : "Metabolic Inhibitors", R. M. Hochster and J. H. Quastel, Eds., Academic Press Inc., N. Y., 119.

Magos, L. (1974): Postgrad. Med. J., 50:22.

Mallik, D.; Sheoran, I.S. and Singh, R. (1992): Carbon Metabolism in Leaves of Cadmium Treated Wheat Seedlings. Plant Physiol. Biochem., 30:223-229.

Mansy, S., T. E. Wood, J. C. Sprowles and R. S. Tobias (1974): J. Am. Chem. Soc., 96:1962.

Marshal, J., L. Jean, E. B. James and W. W. Jeffrey (1984): J. Biol. Chem., 259(5):3033.

Marden, P.; Nystrom, T. and Kjelleberg, S. (1987): Uptake of Leucine by a Marine Gram Negative Heterotrophic Bacterium During Exposure to Starvation Conditions. FEMS Microbiol., Ecol. 45:233-241.

Marschner, H. (1983): General Introduction to the Mineral Nutrition of Plants. In: Lauchiu. a. and Bielski, R.L. (ed.): lnorganic Plant Nutrition. pp. 5-60, Springer-verlag. Berlin Heidelberg, New York-Tokyo.

Mason. A.Z. and Jenkins, K.D. (1991): Effect of Cadmium Bioavailability on the Cytoplasmic Distribution of Cadmium in Nearther arnccdentata. Bull of Marine Science, 48:524-529.

Matin, A.; Veldhuis, C.; Stegeman, U. and Veenhuis, M. (1979): Selective Advantage of a Spirillum sp.in a Carbon-limioted Environment. Accumulation of Poly-β-hydroxybutyric Acid and Its Role in Starvation. J. Gen. Microbiol., 112:349-355.

Matsumoto, H. (1988): Repression of Protein Extrusion from Intact Cucumber Roots and the Proton Transport Rate of Microsomal Membrane Vesicles of the Roots due to Ca^{2+} Starvation. Plant Cell Physiol., 29:79-84.

Matsumoto, H.; Yamamoto, Y.; and Kasai, M. (1992): Changes of Some Properties of the Plasma Membrane-enriched Fraction of Barley Roots Related to Aluminum Stress: Membrane-associated ATPase, Aluminum and Calcium. Soil. Sci. Plant Nutr., 38:411-419.

Matsumura, F.Y. Gotoh and G. M. Bousch (1971): Science, 173:49.

Meharg, A.A. (1994): Integrated Tolerance Mechanisms: Constitutive and Adaptive Plant Response to Elevated Metal Concentrations in the Environmet. Plant Cell and Environ, 17:989-993.

Mehra, R.K. and Winge, D.R. (1991): Metal Ion Resistance in Fungi: Molecular Mechanisms and Their Regulated Expression. J. Cell. Biochem., 45:30-40.

Mehrle, P. M. and F. L. Mayer (1980): Clinical Tests in Aquatic Toxicology : State of the Art. Environ Health Perspect, 34:139.

Mench, M.; Tancogne, J.; Gomez, A. and Juste, C. (1989): Cadmium Bioavailability to *Nicotiana Tabacum L. Nicotiana Rustica, L., and* Zea Mays. L. Grown in Soil Amended or Not Amended with Cadmium Nitrate. Biol. Fertil. Soils, 8:48-53.

Miflin. B.J. and Lea, P.J. (1980): Ammonia Assimilation-ln: Miflin, B.J. (ed.): The Biochemistry of Plants. Vol. 5: pp. 169-202. Academic Press, London, New York.

Miller, D. R. (1984): Chemicals in the Environment, in Effects of Pollutants at the Ecosystem Level. Sheehan, P. J., Miller, D. R., Butler, G. C. and Bourdeau, P., Eds., John Wiley and Sons. Chichester, 7.

Mishra, B. N. and Misra, M. K.(1983): Introductory Practical Biostatistics, Naya Prakash Publications, Calcutta.

Misra, S. R. (1984): Analysis of the Effects of Solid Waste Extracts of a Caustic-chlorine Factory on Growth and Physiology of Rice Seedling's. Ph. D. Thesis, Berhampur University, Berhampur, Orissa, India.

Mitchell, G.A. Bingham, F.T. and Page, A.L. (1978): Yield and Metal Composition of Lettuce and Wheat Grown on Soils Amended with Sewage Sludge Enriched with Cadmium, Copper. Nickel and Zinc./J. Environ. Qual., 7:165-171.

Moore, R. B. (1969): Proc. Int. Seed Test Ass., 34,233.

Mortvedt, J.J. (1987): Cadmium Levels in Soils and Plants from Some Long Term Soil Fertility Experiments on the United States of America. J. Environ. Qual., 16:137-142.

Mukherji, S. and G. Ganguly (1974): Ind. J. Expt. Biol., 12:432.

Mukherji, S. and P. Maitra (1977): Z. Pflanzen. Physiol., 81:26.

Mukherji, S. and P. Nag (1974): Ind. J. Expt. Biol., 171:227.

Mukhiya, Y. K., K. C. Gupta, N. Shrotriya, J. K. Joshi and V. P. Singh (1983): Int. J. Environ. Stud., 20(314): 323.

Mulvihill, J. (1972): Science, 176:132.

Murthy, S. D. S. and P. Mohanty (1991): Plant cell Physiol., 32(2):231.

Nagase, H., Y. Ose, T Sato and T. Ishikawa (1982): Science of the Total Enviroment, 25:133.

Nakajima, a. and Sakaguchi, T. (1986): Selective Accumulation of Heavy Metals by Microorganisms. Appl. Microbiol. Biotechnol, 24:59-64.

Nalewajko, C. (1995): Effects of Cadmium and Metal Contaminated Sediments on Photosynthesis, Heterotrophy and Phosphate Uptake in Mackenzie River Delta Phytoplankton. Chemosphere, 30 (7): 1401-1414.

Nelson, N. T. C. Byerly, A. C. Kolbye, L. T. Kurland, R. E. Shapiro, S. I. Shibko, W. H. Stickel, J. E. Thompson, L. A. Van Den Berg and A. Weissler (1971): Environmental Research, 4:1.

Nriago, J.O. (1979): Global Inventory of Natural and Anthropogenic Emissions of Trace Metals in the Atmosphere. Nature, 279:409-411.

Nose, K. (1976): J. Pestic Sci (Nihon Noyakugaku Kaishi), 1(2):87.

Nystrom, T.; Albertson, N.; Flardh, K.; and Kjelleberg, S. (1990): Physiological and Molecular Adaptation to Starvation and Recovery from Starvation by the Marine Vibrio sp. S14. FEMS. Microbiol. Ecol., 74:129-140.

Nystrom, T. and Kjelleberg, S. (1987): The Effect of Cadmium on Starved Heterotrophic Bacteria Isolated Frommarine Waters. FEMS Microbiol. Ecol., 45:143-153.

Obata. H. and Umebayashi, M. (1993): Production of SH Compounds in Higher Plants of Different Tolerance to Cadmium. Plant Soil.,155/156:533-536.

Obata, H.; Inoue, N. and Umebayashi, M. (1996): Effect of Cadmium on Plasma Membrane Atpase from Plant Roots Differeing in Tolerance to Cadmium. Soil. Sci. Plant Nutr., 42 (2): 361-366.

Opik, H. (1973): J. Cell. Sci., 12:725.

Oser, B. L. (1965): Hawk's Physiological Chemistry. Tata McGraw Hill Publishing Co. Ltd., Bombay, New Delhi, 1472 p.

Overnell, J. (1975): Marine Biology, 29:99.

Padhi, N. P. (1990): Ecophysiological Response of Germinating Rice Seedlings to an Organomercurial fungicide, MEMC, Ph. D. Thesis, Berhampur University, India.

Page. A.L; Bingham, F.T. and Chang, A.C. (1981): Cadmium. In Effect of Heavy Metal Pollution on Plant. Vol. I. Effect of Trace Metal on Plant Function. Ed. N.W. Lepp .pp. 77-109.

Pandey, A. K.(1981): Heavy Metal Toxicity in the Blue-green Algae, *Nostoc Calcicola*. Ph. D. Thesis, Banaras Hindu Univ., Varanasi, India.

Panigrahi, A. K. and B. N. Misra (1978 a): Comp. Physiol. Ecol., 8: 253.

Panigrahi, A. K., M. K. Misra and B. N. Misra (1978) Indian J. Ecol., 5:98.

Parida, R. K. and D. Mishra (1980): Photosynthetics, 14:431.

Patra, R. R.(1993): Eco-physiological Effects of an Organomercury Based Pesticides on a Crop Plant. Ph. D. Thesis, Berhampur University, Berhampur-7 (Orissa).

Petrovic, N. and Kastori, R. (1994): Effect of Sulphur on Nitrogen Assimilation in Young Sugar Beet Plants (*Bete vulgaris,* L.). Biol. Plant., 36 (Suppl.): 201.

Phillip, J. R. (1958 b): Plant Physiol., 33:23.

Piccini, E. (1989): Response to Heavy Metals of Uni-and Multicellular Organisms; Homologies and Analogies. Boll. Zool., 56:265-271.

Pickering, O. H.; Handerson, C. and Lenle, A. K.(1962): Trans. Am. Fish. Soc., 91: 175.

Pilet, P. E. and M. V. Jean, (1981): Z. Pflanzen. Physiol., 104(3): 193.

Polek, B. (1992): The Cd-binding Proteins in the Fat Body of Thelarvae of the *Galleria Mellonella* ln: Bennettova, B.; Gelbic. l.; Soldan, T., (Eds.): Advances in Regulation of Insect Reproduction, IE GAS Ceske Budcjovice, pp. 227-230.

Polek, B.; Feriang, P.; Codocikova, J. and Toth, D. (1995): Effect of Cadmium on Growth and Protein Synthesis in Vibrio S^{14}. Biologia, Bratislava, 50(3):205-209.

Polis, B. D. and O. Meyerhof (1947): J. Biol. Chem., 169:389.

Poljakoff-Mayber, A. and J. Gale (1975): Plants in Saline Environments (Ecological Studies 15). Springer-Verlag. Berlin.

Popovic, M.; Kevresan, S.; Kandrac, J. and Nikolic, J. (1996): The Role of Sulphur in Detoxification of Cadmium in Young Sugar Beet Plants. Biologia Plantarumn, 38(2):281-287.

Pradhan, P. (1998): Eco-toxicological Effects of a Pesticide on a Crop Plant. Ph.D. Thesis Submitted to Berhampur University. Orissa. India.

Puerner, N. J. and S. M. Siegel (1972): Physiologia Pl., 26:310.

Puranik, P.R.; Chabukswar, N.S. and Paknikar, K.M. (1995): Cadmium Biosorption by *Streptomyces Pimprina* Waste Biomass. Appl. Microbiol. Biotechnol. 43:1118-1121.

Rachlin, J. W., T. E. Jensen, M. Baxter and V. Jani (1982): Arch. Environm.Contam. Toxicol., 11:323.

Rai, L C. and N. Khatoniar (1980): Indian J. Environ. Hlth., 22:113.

Rai, L. C., J. P. Gaur and H. D. Kumar (1981 a): Biol. Rev. 56:99.

Rai, L. C., J. P. Gaur and H. D. Kumar (1981 b) : Environmental Research, 25: 250.

Ramade, F. (1977): Ecotoxicologie. Masson. Paris.

Ramamoorthy, S., T. C. Cheng, and ds. J. Kushner (1982): Bull. Environ. Contam. Toxicol., 29:167.

Ramel, C. (1969): Genetic Effects of Organic Mercury Compounds-I, Cytological Investigations on *Allium* Roots. Hereditas 61:208.

Rao, D. M. R.; Devi, A. P. and Murty, A. S.(1980): J. Toxicol. Environ. Health, 6:825.

Rao, D. N. and F. LeBlanc (1966): Bryologist, 69:69.

Rath, P., A. K. Panigrahi and B. N. Misra (1985): Effect of Pesticides on the Photosynthetic Efficiency of a Blue-green Alga, *Westiellopsis prolifica* Janet. Microbios Letters, 29:25.

Rath, S. C. (1991): Toxicological Effects of a Mercury Contained Toxicant on *Anabaena Cylindrica,* L. and Its Ecological Impliations. Ph. D. Thesis, Berhampur University, India.

Rauser, W.E. (1990): Phytochelatins. Annu. Rev. Biochem. 59:61:86.

Reedy, G.N. and Prasad, M.N.V. (1990): Heavy Metal-binding Protein Peptides: Occurence, Structure, Synthesis and Functions. A Review. Environ., Exp. Bot., 30:251-264.

Ricard, A.C.; Daniel, C.; Anderson, P. and Houtela, A. (1998). Effect of Sub-chronioc Exposure to Cadmium Chloride on Endocrine and Metabolic Functions in Rainbow *Trout,Oncorhynchus Mykiss.* Arch. Environ. Coutam. Toxicol., 34:379-381.

Roesijadi, G. and Klerks, P.L. (1989): Kinetic Analysis of Cadmium Binding to Metallothionein and Other Intra Cellular Ligands in Oyster Gills. Journals of Expt. Zool. 251:1-12.

Roesijadi, G. (1972): Metallothioneins in Metal Regulation and Toxicity in Aquatic Animals. Aquatic Toxicol. 22:81-114.

Rogers, R. D. (1976): Methylation of Mercury in Agricultural Soils. Journal of Environmental Quality, 5:454.

Rogers, R. D. (1977): A Biological Methylation of Mercury in Soil. US Environmental Protection Agency, EPH-600/3-77007.

Ros, R.; Morales, A.; Segura, J.; and Picazo, I. (1992): *In Vivo* and *In Vitro* Effects of Nickel and Cadmium on the Plasmalemma ATPase from Rice (Oryza Sativa. L.) Shoots and Roots. Plant. Sci, 83:1-6.

Rothstein, A. (1959): Fed. Proc. Fed. Amer. Soc. Exp. Biol., 18:1026.

Rothstein, A. (1973): In "Mercury, Mercurials and Mercaptans". M. W. Miller and T. W. Clarkson, Eds., Chapter-4, Thomas Books, Springfield, III.

Rwgsegger a; Schmutz, D. and Brunold, C. (1992): Effect of Cadmium on γ-glutamyl Cystenine Synthesis in Maize Seedlings. Plant. Physiol., 99:428-433.

Ryan, J.A.; Pahren, H.R. and Lucas, J.B. (1982): Controlling Cadmium in the Humnan Food Chain: A Review and Rationale Based on Health Effects. Env. Res. 28:251-302.

Sacher, J. A. and P. De Leo (1977): Plant Physiol., 18:101.

Sahu, A. (1987): Lexicological Effects of a Pesticide on a Blue-green Alga : III. Effect of PMA on a Blue-green Alga, *Westiellopsis Prolifica* Janet, and Its Ecological Implications. Ph. D. Thesis, Berhampur University, India.

Sahu, A., B. P. Shaw and A. K. Panigrahi (1990): Microbios Letters, 43:25.

Sai Babu, T. (1998): Eco-physiological Effects of a Pesticide on a Crop Plant. M.Phil. Thesis. Berhampur University.

Sailatha, D., Kabir Ahammad Sahib, I and Ramana Rao, K. V.(1981): Acad. Sci., (Anim. Sci.), 90:87.

Salt, D.E.; Blaylock, M.; Kumar, PBAN; Dushenkov, V.; Ensley, B.d.; Chet, I and Raskin, I. (1995): Phytoremediation: A Novel Stratagy for the Removal of Toxic Metals from the Environment Using Plants. Biotechnology, 13:468-474.

Salt, D.E.; Prince, R.C.; Pickering, I.J.; and Raskin, I. (1995): Mechanisms of Cadmium Mobility and Accumulation in Indian Mustard. Plant Physiokl., 109:1427-1433.

Samantaray, A.C. (1999): Eco-toxicological Effects of Leached Wastes of an Aluminium Factory a Crop Plant. Ph.D. Thesis, Berhampur University.

Sax, I. N. (1974): Industrial Pollution. Van Nostrand Reinhold Company, N.Y.

Schat, H. and Kalff, M.M.A. (1992): Are Phytochelatins Involved in Differential Metal Tolerance Ordor They Merely Reflect Metal Imposed Strain? Plant Physiol., 99:1475-1480.

Scheller, H.V.; Huong, B.; Hatch, E. and Goldsbrough, P.B. (1987): Phytochelatin Synthesis and Glutathione Levels in Response to Heavy Metals in Tomato Cells. Plant Physiol., 85:1031-1035.

Scheller, H.V.; Huang, B.; Hatch, E. and Goldsbrough, P.B. (1987): Phytochelatin Synthesis and Glutathione Levels in Response to Heavy Metals in Tomato Cells. Plant Physiol., 85: 1031-1035.

Schmitz, R. (1967): Arch. Mikrobiol., 56:225.

Schopfer, P., D. Bajraccharya and C. Plachy (1979): Control of Seed Germination by Abscicic Acid. I. Time Course of Action in *Sinapis alba* L. Plant Physiol., 64:822.

Schultz, C.L. and Hutchinson, T.C. (1988): Evidence Against a Key Role for Metallothionein-like Protein in the Copper Tolernce Mechanism of Deschmpsia Cespitosaz (L) Beauv. New Phytol.110:163-171.

Scott, R.; Aughey, E.; Fell, G.S.; and Quinn, M.J. (1987): Cadmium Concentrations in Human Kidneys from the UK. Hum. Toxicolk., 6:111-120.

Semu, E., B. R. Singh, A. R. Selmen-Olsen and K. Steenberg (1985): Plant and Soil., 87:347.

Serrano, R. (1989); Structure and Function of Plasms Membrane ATPase Annu. Rev. Plant. Physiol. Plant Mol. Biol., 40:61 -94.

Sharma, B. K. and H. Kaur (1993): "Environmental Chemistry", Goel Publishing House, Krishna Prakashan Media (P) Ltd. Meerut.

Sharma, S. S. (1985): Environmental and Experimental Botany, 25(3): 189.

Shaw, B. P. (1987): Eco-physiological Studies of Industrial Effluent of a Chlor-alkali Factory on Biosystems. Ph. D. Thesis, Berhampur University, Orissa, India.

Shekour, G. M., C. R. McDavid and R. A. I. Brathwaite (1991): Response of Sweet Corn to Different Rates and Frequencies of Application of PMA and Vapour gard. Trop. Agric. (Trimidad) 68(3):225.

Shekour, G. M., R. A. I. Brathwaite, and C. R. McDavid (1987): Dry Seaseon Sweet Corn Response to Mulching and Anti-transpirants, Agron. J., 79:629.

Shimsi, D. (1963 a): Effect of Chemical Closure of Stomata on Transiparion in Various Soil and Atmospheric Environments. Pl. Physiol. Lancaster, 38:709.

Shimsi, D. (1963 b): Effect of Soil Moisture and Phenyl Merucuric Acetate Upon Stomatal Aprerture, Transpiration and Photosynthesis. PI. Physiol., Lancaster, 38:713.

Sieddleckaa and Bazynski, T. (1993): Inhibition of Electron Flow Around Photosystem I in Chloroplasts of Cd Treated Maize Plants is Due to Cd-induced Iron Deficiency. Physiol. Plant., 87:199-202.

Siegel, B. Z., m. Lasconta, E. Yaeger and S. M. Siegel (1984): Water Air Soil Pollut, 23(1):15.

Siegenthaler, P. A. (1966): Phenyl Mercuric Acetate and Phosphate Control of Light Dependent Shrinkage and Reactions in Chloroplasts. Physiologia. Pl, 19:437.

Siegenthaler, P. A. and L. Packer (1965): Light-dependent Volume Changes and Reactions in Chloroplasts I Action of Alkenylsuccinic Acids and Phenyl Mercuric Acetate and Possible Relation to Mechanism of Stomatal Control. Pl. Physiol. Lancaster, 40:785.

Simkis, K. (1979): Metal Ions in Cells, Endeavour., 3:2.

Simon, E. W. (1967): Types of Leaf Senescence. In : Symposium of the Society of Experimental Biology. XXI : Aspects of the Biology of Aeging (Ed. H. W. Hoolhouse), Cambridge Univ. Press, London, pp.215-230.

Singerman, A. and R. L. Catalina (1969): Proc. XVI. Int. Cogr. Occup. Health. Tokyo, No. 6.

Singh, B. and O. P. Awasthi (1984): Effect of Time of Appliation of Anti-transpirants on the Yield of Rainfed Wheat Under Mid-hill Conditions of Himachal Pradesh, Indian J. Agron., 363.

Singh, B.R. (1994): Trace Elements Availability to Plant in Agricultural Soil with Special Emphasis on Fertiliser Inputs. Environ. Rev., 2, 133-146.

Slade, R. E., W. G. Templeman and W. A. Sexton (1945): Nature (London), 155:497.

Slatyer, R. O. and J. F. Bierhuizen (1964 a): The Influence of Several Transpiration Suppressants on Transpiration, Photosynthesis and Water-use Efficiency of Cotton Leaves. Aust. J. Biol. Sci., 17:131.

Slatyer, R. O. and J. F. Bierhuizen (1964 b): The Effect of Several Foliar Sprays as Transpirant and Water-use Efficiency of Cotton Plants. Agric. Meteorol. 1:42.

Smith, L. and M. Baltscheffsky (1959): Respiration and Light Induced Phosphorylation in Extracts of *Rhodospirillum Rubrum*. J. Biol. Chem., 234:1575.

Smith, G.C.; Brennan, E.G. and Greenhalgh, B.J. (1985): Cadmium Sensitivity of Soyabean Related to Efficiency in Iron Utilisation. Env. Exp. Bot., 25:99-106.

Sokolowska, K., Alicja, et al. (1975): Acta Bio! Craov Ser Bot, 18(2):115.

Sorteberg, A. (1974): J. Scient. Agric. Soc. Finl., 46:227.

Spangler, W. J., J. L. Spigarelli, J. M. Rose and H. M. Miller (1973): Methyl Mercury: Bacterial Degradation in Lake Sediments. Science, 180:192.

Spicket, J.T. and Lazner, J. (1979): Cadmium Concentration in Human Kidney and Liver Tissues from Western Australia. Bull. Environ. Contam. Toxicol., 23:627-630.

Squire, G. R. and M. B. Jones (1971): Studies on the Mechanism of Action of the Anti-transpirant Phenyl Mercuric Acetate and Its Penetration into the Mesophyll. J. of Expt. Bot., 22(73):980.

Srivastava, A. K., V. K. Sharma and K. L. Ahuja (1972): Effect of Salt Stress on Seed Germination and Survival of Soyabean Seedlings. Trop. Ecol.,18:27.

Srivastava, B. J. S. and G. Ware (1965): Plant Physiol., 40:62.

Stobart, A.K.; Griffiths, W.T.; Ameen Bukhariu, I and Sherwood, R.P. (1985): The Effect of Cd^{2+} on the Biosynthesis of Chlorophyllin Leaves of Barley. Physiol. Plant., 63:293-298.

Stobart, A.K.; Griffiths, W.T.; Ameen Bukhari, I. and Sherwood, K.P. (1985): The Effect of Cd^{2+} on the Biosynthesis of Chlorophyll in Leaves of Barley. Physiol. Plant., 63:293-298.

Street, J.J.; Lindsay, W.L. and Sabey, B.R. (1977): Solubility and Plant Uptake of Cadmium in Soils Amended with Cadmium and Sewage Sludge. J. Environ. Quel., 6:72-77.

Soltanpour, P.W. (1991): Determination of Nutrient Availability and Elemental Toxicity by AB-DTPA Soil Test and ICPS. Adv. Soil. Sci., 16:165-190.

Strickland, R.C.; Chaney, W.R. and Lamoreawe, R.I. (1979): Membrane Damage of Cd on Pinus Resionosa Pollen, Effect Oncation Release and Membrane Permeability. Plant Physiol., 64:366-370.

Sugita, M. and Tsuchiya, K. (1995): Estimation of Variation Among Individuals of Biological Half Time of Cadmium Calculated from Accumulation Data. Environ. Res. 68:31-37.

Summers, H.O. and Silver, S. (1978): Microbial Transformation of Metals. Annu. Rev. Microbiol., 32:637-672.

Sussman, M.R. (1994): Molecular Analysis of Proteins in the Plant Plasma Membrane. Annu. Rev. Plant Physiol. Plant Mol. Biol.,45:211-234.

Tamaddon, F. and Hogland, W. (1993); Review of Cadmium in Plastic Waste in Sweden. Water Manage. Res., 11:287-295.

Tayler, G.J.; Stadt, K.J.; and Dale, M.R.T. (1991): Modelling the Phytoxicity of Aluminium, Cadmium, Coper, Manganese, Nickel and Zinc Using the Weukvykk Freqyebnct Distribution. Can. J. Bot., 69:359-367

Thomas, H. and J. L. Stoddart (1980): Ann. Rev. Plant. Physiol., 31:83.

Thurberg, F. P., A. Calabrese and M. A. Dawson (1974): Effect of silver on Oxygen Consumption of Bivalves at Various Salinities. In: Pollution and Physiology of Marine Organisms (Eds. F. J. Vernerg and W. B. Vernberg), p. 67. Academic Press. N. Y.

Toubey, C. L. (1972): Aust. J. Exp. Agric. Anim. Husk., 12(55): 176.

Trim, A. R. (1959): Biochem. J., 73:928.

Tsuzuki, Y., Y. Takamichi and I. Koji (1979): J. Toxicol. Sci., 4(4):417:426.

Turner, N. C. and P. F. Waggoner (1968): Effects of Changing Stomatal Width in a Red Pine Forest on Soil Water Content, Leaf Water Potential, Bole Diameter and Growth, Plant Physiol., 43:973.

Turner, N. C. and P. J. Kramer (1980): Adaptation of Plant to Water and High Temperature Stress, 231-232. Willey Inter-Science, New York.

Turner, M.A. (1973): Effect of Cadmium Treatment on Cadmium and Zinc Uptake by Selected Vegetable Species. J. Environ. Qual.,2:118-119.

Underwood, E. J. (1977): Selenium. In : Trace Elements in Human and Animal Nutrition. P. 302-346. 4th Ed. Academic Press, New York.

Venot, C. and N. Giachhero (1971): C. R. Seances Soc. Biol. Fil., 165(5): 1327.

Venugopal, B. and Luckey, J.D. (1978): Chemical Toxicity of Metals and Metalloids. In Metal Toxicity in Mammals, B. Venugopal and J.D. Luckey,(Eds.) Vol. 2., pp.76-86. Planum, New York/London.

Vernon, L. P. (1960): Spectrophotometric Detrminatkon of Chlorophylls and Pheophytins in Plant Extracts. Anal. Chem., 32:1114.

Vlamis, J. and A. R. Dvis (1943): Germination, Growth and Respiration of Rice and Barley Seedlings at Low Oxygen Pressure. Plant Physiol., 18:682.

Vojtechova. M. and Leblova, S. (1991): Uptake of Led and Cadmium by Maize Seedlings and the Effect of Heavy Metals on the Activity of Phosphoenol Pyruvate Carboxylase Isolated from Maize. Biol. Plant., 33:386-394.

Volkin, E. and W. E. Cohn (1954): Methods Biochem. Anal., 1:287.

Wagner, G.J. (1984): Characterisation of a Cadmium Binding Complex of Cabbage Leaves. Plant Physiol. 76:797-805.

Wagner, J.P.; EI-Ayyoubi, M.A.; Konzen, R.B. and Krohn, J.L (1992): Quantitative Identification of Antimony, Barium, Cadmium and Tin During Controlled Combustion of Plastics. Polymer Plastics Technol. Engineer, 31:73-101.

Wagner, G.J. (1994): Accumulation of Cadmium in Crop Plants and Its Consequences to Human Health. Adv. Agron., 51:173-21.

Wain, R. L. and M. S. Smith (1976): Selectivity in Relation to metabolism. In : L. J. Audus (Ed.), Herbicides, Physiology, Biochemistry, Ecology, Vol. 2, 2nd Ed. Academic Press, London, p.279.

Waisel, Y, G. A. Borger and T. T. Koziowski (1969): Affects of Phenyl Mercuric Acetate on Stomatal Movment and Transpiration of excised *Betula papyhfera* Marsh Leaves. Plant Physiol., 44:685.

Wallace, W.G. and Lopez, G.R. (1996): Relationship Between Subcellular Cadmium Distribution in Prey and Cadmium Trophic Transfer to a Predator. Estuaries, 19(4):923-930.

Ware, G. W. (1980): Effects of Pesticides on Non-target Organisms. In F. A. Gunther (Eds.), Residue Reviews, Residues of Pesticides and Other Contaminants in the Total Environment, Vol. 76. Springer-Verlag, New York, p. 173.

Weaver, R. W., J. R. Melton, D. Wang and R. L. Dable (1984): Environ. Pollut. Ser A. Ecol. Biol., 33(2): 133.

Webb, J. L. (1966): Enzymes and Metabolic Inhibitors. 1st Ed., Vol. II, p. 729. Academic Press, New York.

Webb, M. (1987): Toxicological Significance of Met Allothionein. In Metallethionein II. Experientia Supplementum. Vol. 52. Ed. Kagi, J.H.R. and Kojima, Y, pp. 109-134. Birkhauser Verlay, Basel.

Weigel, H.J. (1985): The Effect of Cd^{2+} on Photosynthetic Reactions of Mesophyll Protoplasts. Phuysiol. Plant. ,63:192-200.

Weiss, H. V., M. Koide and E. D. Goldberg (1971): Science, 174:692.

Westoo, G. (1967): Determination of Methyl Mercury Compounds in Food Stuffs; 2, Determination of Methylmercury in Fish, Egg, Meat, and Liver. Acta Chimica Scandinavica, 21:1790.

White, D. E., M. E. Hinkle and I. Barnes (1970): In : Mercury in the Environment, US Geological Society Professional Paper, 713:25.

White, J. F. and A. Rothstein (1973): Tox. Appl. Pharmacol., 26:370.

Whittakar, J., J. Barika, H. King and M. Burkley (1978): Environ. Pollut, 15:185.

Wiklander, L. (1969): Geoderma, 3:75.

Wilkins, D. A. (1978): The Measurement of Tolerance to Edaphic Factors by Means of Root Growth. New Phytol., 80:623.

Wolk, C. P. (1973): Bacteriol. Rev., 37:32.

Wolken, J. J., A. D. Mellon, and C. L. Greenblatt (1955): J. Protozool., 2:89.

Wolnick, K.A.; Fricke, F.L; Caper, S.G.; Broude, G.L; Meyer, M.W.; Stazger, R.D. and Bonnin, E. (1983): Elements in Major Raw Agricultural Crops in the United States. I. Cadmium and Lead in Lettuce, Peanuts, Potatoes, Soyabeans, Sweet corn, and wheat. J. Agric. Food Chem., 31:1240-1244.

Wong, M.K.; Chauh, G.K.; Koh, L.L., Ang, P.P. and Hew, C.S. (1983): The Uptake of Cadmium by *Brassica Chinensis* and Its Effect on Plant Zinc and Iron Distribution. Env. Exp. Bot., 24:189-195.

Wong, M. H. and A. D. Bradshaw (1982): New Phytol., 91(2):255.

Wood, J. M. (1974): Biological Cycles for Toxic Elements in the Environment. Science, 183:1049.

Wozny, A.; Stronski, A. and Gwozdz, E.(1990): Cell Responses to Cadmium Seria Biologia No: 44, pp. 29. Universitet In.Adama Michienrcza We Poznanu, Poznan.

Xian, X. (1989): Plant and Soil., 113:257.

Xian, X and Shokohifad, G.I. (1989): Effect of pH on Chemical Forms and Plant Availability of Cadmium, Zinc and Lead on Polluted Soils. Water, Air, Soil Pollut., 45:2655-273.

Yamada, M. and K. Tonomura (1972): Formation of Melthylmercury Compounds from Inorganic Mercury by *Closthdium cochlearium.* J. Ferment. Technol., 50:159.

Yannai, S. and Berdicevskuy, I. (1995): Formation of Organic Cadmium Bymarine Microorganisms. Eco-toxicology and Environmental Safety, 32:209-214.

Yost, K.J.; Miles, L.J.; and Parsons, T.W. (1980): A Method for Estimating Contaminants: Cadmium a Case Study. Environ. Interpretation, 3:473-484. Yung, Chi-Tung (1938): Development Anatomy of the Seedling of Rice Plant. Bot. Gaz., 99:786.

Zelitch, I. (1963): The Control and Mechanisms of Stomatal Movement. Conn. Agr. Expt. Sta. Bull., 664:18.

Zelitch, I. and P. E. Waggoner (1962): Effect of Chemical Control of Stomata on Transpiration and Photosynthesis of Intact Plants. Proc. Natn. Acad. Sci. USA, 48:1297-9.

Zia, S. and Aliklan, M.A. (1989): Copper Uptake and Regulation in a Copper Tolerant Decapod Camparus Artoni (Frabricius) (Decopods, Crustacea). Bull.Environ. Contam. Toxicol., 42:103-110.

Zhang, M.; Wang, J. and Bao, J. (1992): Study on the Relationship Between Speciation of Heavy Metals and Their Eco-toixicity. I. Toxicity of Copper, Cadmium, Lead and Zinc in Seawater to Three Marine Algae in the Presence of Different Complexation Agents. Chinese J. Ocean and Limnol., 10:215-222.

Index